Religions in Contempor

MW00657559

Religions in Contemporary Africa is an accessible and comprehensive introduction to the three main religious traditions on the African continent: African indigenous religions, Christianity and Islam. The book provides a historical overview of these important traditions and focuses on the roles they play in African societies today. It includes social, cultural and political case studies from across the continent on the following topical issues:

- Witchcraft and modernity
- Power and politics
- Conflict and peace
- Media and popular culture
- Development
- Human rights
- Illness and health
- Gender and sexuality

With suggestions for further reading, discussion questions, illustrations and a list of glossary terms this is the ideal textbook for students in religion, African studies and adjacent fields approaching this subject area for the first time.

Laura S. Grillo earned her PhD in History of Religions from the University of Chicago and is Affiliated Faculty at Georgetown University. Her book, *An Intimate Rebuke* (2018), was supported by a Research Fellowship at Harvard Divinity School.

Adriaan van Klinken is Associate Professor of Religion and African Studies at the University of Leeds (United Kingdom). He holds a PhD in Religious Studies from Utrecht University (the Netherlands) and was a postdoctoral fellow at SOAS University of London.

Hassan J. Ndzovu is a Senior Lecturer of Religious Studies at Moi University, Kenya, with a PhD degree from the University of Kwazulu Natal, South Africa. Ndzovu has also held two postdoctoral positions at Freie Universität Berlin and Northwestern University, USA.

Religions in Contemporary Africa

An Introduction

Laura S. Grillo, Adriaan van Klinken and Hassan J. Ndzovu

Routledge
Taylor & Francis Group

LONDON AND NEW YORK

First published 2019
by Routledge
2 Park Square, Milton Park, Abingdon, Oxon OX14 4RN

and by Routledge
52 Vanderbilt Avenue, New York, NY 10017

Routledge is an imprint of the Taylor & Francis Group, an informa business

British Library Cataloguing in Publication Data
A catalogue record for this book is available from the British Library

Library of Congress Cataloging-in-Publication Data
Names: Grillo, Laura S., 1956- author. | Ndzovu, Hassan J., author. |
Van Klinken, A. S., author.
Title: Religions in contemporary Africa : an introduction / Laura S. Grillo,
Hassan J. Ndzovu, Adriaan van Klinken.
Description: New York, NY : Routledge, 2019. | Includes bibliographical
references and index.
Identifiers: LCCN 2018052723 (print) | LCCN 2018054126 (ebook) |
ISBN 9781351260725 (eBook) |
ISBN 9780815365778 (hardback : alk. paper) | ISBN 9780815365792
(pbk. : alk. paper)
Subjects: LCSH: Africa--Religion.
Classification: LCC BL2400 (ebook) | LCC BL2400 .G75 2019 (print) |
DDC 200.96--dc23
LC record available at https://lccn.loc.gov/2018052723

ISBN: 978-0-815-36577-8 (hbk)
ISBN: 978-0-815-36579-2 (pbk)
ISBN: 978-1-351-26072-5 (ebk)

Typeset in Sabon
by Taylor & Francis Books

Contents

vi   *Contents*

Figures

Tables

Boxes

List of abbreviations

AACC	All Africa Conference of Churches
ACHPR	African Charter of Human and Peoples' Rights
AICs	African Independent (or Instituted, or Initiated) Churches
AIDS	Acquired Immuno-Deficiency Syndrome
AU	African Union
CCC	Celestial Church of Christ
FBO	Faith-based organizations
HIV	Human Immunodeficiency Virus
IPK	Islamic Party of Kenya
LGBT	Lesbian, Gay, Bisexual and Transgender
NGO	Non-governmental organizations
NTRM	Neo-traditional Religious Movements
PEPFAR	President's Emergency Plan for AIDS Relief
UMA	United Muslims of Africa

Introduction

Why and how this book helps you understand religions in Africa

Who are we?

With the reading of any text, a relevant question to ask is who the author is and what the objective for writing it was. So as you begin reading this book on religions in contemporary Africa, we would like to introduce ourselves, tell you how this work came about and share with you our motivation for writing it. We hope you don't mind our conversational style, deliberately adopted in this section to ease you into this book and its subject.

This is a collaborative effort of three of us, all academics with a great interest in religion as well as in Africa: Laura Grillo, Hassan Ndzovu and Adriaan van Klinken. Each of us holds a PhD in the academic study of religion in Africa, and has a record of teaching, researching and publishing in this subject. Our academic specializations in this area are closely connected to our respective biographies.

Laura grew up in the United States. When she was an undergraduate her involvement in an international student organization led her to meet and eventually marry a fellow student from Côte d'Ivoire. She lived and taught in that country as well as in Kenya, where she also worked for the All Africa Conference of Churches. When she returned to the US to complete a Masters of Divinity degree, she was troubled that African religions were not included among the "world religions" she studied. Her thesis on an Ivoirian ritual of initiation, possession trance, self-wounding and instantaneous healing led her to pursue a PhD in history of religions at the University of Chicago, pioneering the study of African indigenous religions in that field. Her work emphasizes the vitality of these traditions as a critical part of the social imaginary, and the timely contributions they make to civil society and politics today. Her current focus is the heritage of African women's power and the history of women's use of ritual to enforce an ethical check on political villainy. Even after her second marriage, Laura's close ties in Côte d'Ivoire endure and it remains her "home base" in Africa.

Hassan was born and grew up on the east coast of the African continent, in coastal Kenya. Raised in a Muslim family and living in an area where there is a strong historical presence of Islam, he soon became aware that in Kenya as a whole, Islam is a minority religion vis-à-vis a Christian majority. While training to become a high school teacher in Islamic religious education, he realized that there is a paucity of university experts in Islamic studies in the country. This inspired him to immediately enrol for a master's degree in religious studies, upon completion of his undergraduate studies, providing him the prospects to fill in the gap, to realize his potential as well as sharpening his critical thinking skills in the field of religious studies. Subsequently, he got the opportunity to pursue his PhD in a collaborative programme between a university in South Africa and in Germany, writing a dissertation on the politicization of Islam in Kenya. Teaching and researching on Islam in Africa, his current interest focuses on Muslims and politics including Salafi-jihad-minded movements that have emerged in various parts of the continent and their socio-political significance.

Adriaan is from the Netherlands. Out of a personal interest in matters of faith, he went to study religion at university, where he soon learned that religious texts, practices and beliefs are much more ambivalent, complex and diverse than he had realized before. One of his professors sparked his interest in Africa – a continent where religion seemed so much more vibrant and dynamic than in Western Europe. Being offered the opportunity to study in South Africa for a semester in 2006, he ended up writing his MA dissertation on religious responses to the HIV epidemic. He pursued this subject further for his PhD, with a strong focus on issues of gender, for which he conducted fieldwork in Zambia. More recently, he has carried out research in Kenya, focusing on religion, homosexuality and LGBT activism. His overall interest is in contemporary forms of Christianity and their social, public and political roles in African societies. He has established warm friendships in various countries on the continent, and has come to appreciate many things that Africa offers, such as delicious food, incredible music, lively markets, and buzzing street life.

From these personal introductions it is clear that the three of us complement one another in several respects: we come from three different continents (North America, Africa, and Europe) and have taught religion in those contexts; we have lived experience and direct knowledge of various regions of the African continent (West, East, and Southern Africa); finally, we have expertise on the three major religious traditions of Africa (indigenous religions, Islam, and Christianity). Because of this complementarity, writing this book collaboratively has been such an enriching academic experience through which we ourselves have learned a lot. What we have in common is an approach to religion that is critical yet empathetic, and a fascination for Africa and for the role of religions in African cultures and societies.

Each of us is academically located in religious studies, which is an interdisciplinary field making use of anthropology, history, politics, sociology, theology, as well as of critical theory (e.g. postcolonial, gender, sexuality studies). We also situate our work in the field of African studies, which equally makes use of multiple disciplinary perspectives in order to understand the rich complexity and diversity of African cultures, societies and politics. Where religious studies is problematic for us because it has historically privileged Western contexts and traditions, African studies is so because it has historically tended to overlook religion as a primary category of analysis. We maintain that one cannot understand "religion" fully without studying the ways in which it is practised and manifested in African contexts. Likewise one cannot fully understand "Africa" without taking into account the salience and significance of religious beliefs, practices and worldviews. Therefore in this book, we constructively and creatively engage various approaches, which we believe are vital to understanding the complex meanings and significance of religion in Africa.

Why did we write this book?

As soon as he started teaching at the University of Leeds in 2013, Adriaan discovered that there was no adequate text-book available for his undergraduate course on religion in Africa. No one book covered indigenous religions, Christianity and Islam in contemporary African contexts. Either they focus on one of these religious traditions instead of putting them in a comparative perspective, or they offer more historical than contemporary studies. The existing edited book volumes on religion in Africa are written at a level not suitable for undergraduate students (e.g. Bongmba 2012) and/or have become a little dated, not giving a current overview of religion in Africa (Blakely, van Beek and Thomson 1994; Olupona 2000; Ray 2000). Hence, he started playing with the idea of writing an undergraduate textbook on religions in Africa, including indigenous religions, Christianity and Islam, and focusing on contemporary contexts and the role of religion in society. However, writing such a book could never be an individual endeavour; the African continent is simply too large, and the diversity and complexity of its religious traditions too vast, to be adequately covered by one individual. Luckily, Adriaan found Laura and Hassan agreeing on the need for a comprehensive and up-to-date introduction to religions in Africa, and willing to join the bandwagon and write such a book together.

How did this book come about?

Laura and Adriaan knew each other through the American Academy of Religion, where they both are involved in the African Religions unit. Hassan and Adriaan knew each other from a publishing project in which they both had been involved. As soon as the three of us formed a team, early 2017, we drafted a book proposal. The publisher sent this outline of the book and abstracts of each chapter to three anonymous reviewers, who each made comments and suggestions for the book from which we benefited in the process of writing.

From the beginning, we intended this project to be a collaborative effort. So, although each of us drafted a number of chapters, assigned on the basis of our expertise, these drafts were exchanged by email. The other two team members gave detailed comments and feedback, and in many cases also contributed paragraphs or sections on the basis of complementary expertise. We soon realized that for the project to be truly collaborative, communication by email and skype did not suffice. Practically, skype meetings were difficult because of the time differences between our geographical locations, and because of technical limitations (the internet is not as fast as one would wish in the Kenyan city where Hassan is based). Email, on the other hand, is useful for exchanging and commenting on drafts but does not allow for in-depth discussion of the critical issues that emerged from the draft chapters. Hence we planned a writing retreat, which Laura hosted in her lovely house in Durham, North Carolina. Working together there for a week, we had sufficient time to talk through all the chapters (which by then had already been revised for the first time) in great detail, and to agree on further additions and revisions. Our own debates helped us draft questions for discussion included at the end of each chapter.

Why do we want you to learn about religions in Africa?

We are convinced that studying religions in Africa is essential for understanding Africa, whose young and growing population has an ever-increasing influence in world affairs. Thus, we hope that this book will be read by students in religious studies and African studies, as well as fields like global studies, women and gender studies, development and political studies.

The study of Africa itself is perhaps more important now than ever, for a variety of reasons. First, the continent has a long and rich history, and has been home to great civilizations and cultures (Parker and Rathbone 2007). Second, as the second largest continent in the world, Africa is enormously diverse; it presents a great variety of cultural and artistic traditions, beliefs and values, forms of social organization and political structures. Third, through the centuries Africa has been involved in trans-continental exchange and interaction, informing Europe, the Middle East, Asia, and the Americas (Reid 2012). Fourth, today Africa is a vital part of the contemporary world, commanding an ever-increasing cultural, economic and political significance. This is indicated, for instance, by China's strong interest and investment in Africa in recent years, which has been referred to as a new "scramble for Africa" (Carmody 2011), following the pattern of Europe's 20th century colonial engagement with the continent. Also, Africa has a rapidly growing population with a comparatively young demographic. In 2018, the continent's population was about 1,300,000,000, which is 17 per cent of the total world population. It is expected to almost double to over 2,500,000,000 by 2050 (Worldometers 2018). Currently, the median age in Africa is 19.4 years, meaning that half of the population is even younger, making Africa the youngest continent in the world. This demographic situation will not only stimulate new cultural production, economic activity and social change on the continent, but could also intensify migration from it. It is also likely to increase social tensions and political conflict about scarce economic resources. Fifth, unfortunately there exist many stereotypes and misrepresentations of African cultures and societies, especially in Europe and North America where the relationship to the continent is built on the history of the slave trade and colonization. Ironically such distortions are also prevalent on the continent itself where many people, especially youth, are ignorant of African history and alienated from its traditions.

In addition to the general importance of studying the African continent, we believe it is of vital importance to learn about *religions in* Africa for a variety of reasons. First, the continent is home to a rich diversity of religious traditions. The beliefs, rituals and practices of indigenous religions differ among the ethnic groups of any given country, and vary even more widely from region to region. Christianity and Islam both have a long history and strong presence in Africa, and have also been shaped by African cultural, social and political contexts. All religious tradition is subject to the complex processes of religious change over time, and religions in Africa remain relevant to the changing circumstances on the continent.

Second, religious practice in Africa is deeply intertwined with other spheres of life, such as cultural production, social organization, political institutions and economic activity (Ellis and Ter Haar 2004). Thus, understanding religion is key to understanding African societies generally. Religion is so much a part and parcel of African life that we even dare to say that one cannot understand African politics, media, popular culture and so on without engaging with religious thought and practice.

Third, as a result of the transatlantic slave trade and more recent patterns of migration and globalization, the religious traditions of Africa – indigenous religions as well as African forms of Christianity and Islam – have spread globally and have a profound impact on religious cultures worldwide. Thus, knowledge of the African religious climate is crucial to understanding the ever-expanding plurality of religions in our globalizing world.

Fourth, the concept of religion itself – what we think "religion" is and does – has historically been defined by Western traditions, and therefore can be enriched, nuanced and complicated by the study of religious thought and practice in African societies.

What do we want you to know about religions in Africa?

This book is organized in two main parts. Part I introduces the three major religious traditions featured in the book: African indigenous religions, Christianity and Islam. The history, development and characteristics of these traditions are discussed in separate chapters. These are followed by three complementary chapters that focus on the dynamics of religious change, exploring neo-traditional, Pentecostal Christian and Islamic reform movements respectively. Thus, the six chapters in the first part of the book help you understand the three major religions on the African continent from a historical perspective as well as contemporary trends.

Although these religions are discussed separately, the chapters also highlight interactions and interconnections among them. We believe that it is of critical importance to study the three major religious traditions of Africa together in one book. First and foremost, it presents them as commensurate systems of thought and ritual practice. Historically, religious studies bifurcated religions into two categories, diametrically opposed: "world religions", such as Christianity and Islam and "the primitive" indigenous religions. It excluded indigenous oral traditions, promoting the misconception that without text there could be no philosophy, historical consciousness, or appeal beyond the immediate cultural context. In short, African indigenous religions were not considered "religion" at all. Our treatment rectifies these longstanding misconceptions and underscores that they are comparable: fulfilling the same spiritual and social functions, shaping the history of the continent today as much as in the past, and equally capable of addressing the pressing issues of today's complex, globalizing world. Secondly, it challenges the idea that Christianity and Islam are foreign to Africa. The book traces the extensive history of both religions on the continent and underscores their complex interface with African traditions.

Part II, the larger section of the book, is organized thematically, to demonstrate how religious thought and practice in Africa affect other spheres of life especially pertinent today. Each of the nine chapters addresses a critical theme: witchcraft, politics, conflict and peace, development, human rights, illness and health, gender, sexuality, and finally, media and popular culture. These themes were selected because they are broad and diverse enough to cover a wide range of cultural, social and political issues in contemporary African societies that are impacted by religion. It is fair to say that our choice of themes, of course, also reflects our specific research interests, allowing us to share with you our expertise on these subjects. The objective of these chapters is to provide a broad context and background, but each chapter also includes "Features" that focus on a specific cases or issues, treating these in-depth.

Together, the two parts of the book give you a comprehensive understanding of the diversity of religious traditions in Africa, their historical backgrounds, and the role they play in African societies today. We also invite you to reflect upon how the manifestation of these religions provides you a deeper understanding, of both that place called "Africa" and that thing called "religion". Overall, we believe that there is a deeply humanistic value in studying religions in Africa. Such a study demonstrates that there is no universal way of being human: both Africa and religions in Africa make us aware of the rich diversity of human existence.

What do we mean by "Africa"?

The name "Africa" is usually traced back to the Latin term "Afri" that was used to refer to the inhabitants of the land south of the Mediterranean Sea (in particular, contemporary Libya and Tunisia). This word first appeared in Roman writings in the 3rd century BCE. The region where these so-called Afri lived was referred to by the Romans as *Africa terra*, that is, land of the Afri. In the 2nd century BCE, the Roman Empire established a province in this region which they called *Africa Proconsularis* (Province of Africa). There are various theories about the etymological origins of the word *afri*: it might originate from the Greek word *aphrike* ("land without cold"), the Latin word *apri* (sunny), the Phoenician word *afar* (dust) or the Berber word *ifri* (cave) (cf. Benjamin 2006,

73; Stokes 2009, 764). Only much later in history, in the period of European explorations starting in the 15th century, did Europeans realize the real extent of the land mass referred to as Africa and began to expand their knowledge of the continent and its inhabitants.

Two things stand out already from this short overview of the name "Africa". First, historically speaking, the name first and foremost referred to North Africa. This is interesting because this part of the continent nowadays is frequently considered part of the Middle East, with the name Africa in fact often used to refer to the sub-Saharan part of the continent only. This raises questions about the unity of the continent, not only about whether Africa can be understood as one geographical entity, but especially about how it can best be understood culturally, socially and politically. Second, and again historically speaking, the name "Africa" was not a self-identifier, but a term used by others – in this case, the Romans – to name the continent. On the one hand, this illustrates the point that far from being isolated, Africa has long maintained connections with other parts of the world. On the other hand, it raises the critical question of who has the power, not only to name the continent but also to produce knowledge about it. As Congolese philosopher V.Y. Mudimbe (1988) argues, "Africa" is an invention, or a construct, fashioned by non-Africans, especially Europeans, as a "paradigm of difference", by means of which Europe contrasts itself and considers itself superior. A similar point is made by Cameroonian philosopher Achille Mbembe when he writes:

> Africa as an idea, a concept, has historically served, and continues to serve, as a polemical argument for the West's desperate desire to assert its difference from the rest of the world. In several respects, Africa still constitutes one of the metaphors through which the West represents the origin of its own norms, develops a self-image, and integrates this image into the set of signifiers asserting what it supposes to be its identity.
>
> (Mbembe 2001, 2)

Only in the 19th century, Africans themselves – especially intellectuals in the diaspora – "began to appropriate the idea of Africa" and lay "the foundations of what came to be known as pan-Africanism" (Parker and Rathbone 2007, 4). Interestingly, pan-African ideology often centred on race as a central category, which is understandable against the traumatic history of the trans-Atlantic slave-trade and European colonization of the continent. Yet by taking race as the starting point for defining Africa, the focus tended to be on sub-Saharan or "black" Africa, with the northern part of the continent (with a largely lighter-skinned and Arab-speaking population) being made relatively marginal to it as a cultural, political or religious entity. Not only pan-African ideology, but also African studies as an academic field has often limited its scope to sub-Saharan Africa.

Obviously, the matter touched upon here is a complicated one and cannot be adequately discussed in this introduction. We raise it to explain certain choices we made regarding this book. We opted to focus our discussion, especially of the contemporary situation, on sub-Saharan Africa. This is a way of acknowledging that the religious, cultural and political dynamics in North Africa today are quite different from the rest of the continent and tend to be informed by the Arab world. At the same time, our discussions acknowledge that historically speaking, societies in sub-Saharan Africa have experienced (and still experience) considerable influence from, and have maintained (and still maintain) close ties to the northern part of the continent. Especially in our introduction to the histories of Christianity and Islam on the continent, considerable attention is paid to these longstanding connections.

Africa being a vast and highly diverse continent, it is impossible for a book like this to cover all cultures, societies and countries in depth, or indeed to even mention them all. We have sought, however, to give a representative and relatively balanced discussion of countries in the major regions of sub-Saharan Africa: West, Central, East, and Southern Africa, as well as the region known as the Horn of Africa in the north-east. In total, over 40 (of the 54) independent African states are mentioned in this book, and many of them are discussed in more detail. Obviously, the countries and regions that receive most attention are those with which we are most familiar, yet we have endeavoured to extend our reach to include accounts of cases beyond our areas of expertise. Including examples and discussing cases from a range of countries across the continent has also helped us to avoid simplistic generalizations about Africa – although we recognize that in an introductory textbook such as this some level of generalizing cannot be avoided.

What do we mean by "religion"?

It is now a well-established truth that the "academic study of religion has its roots outside the [African] continent" and that "the very category of religion itself has a European history" (Chitando, Adogame and Bateye 2012, 1). One legacy of the European roots of the study of religion is that the concept of "religion" itself is shaped by Western religious traditions, in particular Christianity. Moreover, the way the concept has been operationalized in Africa is historically shaped by colonial, Western-superior modes of thought (e.g. see Chidester 1996). From this perspective, religions are traditions with a historical founding figure (e.g. Jesus), a canon of sacred scripture (e.g. the Bible), with doctrines about the nature of God (e.g. the Trinity) and God's relation to humankind (e.g. redemption in Jesus Christ), with institutionalized forms of authority (e.g. the pope or church synods), and with permanent structures of worship (church buildings). This idea of what religions are is then applied to other traditions than Western Christianity – traditions that may only fit partly, or hardly at all, in this mould and which are therefore considered as inferior, "primitive" or even "superstitious" forms of religiosity.

Indeed, historically, scholars of religious studies have been slow to acknowledge and classify African indigenous systems of belief and practice as "religion" (Chidester 1996). These systems simply did not appear to fit the Western image of what "religion", conceived as institutionalized doctrine existing apart from the rest of social life, should look like. As will be pointed out in Chapter 1, African indigenous religions do not have historical founders or an ultimate religious authority, they have no sacred scripture, nor are they concerned with capturing the truths about sacred realities in a set of doctrines of faith. Instead of being preoccupied with the question of *orthodoxy* (the correct doctrine), they are more concerned with *orthopraxis*, that is, the correct practice of rituals. It is not adherence to abstract belief, but the participation of adherents that is central to them. Ritual actively serves to maintain harmony in the relationship with the sacred and divine realm, which is believed to be the source of the spiritual power that ensures the ongoing life of the community. Likewise, Christian and Islamic traditions in Africa tend to be more concerned with accessing spiritual power than with doctrinal matters (as a result of which these traditions are sometimes seen as un-orthodox, and not "truly" Christian or Islamic, by adherents of the same faiths outside the continent).

Focusing on pragmatic matters of religious practice rather than doctrine, the boundaries of African religions are not as rigidly controlled, and participation tends to be inclusive rather than exclusive. Often participants practice across the boundaries of different faith traditions, or put differently, the boundaries themselves tend to be fluid and ambiguous. Scholars often refer to this phenomenon as religious hybridity (a mixing of what should ostensibly remain pure), syncretism (the simultaneous practice of two supposedly distinct traditions), or pragmatism (taking care of immediate spiritual needs without regard to religious allegiance). Each of these terms gives a slightly different sense of the dynamics in play, but they all allude to the same reality: religious identity and practice are often not as straightforward as they may appear at first sight. Individuals may engage in indigenous religious traditions while at the same time considering themselves Christian or Muslim. Although Christians and Muslims may denounce indigenous religious practice as "backward", many visit a diviner or healer in times of crisis nevertheless. Many families are religiously mixed, with members practising indigenous ritual, Christianity and/or Islam relatively harmoniously alongside one another. Moreover, people often consider the term "religion" to refer exclusively to Christianity or Islam. They associate indigenous religious practice with "culture" or "custom", rather than with "religion". One consequence of this is that statistics about religious adherence are of limited use, especially because – in response to a question about their religion or faith – people are likely to consider only Christianity or Islam.

According to Ezra Chitando, Afe Adogame and Bolaji Bateye (2012, 6),

> whereas the study of religion in Europe [and America] has tended to be caught up in recondite methodological debates, the study of religion in Africa has been keen to describe religious vitality on the continent. Indeed,

contemporary Africa is the researcher's paradise: the numerous religions and ideologies of the world jostle for attention in a thriving market.

In this book, we follow this trend by not being preoccupied with the methodological and theoretical question of what religion *is*, but instead focusing on what religions *do* – both in the lives of practitioners and adherents, and of the community and society in which they are practised. This focus on what religions do is further introduced in Chapter 1 in relation to African indigenous religions, but we maintain that it is also useful to understand Christian and Islamic practice on the continent. One major advantage of this approach is that it immediately demonstrates that religions in Africa cannot be analysed in a Western secular framework that considers religion to be a distinct sphere of life, separate from, for instance, politics, economics, or popular culture. As Jacob Olupona argues, even if in Europe the separation of religion and politics, and of church and state, in many cases is more theoretical than actual,

> the fact that it is even believed to be possible – or desirable – reveals important Western assumptions about the nature of religion, especially as it pertains to communal life. … Religion in Africa remains the pulse of the private and public sphere … [and] it pervades the daily affairs and conduct of African societies.
>
> (Olupona 2014, 2)

The study of religion in Africa, according to Jan Platvoet's historical overview, has passed through a stage of "Africa as Object", where scholars from outside the continent tried to make sense of religious phenomena on the continent, to the stage of "Africa as Subject", where African scholars themselves increasingly participate in the production of knowledge about the religious traditions on the continent (Platvoet 1996). This development has given rise to a quest to define "African traditions in the study of religion in Africa", traditions that according to Chitando, Adogame and Bateye (2012, 9) centre on "rejecting and adjusting current theories and suggesting new approaches to the study of religion in the light of religious data in Africa", as well as on an "unrelenting focus on African issues". As an example of theories that need to be questioned, they refer to Western theories of secularization that are of very limited use in African contexts. Instead of being preoccupied with secularization, they argue that the study of religion in Africa should be focused on the vitality of religion and dynamics of religious change on the continent, as well as the interplay of religion and concrete social and political questions.

Although two of the three authors of this book cannot claim to be "African" themselves, we all are sympathetic to the "Africa as Subject" approach, develop theories and methodologies that emerge from the religious realities in Africa, and emphasize the significance of these realities for the understanding of "religion" more broadly. Hence, in various chapters we question dominant, Western-centred interpretations of certain phenomena. We also have endeavoured to acknowledge the contribution of African scholars to the study of religion on the continent by making use of their work.

How does context shape religions in Africa?

The premise of this book is that religions in Africa cannot be understood as separate from the cultural, economic and political spheres of life. This means that in order to understand religious realities, one has to engage the fuller picture of how African societies have evolved throughout history up to the contemporary moment. The chapters in this book make considerable reference to colonialism, because the history of European political domination in Africa has had a profound impact on African societies and political systems, as well as on religious practice. One important example was the pressure to convert to missionary Christianity as a means to entering the so-called modern world, in particular colonial education and employment opportunities. Today similar pressures to abandon traditional ideas and customs are part of the on-going process of globalization, in particular the extended reach of Western culture and interests.

We use the term post-colonialism to refer both to the period after independence, and to the body of critical theory concerned with understanding the lasting impact of colonization, as well as the ongoing colonial-like patterns in Africa. The book discusses several examples of the role that religions have played in colonial liberation movements as well as in shaping conceptions of African post-colonial identity. This brings us to the terms neo-colonialism and imperialism, which refer to the ways in which global economic and political power relations continue to shape the unequal relationships between Africa and "the West". In the discussion of economic issues in this book, the term neoliberal capitalism is frequently used. It refers to the global economic order in our contemporary world, characterized by economic liberalization policies such as deregulation, privatization, free trade and reductions in government spending, all of which aim to increase the role of the private sector in the economy and in society generally. These policies have often been imposed on Africa by Western institutions such as the World Bank and the International Monetary Fund, which in the 1980s forced debt-ridden African governments to accept so-called structural adjustment measures in order to reorganize their economies. Structural adjustment policies meant that African currencies were devalued overnight, leaving national economies practically bankrupt and creating major economic challenges for their people; simultaneously, the state governments were required to withdraw from providing social services in order to make room for "the market". The severe economic crises resulting from structural adjustment are often seen as a major cause of social unrest and political instability in Africa. They also represent the context that helps explain the emergence and widespread appeal of neo-traditional religious groups, revivalist Christian movements and reformist Islamic movements (see Chapters 4, 5 and 6).

What more is there to explore about religions in and from Africa?

A textbook like this is by definition introductory in nature. Although this book has sought to offer a comprehensive overview to religion in contemporary Africa, it remains an overview. As you may have noticed, this book lacks a concluding chapter. This is deliberate, to signal that we leave it to you to engage with the material – think about it, do further reading, discuss it, and reflect upon it. Leaving the material somewhat open-ended also serves to signal that the subject matter – religions in contemporary Africa – itself is highly dynamic, and that future developments are difficult to forecast. Thus, rather than "concluding" the book, at this point in the introduction we would like to suggest a few lines of inquiry that you could pursue in further studies.

First, each of the three major religious traditions covered in this book – indigenous religions, Christianity and Islam in Africa – presents a rich history and a fascinating diversity, which the chapters in this book have only begun to unfold. For any of these traditions, you could undertake a deeper study on their wide-ranging expressions of belief, ritual or other practice, and examine some of the complex ways in which they continue to play social, public or political roles in their contexts. In so doing we encourage you to avoid any monolithic representation of indigenous religions, Christianity or Islam, and to acknowledge instead the internal plurality of these traditions on the continent.

Secondly, in addition to these three major traditions, there are minor religious communities present in various parts of the continent, some of which have been there for a while, and others are relatively recent. Buddhism, Hinduism and Judaism are among the so-called world religions with a presence in Africa, and so are the Baha'i faith, Jainism and various Chinese and Japanese religions. Their consideration was beyond the scope of this book. The presence of these traditions in Africa is often the result of migration of adherents to the continent, but frequently they also attract a following among the local African population. Africa may be seen as a religious market place, a cross-roads of ideas and practices. Therefore, the longer-term potential of these minority religions to firmly establish themselves on the continent cannot be predicted.

A third line of inquiry that is also beyond the scope of this book but certainly noteworthy is the consideration of African religious thought and practice outside the continent. The major religious traditions on the continent – African indigenous religions, Christianity and Islam – have all spread to other parts of the world as a result of the transatlantic slave trade as well as more recent migration patterns (Trost 2007). African indigenous religions have given rise to fascinating religious cultures in the Americas and Caribbean, such as Candomblé (Brazil), Santería, also known as Lukumi (Cuba), Vodou (Haiti), to name only a few. These burgeoning traditions, collectively known as religions of the "African diaspora", are increasingly practised across the United States today by immigrants and converts alike. Likewise, the particular beliefs and practices of African Christians and Muslims have travelled with African migrants and settled with them in their new homes. African Pentecostal churches have actively sought to expand through mission activities and attain a global reach, a phenomenon sometimes referred to as "reversed mission". Olupona (2014, 112) refers to religions grounded in African indigenous traditions as "African diaspora religions" and to African-inflected Christianity and Islam as "African immigrant religions", although recognizing that these categories are "distinct but not entirely separate" from one another.

Finally, one might consider the theoretical implications of religious phenomena in Africa. In other words, one may profit from asking how they impact (or should impact) the understanding of the category of religion more generally, and what Africa contributes to the study of religion as an academic field. These are questions that this book has only begun to address.

What did we learn by writing this book?

As authors we learned a lot through the process of writing this book. We learned from one another, as our expertise was complementary both in terms of religious traditions, regional contexts and specific topics and approaches. Even when writing on matters with which we were familiar, working on this book as a teaching tool forced us to engage with the latest research and develop new insights. New knowledge is constantly being produced, and each new study of particular aspects of religious life in contemporary Africa enriches and nuances existing knowledge. Where academic scholarship, including our own research, tends to be very niche – that is, concerned with very specific issues, localities and traditions – writing this book challenged us to develop a broader understanding of our work and situate it in a general overview. Putting it in a broader continental perspective and discovering historical dis/continuities as well as dis/similarities among regions has been very rewarding, and our specialist knowledge and understanding was enriched.

Thus, writing a textbook which by its very nature is an overview has forced us to keep an eye on the general picture while bringing our specializations to the work. It has also helped us to develop a fuller understanding of the inter-relationship among the religions in African societies in relation to a whole range of critical and current issues, such as development and politics, gender and sexuality.

We hope that reading the fruit of our labour will be equally rewarding for you, that it will help you develop an understanding of religions in contemporary Africa and a more comprehensive view of why they matter. Above all, we aimed for this book to be an invitation for a continued engagement with this fascinating subject. We invite you to think about the role of the religions that we present here while watching the news and hearing about current affairs on the continent. We invite you to think about the representation of religion while enjoying the increasing body of African literature, music or films produced on the continent. We invite you, while planning your next holiday, to consider travelling to any part of the continent and to discover yourself the realities, particular religious histories and contemporary dynamics of the religions of Africa.

References (*indicates recommended reading)

Benjamin, Jesse. 2006. "Antiquity." In *Encyclopedia of African American History, 1619–1895* (vol. 1), edited by Paul Finkelman, 73–77. Oxford: Oxford University Press.

Blakely, Thomas, Walter van Beek, and Dennis Thomson, editors. 1994. *Religion in Africa: Experience and Expression*. London: James Currey.

*Bongmba, Elias, editor. 2012. *The Wiley-Blackwell Companion to African Religions*. Malden: Wiley-Blackwell.

Carmody, Pádraig. 2011. *The New Scramble for Africa*. Cambridge: Polity Press.

*Chidester, David. 1996. *Savage Systems: Colonialism and Comparative Religion in Southern Africa*. Charlottesville: University Press of Virginia.

Chitando, Ezra, Afe Adogame, and Bolaji Bateye. 2012. "Introduction." In *African Traditions in the Study of Religion in Africa*, edited by Ezra Chitando, Afe Adogame and Bolaji Bateye, 1–16. Farnham: Ashgate.

Ellis, Stephen, and Gerrie ter Haar. 2004. *Worlds of Power: Religious Thought and Political Practice in Africa*. London: Hurst & Co.

Mbembe, Achille. 2001. *On the Postcolony*. Berkeley: University of California Press.

Mudimbe, V.Y. 1988. *The Invention of Africa: Gnosis, Philosophy and the Order of Knowledge*. Bloomington: Indiana University Press.

Olupona, Jacob, editor. 2000. *African Spirituality: Forms, Meanings and Expressions*. New York: Crossroad.

Olupona, Jacob. 2014. *African Religions: A Very Short Introduction*. Oxford: Oxford University Press.

Parker, John, and Richard Rathbone. 2007. *African History: A Very Short Introduction*. Oxford: Oxford University Press.

Platvoet, Jan. 1996. "From Object to Subject: A History of the Study of Religions of Africa." In *The Study of Religions in Africa: Past, Present and Prospects*, edited by Jan Platvoet, James Cox and Jacob Olupona, 105–138. Cambridge: Roots and Branches.

Ray, Benjamin. 2000. *African Religions: Symbol, Ritual, and Community*. Upper Saddle River: Prentice Hall.

*Reid, Richard. 2012. *A History of Modern Africa: 1800 to the Present*. Malden: Wiley-Blackwell.

Stokes, Jamie. 2009. "The Geography of Africa." In *Encyclopedia of the Peoples of Africa and the Middle East*, edited by Jamie Stokes, 764–767. New York: Facts on File.

Trost, Theodore Louis, editor. 2007. *The African Diaspora and the Study of Religion*. New York: Palgrave Macmillan.

Worldometers. 2018. Africa Population. http://www.worldometers.info/world-population/africa-population/ (accessed 26 June 2018).

Part I

Religious Traditions and Trends in Africa

1 African indigenous religions

Problems of terminology and approach

As we begin considering the indigenous religious traditions of Africa, the first order of business is to recognize that scholars and students bring certain assumptions to the study, largely introduced through the terms we use unself-consciously. Unless we take note of these terms and their nuances, we risk importing distorting biases.

Some literature refers to African Traditional Religion in the singular, often using the abbreviation ATR. Pioneers on the subject, like E. Bọlaji Idowu (1973) and John S. Mbiti (1975), defined the subject in this way. They attempted to consolidate the many diverse traditions on the continent to show them as offering a systematic philosophy that is commensurate with other world religions. Seemingly more intent on fostering respect for Africa than conveying the substance of its religious realities, they emphasized features consistent with Christian doctrine, such as belief in a Supreme Being, and characterized "African Religion" as essentially monotheistic. They also underplayed the degree to which religious identity and ethnicity are inextricably entwined, and the multiplicity of religious ideas and practices on the continent. By contrast, in this chapter, we intentionally refer to African indigenous religions in the plural. Although there are common features or themes among them, Africa's innumerable traditions demonstrate the tremendous capacity of the religious imagination to create diverse but equally meaningful and effective systems of belief.

The use of the term "traditional" is also problematic. It suggests that African religions are fixed and timeless, or not part of modernity. In reality, African religions are dynamic and reflect the historical circumstances and lived experiences of their practitioners. Moreover, they are still a vital part of contemporary Africa. Therefore we prefer the term "indigenous".

"Indigenous" refers to that which is original and intrinsic to a place. What is indigenous is local, as opposed to imported or transplanted, foreign, or alien; locality lends a distinctive and deeply rooted character to all that naturally belongs to it. Indigenous does not mean "primitive", in the sense of crude, rudimentary, undeveloped or unsophisticated. In the past other terms adopted to refer to the local nature of the religions of Africa were tainted by this nuance.

"Native" is one of them. It too means, "originating in the place where found". Narratives of explorers, missionaries and colonialists about "natives", depicted as unsophisticated and credulous people, created the sense that all things native are necessarily simplistic. Native practices and indigenous traditions are not inferior or embryonic forms of greater ones. Nor are African traditions obsolete and destined to be surpassed. Although some scholars predicted that indigenous religions would disappear in the wake of the impact of so-called world religions and their cosmopolitan influence, history proved them to be wrong. Quite to the contrary, indigenous religions showed themselves to be innovative, adaptive and therefore tenacious (see Chapter 4). The beliefs and values, customs and rituals that have been so critical to the establishment of ethnic identity are as important as ever for establishing a meaningful orientation in an ever-changing world. They continue to inform the contemporary social imaginary. They constitute an active heritage that is self-consciously responsive to history.

What may be most surprising is that another problematic word is "religion". Scholars of religious studies were slow to acknowledge and classify African indigenous systems of belief and practice as "religion". They simply did not appear to fit the Western image of what "religion", conceived as institutionalized doctrine existing apart from the rest of social life, should look like. Criteria that supposedly define religion are absent from African religions:

1   There are *no historical founders* (like Jesus or the Buddha); instead anonymous ancestors are recognized as the founders and guardians of the moral order.
2   Although there are religious specialists, like priest(esses), diviners and healers, there is *no ultimate religious authority* (such as the Pope or an Imam) that protects orthodox claims or maintains an exclusive circle of the faithful. The focus of African religions is not doctrine but adherence to communal ritual practice, which favours inclusive participation.
3   There are *few permanent structures of worship* such as temples, mosques or churches; shrines and altars are typically not imposing or permanent structures.
4   There are *no sacred scriptures*. Oral literature including mythology, epic tales, praise poetry, and proverbs are integral to African traditions. They relate sacred histories, laud culture heroes, relate critical values and transmit wisdom, but they are first and foremost embodied and performed in ritual contexts.

While the differences of form are significant, rather than disqualifying African traditions because they do not fit the Western category of what religion should look like, it is more profitable to shift the criteria by which we understand the category "religion". Religions are complex systems of thought and practice that convey foundational ideas in ways that allow adherents to experience them as a compelling ground of being. Instead of asking what religions *are*, we focus on what religions *do*: (1) They *orient* practitioners to what is sacred and significant; (2) they *reveal and engage* the invisible sources of spiritual power; (3) they *distinguish adherents* by establishing their unique identity in relation to divinity, and (4) they *empower practitioners* to act as self-conscious, ethical agents, allowing them to shape and transform their lives in conformity with ultimate values.

Viewing religion as a dynamic and coherent system organized to achieve such ends can make it clear that African indigenous religions are indeed comparable to the so-called world religions. It also allows us to identify common ways of knowing and being without suggesting that Africa's traditions are all the same. It helps us avoid reifying "religion" as if it were a concrete institution, a thing apart from actual practice or separate from the living cultures in which they are embedded. It underscores that African religions are not fixed or timeless but vital and timely, shaped by experience and history.

Worldly and embodied

It is an often-repeated truism that African religions are pragmatic. Instead of looking forward to meeting God in heaven, devotees call divinity into *this world* to support them and their community. Rather than promises of rich rewards in the afterlife, the greatest spiritual blessings are this-worldly: health and long life; prosperity and proper social standing; fertility and offspring. African mythologies offer more than imaginative explanations of the world. They are a mode of reflection on its complex dynamics and the place of the human being in it. A Yoruba proverb says, "The world is a marketplace". It is a crossroads of divine and human activity and a place of constant negotiation. African indigenous religions provide systems of ethical guidance and choice, initiatory insight and teaching, healing and reconciliation. In other words, their complex systems of thought are oriented towards sustaining the human community and supporting its spiritual anchors.

Just as African indigenous religions are worldly, they are also embodied. The physical world is considered a manifestation of the invisible spiritual realm. It may well be that this emphasis on the intrinsic value of the physical world is one of the most distinctive contrasts between the "world religions" in Africa (Christianity and Islam), and indigenous religions. The "religions of the Book" give primacy to *time* as the sphere in which God is revealed. Their sacred scriptures chronicle human *history* as a means of tracing God's presence and knowing the divine will. By contrast, African indigenous religions look to *space* as the medium of divine revelation. The *cosmos* and the material world, including the human body, are imbued with significance as the locus of God's presence and the medium of divine guidance.

Ritual and the visual arts, concretely grounded in space, are therefore foundational to indigenous religions. Altars and power objects, like carved statuettes, do not only represent gods and spirits, but are mediums for making them appear and channel their power. They are not idols or icons, but "the material incarnation of the spirit itself" (Landry 2016, 55). Ritual's imaginative dynamics appeal to the body to enable participants literally *to make sense* of themselves and the world, and to situate themselves in it meaningfully (Grillo 2012). African rituals are replete with the sounds of drumming and song, the visual splendour of fantastic costumes, masks, painted bodies, or lavish adornment. Special foods and offerings are shared in feasts, or participants are required to fast. Some rituals inflict pain and permanently mark or transform the bodies of practitioners. African mythologies do not exist as a disembodied corpus, either. Myths are embedded into living practices and transmitted in vibrant spectacles, like masquerades. Through these embodied arts, abstract thought is transformed into tangible, lived experience that makes religious principles vivid and real. They are the means by which they are most effectively transmitted, not as transcendent ideals but as palpable truths and substantial commitments. Ritual is not devoid of thought; it is a form of reflection through bodily ways of knowing.

In what follows, we present some characteristic examples of the material and embodied forms of African religious thought, showing what the traditions *do* for practitioners and how they achieve the common aims of all religion. While many common ritual practices – like divination or masking – are detailed here, the aim is to show how they fit into an overarching religious system of thought. These practices should not be viewed as entirely separate or unconnected, but as components of an overarching way of understanding the world and being in it.

To orient: God, cosmos and the place of human beings

African cosmologies, myths about the creation of the world, underscore that God and the world exist together inextricably as "the spatio-temporal 'totality' of existence" (Wiredu 1998, 29). They resist the idea of a creator who generated the world directly and from nothing (creation *ex nihilo).* Rather than an abstract being acting outside of creation, God is the matrix of nature, time and space. No one overarching orthodoxy, text or set of mythologies provides this guiding orientation. But the innumerable myths of countless traditions reiterate similar concepts.

The Yoruba peoples of Nigeria are the largest ethnic grouping in that most populous nation in the most densely populated sub-region of West Africa. Yoruba thought maintains that *Olodumare*, the Supreme Being, is the coordinator of the dynamics of the universe. Invisible and so unfathomable as to be beyond identification with any particular place, Olodumare has no direct cult. By contrast, there are said to be 401 divinities (*orisha*) in the Yoruba pantheon to whom devotees may turn for spiritual support, a number meant to suggest that the divinities are ubiquitous and everywhere active in human affairs. The first 16 are said to have descended from the sky to the centre of the world to found the holy city, Ile-Ife. The secondary divinities may be local deities and spirits identified with sacred places such as important rivers, or associated with natural phenomena such as thunder. Or they may be deified culture heroes, legendary founders whose acts definitively shaped society. Constantly solicited for personal and collective welfare, their central place in the community is visible in the many shrines and altars consecrated to them.

The Akan peoples of Ghana and Côte d'Ivoire call God *Nyame*, meaning "Absolute satisfier", or *Onyankopon*, which means, "One who is alone great" (Wiredu 1998, 29). Such divinity is beyond personification or gender. Proverbs, legends and myths that constitute the body of Akan religious wisdom as it was revealed by the spirits and transmitted by ancestors are encoded in distinct designs of brass weights and figurines. The collection of these emblems, *thedja*, is wrapped in a package and treated as a sacred relic (Niangoran-Bouah 1973, 211–12). Despite such rich material imagery of spiritual power in Akan tradition, the creator God is never represented concretely. The strong belief that "the one who dwells on high" or "the High One" cannot be represented or contained was also dramatically demonstrated in Southern Africa by the open protest of the Batswana people against the missionaries' building of the first churches, for "there is no God (*Modimo*) for whom a house has to be built" (Ntloedibe quoted by Dube 2012, 127).

Early European writers surmised that the absence of a formal cult to the Supreme Being indicated that Africans believed that God was indifferent to the fate of human beings. That claim is clearly belied by the pivotal role that divination plays in African indigenous religions. Among the Yoruba, for example, *Olodumare* is the ultimate source of every individual's personal destiny, a path chosen before birth by the human soul. Divination provides the means to remember that destiny and get the spiritual guidance needed to fulfil it. Therefore the goodwill of God is not in doubt. Many African societies tell a strikingly similar, witty tale to explain why a benevolent God is nevertheless remote from human society. In West Africa, the Ashanti say that once the realms of heaven and earth touched, but whenever women pounded yams for food the upward thrust of the pestle knocked against the sky. Constantly annoyed by this, God retreated. Across the continent in East Africa, the Dinka have an almost identical story. Therefore, like the Ashanti, they call on the Creator only at the most dire of moments, turning more regularly to the lesser divinities for daily support. Nevertheless, the Ashanti Supreme Being *Nyam* is honoured with regular libations.

In many African cosmologies, the fullness of God is represented as a *twinned being*, simultaneously male and female, united in self-generating force. For the Ga people of Ghana, the name of this Supreme Being is *Ataa-NaaNyonmo*, or "The Male-Female One" (Oduyoye quoted by Dube 2012, 134). The idea of a *dual-gendered God* is widespread among Bantu groups in Central and Southern Africa too. Accordingly, *Maweja* created the world in two successive creations, a rainy season and a dry one, during which male and female beings were fashioned and paired as brother and sister, husband and wife (Mudimbe and Kilonzo 2012, 51). According to the mythology of the Chewa of Malawi, God is both male (in the sky) and female (in the earth). God is referred to both as *Chiuta*, the great rainbow, and *Namalango*, the earth-as-womb where seeds germinate and bear new life.

This motif of primordial twinship is prevalent in the mythology of Vodou, the religion of the Fon of Benin and Togo. *Nana Buluku* is the supreme deity who gave birth to *Mawu* the moon, *Lisa*, the sun, and the whole material universe. In other versions divinity was originally androgynous but split into the double-gendered Mawu-Lisa whose union generated seven other pairs of twins. These became the principal vodou, the gods on whom devotees call for succour. The last of the vodou to be born was Legba, a trickster associated with divination (see below). Yet more variations underscore that Mawu-Lisa shaped or ordered the world with the aid of the deity Da Ayido Hwedo, the rainbow serpent. It is not uncommon for multiple mythic versions and varying ideas about the nature of the creator god to exist simultaneously. Often more sophisticated ideas about divinity, creation and the place of the person in the cosmos are only revealed to those initiated into deeper levels of knowledge.

Despite the fact that African languages generally lack a gendered pronoun, Europeans consistently used the masculine pronoun "he" when they transcribed African myths about God. However, wherever myth refers to a self-generating God, that being brings forth elements and other beings from the primordial *womb*. An example is the mythology of the Luba, one of the largest ethnic groups from the Democratic Republic of the Congo, with roots in an ancient kingdom dating to the 5th century. It depicts *Kalowa* as "a She-God, unique and omnipotent … [as] the incarnation of knowledge" (Mudimbe and Kilonzo 2012, 51). That God is conceived to be variously gendered in African religious thought is significant. It is the foundation for alternative understandings of power in gender and relations between men and women (see Chapter 13). Beyond providing mere explanation (in the style of a "Just-so" story), myths are a form of religious thought with considerable consequence.

Tricksters: Co-creators and mediators

The famous myths of the Dogon of Mali include the motifs of God's originating womb, successive attempts at creation, and primordial twinship. They depict the cosmos as imperfect and relate that the creation is an ongoing dynamic in which humans continue to take part. Its corpus also presents a classic example of the trickster figure.

Feature: A Dogon Orienting Myth

According to Dogon mythology, creation was set in motion when sound made the primordial elements stir in the womb of God, *Amma*. This first attempt at creation failed because it lacked moisture. Amma's second attempt generated four sets of primordial twins, the *nommo*. One of them, the restless and disobedient *Ogo*, broke away from the womb prematurely. Dancing on a piece of the placenta, he fashioned a world of his own making. The complex mythology traces Amma's repeated attempts to rein in this cunning character who wreaks havoc on the original plan for the order of existence. Rather than destroy the desecrated world, Amma sacrificed Ogo's twin. This nommo's body was dismembered and scattered to form the cosmos. The sacrificial blood redistributed *nyama*, the vital force, to make this new world fecund and habitable. Amma punished Ogo by depriving him of teeth, tongue and speech – the source of the original creative stirring. Further abased, he was transformed into Yurugu, a fox. But ultimately, the mute Ogo was given an important role in the ongoing dynamic of the world. He serves as the harbinger of divination, the "language" through which God speaks to human beings and provides guidance. The Dogon call divination the "speech of Yurugu", and it involves the interpretation of paw prints left by an actual fox on divinatory tables traced in sand.

Ogo is a trickster, a type of mythic figure that is a divinity, cultural founder, and amusing folktale hero all in one. One of the most distinctive features of African mythology is the prominence of such tricksters as defining players in the cosmic drama. Embodying qualities of unpredictability, like deceit, humour, lawlessness and ribald sexuality, the trickster rebelliously disrupts the divinely ordained order and introduces chaos. But this audaciousness is not tragic. It ultimately brings forth new possibilities for creation.

A shape-shifting primordial being, the trickster is often associated with an animal form, like the crafty fox or the marvellously creative weaver, the spider. For the Akan, the most important mythological tales are called *anansesem*, stories of Kwaku Ananse, the spider trickster. However, the trickster is also the most like the human being in temperament: distrustful of and disobedient to God's will and always attempting to carve out a path of his own making. Tricksters stir up the unpredictable, interject the unexpected and thereby open the way to transformation. Therefore, they are often associated with divination. The Yoruba trickster, Eshu, is carved on the rim of all wooden divining trays, because Eshu is the messenger of the *orishas* and opens the way for these divinities to reveal the dynamics that are in play in the life of the client. The Fon trickster Legba also presides over divination. He translates for humans the otherwise cryptic message of *Mawu*.

The trickster is notoriously libidinous, with an insatiable sexual appetite, and in statuary is represented with an erect phallus. Legba is said to have penetrated the primordial goddess of destiny, Gbadu, who sat atop the palm tree.

[This] cosmic tree, whose roots are in the bowels of the earth and whose uppermost branches are in heaven, the axis mundi, which pierces through and joins together all levels of reality and ensures their harmonious movement around a single centre, is revealed to be nothing more or less than Legba's upright penis.

(Pelton 1992, 123)

The trickster is a clever fool, at once outrageously disruptive and creative, funny and full of earnest pathos. Ultimately, he is a co-creator who paves the way for humans to follow suit. The trickster figure, which features so widely in African mythologies and religious ritual traditions, orients adherents to a view of the universe as imperfect and unpredictable, subject to negotiation and modification, and a place of constant struggle and celebration.

To reveal and engage the invisibles

God and the divinities, ancestors and spirits are invisible, but they are revealed and engaged through vital ritual experience and powerful visual media. This section reviews common phenomena of this kind in African indigenous religions that actively connect spiritual and human realms: *divination; libation and sacrifice; statuary and power objects; and masquerades and secret masking societies.*

Divination

Divination is a complex and compelling system of thought as well as a pragmatic practice. In divination a ritual specialist (diviner) interprets or "reads" material signs or omens in order to obtain insight into troubles and determine a remedy for suffering. The methods vary and include the casting and interpretation of the pattern of the strewn objects (cowrie shells, kola nuts, stones, or bones), and sand-cutting in which the diviner interprets marks that he spontaneously draws in sand. Kuranko diviners in Sierra Leone cast river pebbles to "see" the sacrifice that must be performed to alleviate suffering. The Dogon of Mali read the paw prints of a fox left on divinatory tables traced on the ground. The Baulé of Côte d'Ivoire manipulate leather cordlettes on which are strung beads and other symbolic emblems. Another of their techniques is to read the gnawed grains left by a mouse in a diviner's carved vessel. In all cases diviners understand seemingly random physical arrangements to be messages from the gods intended to help the consulting client find the path to discernment and moral decision-making, to healing and the alleviation of suffering, to reconciliation, prosperity and other forms of social well-being.

More than mere fortune-telling, divination offers a client a diagnosis of the cause of his or her problems. A rupture within one's immediate family, a witch's spell, or a displeased ancestor may cause sickness or overturn fortunes. Spirits, which usually inhabit rivers, sacred groves, or other natural sites, are deemed to protect persons or lineages with whom they have made a pact. But they too may demand attention by bringing misfortune or come in dreams to disturb the mind. The gods provide protection, but if they are neglected or displeased, they can also disrupt devotees' lives. Therefore, every consultation ends with a prescription for sacrifice to repair relations and restore well-being. As Karamongo Abdoulayé, a diviner from Burkina Faso, explained, "Sacrifice is very important. Sacrifice – even one kola nut – can throw off the misfortune heading your way. Sacrifice sweeps away everything [evil] that might happen to you. It will cleanse you and keep you far from harm" (Grillo 2009, 931). Therefore, destiny is not a fixed fate. Divination allows one to navigate life's challenges. It shows that in African religions, persons have agency. Even the choice to consult a diviner is strategic. A consultation allows a client to envision new possibilities and to move "from inertia to purposeful activity" (Jackson 1989, 63). In other words, divination is empowering.

Feature: Ifa divination in Yoruba tradition in Nigeria

The Yoruba diviner is called the Priest of Ifa, and bears the title *babaláwo*, "father of secrets". The object of Ifa divination is to determine which of these divinatory signs apply to the situation of the client. In the most traditional form of Ifa, the diviner manipulates 16 palm nuts (*ikin*) to obtain the sign. After shaking the ikin between his cupped hands, he attempts to grab them all with the right hand. Invariably, some remain in the left. If two palm nuts remain, he makes a single mark on the divining tray which is sprinkled with sand or termite dust. If one palm nut remains, he will make a double mark. This is repeated until two rows of four marks are drawn on the tray's surface. The resulting paired arrangement is one of 256 possible signs, called *Odu*.

Each half of the sign is one of the 16 principal figures, named after the 16 primordial beings who descended to earth to do the bidding of the Creator God, *òrúnmìlà*. This pantheon of divinities became Yoruba ancestral kings and culture heroes, and their personal trials established the precedent for all human experience. The complete Odu is, in effect, an image of a meeting between two of these beings (yielding 256 possible alternatives). After casting the odu, the diviner recites the verses he knows that are associated it. The verses narrate the dynamic of the meeting between the two figures, and their struggles. They always include a description of the sacrifice that was offered to rectify their dilemma. Correlating the verses with the problem of the client, the babaláwo prescribes that same sacrifice. Therefore, knowledge of the verses is a critical aspect of a diviner's training.

A pioneering scholar of Yoruba divination, William Bascom, considered the verses to be the central component of the Yoruba divinatory enterprise, arguing that they "constitute their unwritten scriptures" (Bascom 1991, 11). However no one diviner knows a fixed set of verses. Rather what comprises Ifa's complete and fixed system is the order and arrangement of the odu. They are the "canon", the authoritative source for divine guidance and prescription for moral action (Grillo 2016). (See Figure 1.1.)

Not all African diviners are men. Among the Senufo, an ethnic group whose populations extend across northern Côte d'Ivoire, Burkina Faso and Mali, divination is a female enterprise governed by the *Sandogo* women's association (Hackett 1996, 122). In contrast with public divinatory displays conducted by men, *Sandogo* consultations are private.

Figure 1.1 Consulting Ifa with Babalawo Fayemi Fatunde Fakayode in Ile-Ife, Nigeria
(courtesy of Oluwabunmi Bernard, 2017)

Libation and sacrifice

Libation, the pouring of water or alcohol as a sacrificial offering, is a common
and daily practice. It is a way to recognize and honour the debt owed the
ancestors who peopled the world and transmitted their wisdom. Moreover, it is

a means of activating their spiritual power, and calling for their ongoing sustenance.

Given the regular and ubiquitous invocation of the ancestors, African indigenous religions have often been classified as "ancestor worship". While honouring them is critical for maintaining reciprocal relations between humans and the spiritual realm, these complex religious systems of thought and practice cannot be reduced to ancestor worship. The ancestors are considered the inaugurators of the founding moral order and acts of veneration stir the moral imagination and evoke ethical engagement.

Not all the dead become ancestors or are revered. Only those who lived a full measure of life, left descendants, cultivated moral values and achieved social distinction can attain this status. Those recently deceased who are still remembered are called the "living-dead" because they are believed to actively protect their kin. The more remote and anonymous ancestors ensure the continuity of the human community, granting fertility and bestowing blessings. They also bring misfortune, illness or even death to those who neglect or defy ethical mandates. Libation and sacrifice appease them and facilitate harmonious relations in the community.

Offerings are not necessarily blood sacrifices. For example, through much of West Africa, the first yam harvest is offered to the ancestors and local spirits in sacrifice. However in indigenous religions blood is the life force that "feeds" the spirits. A central tenet of the Vodou religion is the concept of *hun*, the vital force active in God, heart, blood, drums and bellows alike. "Like the circulation of blood and the [sound of the] beating of the heart ... *hun* is seen to be essential to human life and vitality" (Blier 1995, 82). Therefore, animal sacrifice is performed to activate, animate and renew the world, and to feed the spirits so that the human community can engage them.

Activating power objects

Africa is known for its figurative carvings. Their purpose is to give material substance to invisible spiritual intermediaries. More than just represent them, such objects channel their forces. Their power is activated by blood sacrifice or other acts that consecrate them.

In the Vodou religion, carved wooden statues, *bocio*, harness the power of ancestors and other spiritual beings for protection. Metal objects are attached to them to attract the spirits. The bocio are enhanced with "medicines", substances considered to possess magical properties. They are rubbed with palm oil as a propitiatory offering, giving these objects a polished patina. The Lobi of Burkina Faso also carve figures, called *bateba*, that channel the power of spirits. Once activated, the bateba are believed to be actual living beings able to act on behalf of their owners for aid and protection, or to harm enemies. But if they are neglected, they "die" (Hackett 1996, 52). An *nkisi* (plural, *Minkisi*) is a similar power object made by the BaKongo (Democratic Republic of the Congo). (See Figure 1.2.) These figures do not necessarily have human form, but

Figure 1.2 An Nkisi, power object, Republic of the Congo, mid-19th century (©The Art Institute of Chicago/Art Resource, NY)

are rather containers or supports for spiritually charged substances, such as amulets that contain grave-dirt to incorporate the dead, or other medicine bundles (MacGaffey 1988, 190). One striking type of nkisi has nails driven through it to activate its power. Considered particularly aggressive, these are thought to hunt and punish evil-doers. Minkisi are both portable altars and tools of ritual specialists who defend against witchcraft (see Chapter 7).

In Yoruba tradition human twins are considered living *orisha*, secondary divinities. They are believed to possess special powers and to bring good fortune to those who honour them properly. If one or both twins die, one or two memorial figures, *Ere Ibeji*, are commissioned under the guidance of an Ifa diviner, and cared for by the surviving twin or the mother. Treated as if they were alive, they are fed, clothed, sung to and prayed to. "They may be washed, oiled, rubbed with various substances ... adorned with jewellery, clothes ... and amulets" (Hackett 1996, 41). Such nurturing ritual attention assuages the twins' spirits and in return the *Ere Ibeji* protect and bless the family.

Nonfigurative art objects also mediate spiritual power. The stools of the Ashanti are venerated as the literal seats of the soul, imbued with the spiritual essence (*sunsum*) of its owner. Made of wood from a tree believed to be the abode of spirits, the stools are ceremonially blackened with a mixture of kitchen soot, spiders' webs, and eggs representing respectively wisdom, the subjugation of enemies, and peace (cf. Grillo 1999). Stools, like altars, bond and mediate the living and dead. Ancestral stools are the abode of the spirit of the departed and are blackened with egg yolk, soot, and sheep's blood in private domestic rituals (Patton 1979, 77). The famous Ashanti Golden Stool is the emblem of the nation, but it is not a literal seat or throne. Rather it is its spiritual support, enshrining fundamental Ashanti values.

All these examples demonstrate how ritual objects represent invisible spiritual entities, powers and ideals, and that they are used to empower adherents to engage them in support of the moral order. They embody otherwise abstract religious thought, and engage effective action.

Masks and secret masking societies

The performative art form for which Africa is perhaps most renowned is masking. Their dynamic appearance in masquerades embodies religious thought in visual form. Ancestors and other spirit beings may be represented in masking traditions, but contrary to popular thought, those who wear the masks do not always impersonate spirits, they are not possessed, nor is masked dancing a cathartic release. Usually the right to wear a mask is earned through initiation into a masking society in which one learns the meaning of its iconography, techniques for fabrication and the dance steps that must be rigorously followed. This knowledge constitutes the secret that the initiated members of the societies protect. Masking is therefore a sacred duty, not a frenzied liberation (Pernet 1992).

Masks are an important way of representing invisible spiritual beings and conceiving their powers. A widespread and important ritual in the Yoruba liturgical calendar is the annual festival, *Odun Egungun*, which honours patrilineal ancestors. Masks depicting them, the *Egungun*, are not carved face coverings, but full body costumes made of multiple layers of colourfully appliqued cloth. When they dance in swirling movements, the lifted layered skirts form changing visual patterns. Other maskers "magically" reverse the draped cloth of their costume while wearing it without revealing themselves underneath. The feat is meant to portray the ancestors' transformative power.

Many masks have no human features at all, for rather than representing beings of any kind, they transport complex religious ideas. Instead, masks are merely vehicles to carry and animate ornate carvings (Pernet 1992). These super structures allude to primordial beings, or visually convey critical ideas about the nature of power and its secret source. The costumes are equally important. The most spiritually charged part of the sacred *sirige* mask of the Dogon (Mali) is not the face covering but its red dyed raffia skirt that represents the potency of women's blood (Grillo 2012). Although the masquerades include dances and performances, they do not literally enact the stories of myth. For example, Dogon masked dancers reproduce primordial dynamics. They make towering masks seesaw back and forth and then swing in a circle to depict night and day and the spiralling that set creation in motion. It is a visual depiction of the ordered universe.

Another renowned masking tradition that does so is the *Gule Wamkulu* (Great Dance) of the Chewa and Mang'anja peoples of central Malawi and eastern Zambia. Its many different masks of humans, animals and spirits represent the unity of the whole world. Early missionaries documented their masquerades in 1862, describing them as "a powerful and frightening demonstration of the strength of Mang'anja religion" (de Aguilar 1994, 5).

The masking society, *nyau*, performs the *Gule Wamkulu* on the occasions of funerals, funerary memorials for the ancestors and initiations. Its masks portray the dead that return from their graves in tattered clothing (Yoshida 1993, 35). During the funerary period, women brew beer for the ceremony and joke with them to cajole the spirits of the deceased to depart (Yoshida 1993, 37). This enactment reveals and engages the invisibles, but moreover signifies the necessary distinction between the dead and the living.

Chewa oral histories date certain mask types to the 16th century Maravi (Malawi) Empire (de Aguilar 1994, 8). After the decline of the empire, the nyau secret society offered social stability, forging order on the basis of religious principles and moral sanctions. During the 19th century, the expanding slave trade further threatened social stability, as did the spread of Christian missionary teaching, the incursion of Swahili-Arabs, and British colonization. In this context the nyau secret society served to counter foreign domination and revive indigenous traditions. It was transformed from a masking society that was open exclusively to married men, to an institution that initiated all boys. The initiation was based on the girl's *chinamwali* initiation rite, which grounded Chewa matrilineal society (Kachapila 2006, 333). This history demonstrates that "traditional" societies remain fluid and resilient, but shows that adaptations are not necessarily always positive, however. "Chewa women seem to have lost their social status, and to an extent power, to men through nyau's involvement in chinamwali" (Kachapila 2006, 334). The men ceased to honour women, physically harassed and subjugated female initiates, and made them reveal the secrets of women's knowledge.

To distinguish adherents

Like all religions, African indigenous traditions *distinguish their adherents by establishing a special relationship between them and divinity.* This is typically accomplished through initiation, a prolonged rite of passage during which youth are made to understand and experience the power of the religious system. Initiatory rites are not necessarily conducted at the onset of puberty. Nevertheless, they are considered the means by which girls are made into women and boys made into men, that is to say cultivated persons prepared for the duties of adulthood and capable of handling spiritual knowledge. A ritual specialist or spiritual authority oversees this process. They are charged with protecting the initiates who are vulnerable during this ontological transition, a change from one state of being to another.

Initiates' radical shift into new being is likened to death. Indeed, the process may be physically dangerous. Often the neophytes' bodies are marked to signal the embodiment of their new knowledge and way of life. Some rites include scarification, an intentional design patterned on the skin to distinguish initiates' belonging to a particular group and as a permanent sign of their new identity in relation to divinity. Circumcision and excision ("female genital mutilation") are also common components of initiation (see Chapter 13).

Feature: The cinamwali female initiation

The Chewa girls' initiation ceremony, *cinamwali*, is a rite of passage that differentiates the genders by defining the exclusive domain of womanhood and its spiritual significance. Initiates are secluded in a special house for a period of time during which they are taught about sex and childbearing as well as sacred qualities of womanhood. It includes the injunction never to let men see the menstruation cloth, for women's blood is considered especially powerful and therefore dangerous (Harding 2013; see Chapter 13).

In the past, girls were instructed in making clay figures (*vilengo*) and the initiates would dance around them. Most figures were related to water, widely considered the abode of spirits and the domain from which women, too, emerged: the amphibious python, snake, crocodile, and tortoise. The python is also a messenger of God who brings rain to ensure the fertility of the land, and by association fecundity to women. Girls also made vessels for drawing water used to channel the reincarnation of ancestral spirits into the wombs of new brides (Hackett 1996, 110–11). These were among the "secrets" divulged to *Nyau* when the male masking society incorporated the rite of initiation for boys into its practice.

One of the best known of the secret initiatory societies in West Africa is *Poro* and its female counterpart, *Sande*, because it is a multi-ethnic, trans-national phenomenon extending across the western sub-region. It is so pervasive and influential as to have been considered a self-governing "stateless society" in its own right. Although Poro and Sande likely originated with the Mande people of Sierra Leone, neighbouring ethnic groups in Sierra Leone as well as Liberia, Guinea and Côte d'Ivoire adopted them. Sande is especially renowned because it is the only female masking society in the whole of Africa (see Chapter 13).

To empower

Religions honour the gods and ancestors, but they are also organized to empower practitioners. Adherents access sources of spiritual power, share in sacred knowledge, and benefit from the guidance necessary to shape their lives in accord with religious values. Of course divination, initiation, sacrifice, and masking traditions all empower individual practitioners this way. However one phenomenon, common in indigenous religions, stands out as a remarkable instance of empowerment: possession trance.

Possession trance

The most dramatic and intimate contact between devotee and divinity is possession. Entering a dissociative trance, the personal identity of the devotee is displaced, and succumbs to the influence of the spirit. The possessed is unaware of what transpires during this state and has no memory of events afterwards. Therefore possession does not immediately empower the individual. Instead, he or she acts as a conduit for the divinity to engage and serve the community.

The state of possession may be spontaneous and undesired. In such cases it is not considered evil, but is understood to be an affliction brought about by an attention seeking spirit. Submitting to the call to serve as a medium is the only cure. Muchona, an Ndembu informant (Zambia) described being seized by spirit possession:

> I was thrown on the mat by violent quivering. I jerked about very much. I did not know how I was doing it. It was on account of the power of *Kayong'u* which attacked me suddenly there … A person in this state [breaths with difficulty]. His ears are completely blocked. His eyes and his whole body are like those of a man who has drunk beer. He slips onto the ground in an epileptic fit.
>
> (Turner 1975, 256)

In many cases, ritual specialists rely on possession trance to do their spiritual work. In Central Africa, this is the case for the ritual healer, the *nganga*. Possession may be induced by absorbing psychotropic properties of "medicinal" plants, or through techniques that facilitate altered states of consciousness: rhythmic chanting, drumming and dance. For the Fon of Benin, the gods (*vodun*) are elicited in this way. Their devotees are called "horsemen" because when they fall into trance, the vodun "mount" them, taking possession of their bodies. When this happens the possessed subject behaves in accordance with mythology about the character of the god in question. The congregation recognizes, welcomes and honours the possessed as such. The embodied divinity interacts with the congregation, dancing with them and offering blessing and advice. Possession trance is therefore the palpable expression of the close, reciprocal relation between the devotee and the gods. In this state the devotee can be considered a "living altar".

Conclusion

African indigenous religions are diverse and complex systems that show this world to be a dynamic one in which divinities and humans are engaged as mutually dependent co-creators. Pragmatic and worldly, the traditions provide means for adherents to identify with spiritual sources of power, and to harness and channel that vital force for their own well-being and for that of the community. African religions endure as vital realities on the contemporary scene. Their concepts and practices have not disappeared with "modernity", but continue to adapt, thrive and even influence the practice of other religions on the continent and around the world.

Questions for discussion

- What is the difference between religion and cultural custom? If an African Christian or Muslim pours libation to honour the ancestors, is s/he practising African indigenous religion? Is it an act of worship?
- How do Christianity and Islam *orient* adherents, *reveal* divinity, *distinguish* practitioners and *empower* them? What aspects are unique or comparable to African indigenous religions?

References (*indicates recommended reading)

*Bascom, William. 1991 [1969]. *Ifa Divination: Communication between Gods and Men in West Africa*. Bloomington: Indiana University Press.

*Blier, Suzanne. 1995. *African Vodun: Art, Psychology, and Power*. Chicago: University of Chicago Press.

de Aguilar, Laurel Birch. 1994. "Nyau Masks of the Chewa: An Oral Historical Introduction", *The Society of Malaŵi Journal* 42/2, 3–14.

Dube, Musa. 2012. "Postcolonial Feminist Perspectives on African Religions." In *The Wiley-Blackwell Companion to African Religions*, edited by Elias K. Bongmba, 127–139. Malden, MA: Wiley-Blackwell.

Grillo, Laura. 1999. "African Religions." *Encyclopedia Britannica Online*. Chicago: Encyclopedia Britannica, Inc. https://www.britannica.com/topic/African-religions

Grillo, Laura. 2009. "Divination: Epistemology, Agency and the Construction of Identity in Contemporary West Africa", *Religion Compass* 3/6, 921–934.

Grillo, Laura. 2012. "African Rituals." In *The Wiley-Blackwell Companion to African Religions*, edited by Elias Bongmba, 112–126. Malden: Wiley-Blackwell.

Grillo, Laura. 2016. "Signs, Doors and Games: Divination's Dynamic Visual Canon." In *Ifá Divination, Knowledge, Power, and Performance*, edited by Jacob K. Olupona and Rowland Abiodun, 308–324. Bloomington: Indiana University Press.

*Hackett, Rosalind. 1996. *Art and Religion in Africa*. New York: Cassell.

Harding, Frances. 2013. *The Performance Arts in Africa: A Reader*. Abingdon: Routledge.

Idowu, Bọlaji. 1973. *African Traditional Religion: A Definition*. Maryknoll, NY: Orbis Books.

Jackson, M. 1989. *Paths toward a Clearing: Radical Empiricism and Ethnographic Inquiry. African Systems of Thought*. Bloomington: Indiana University Press.

Kachapila, Hendrina. 2006. "The Revival of 'Nyau' and Changing Gender Relations in Early Colonial Central Malawi", *Journal of Religion in Africa* 36/3–4, 319–345.

*Landry, Timothy. 2016. "Incarnating Spirits, Composing Shrines, and Cooking Divine Power in Vodún", *Material Religion* 12/1, 50–73.

MacGaffey, Wyatt. 1988. "Complexity, Astonishment and Power: The Visual Vocabulary of Kongo Minkisi", *Journal of Southern African Studies* 14/2, 188–203.

Mbiti, John. 1975. *Introduction to African Religion*. London: Heinemann Educational.

Mudimbe, V.Y., and Susan Mbula Kilonzo. 2012. "Philosophy of Religion on African Ways of Believing." In *The Wiley-Blackwell Companion to African Religions*, edited by Elias Bongmba, 41–61. Malden, MA: Wiley-Blackwell.

Niangoran-Bouah, Georges. 1973. "Symboles institutionnels chez les Akan", *L'Homme* 13/1–2, 207–232.

Patton, Sharon. 1979. "The Stool and Asante Chieftaincy", *African Arts* 13/1, 74–99.

Pelton, Robert. 1992. *The Trickster in West Africa: A Study of Mythic Irony and Sacred Delight*. Berkeley: University of California Press.

Pernet, Henry. 1992. *Ritual Masks: Deceptions and Revelations* (transl. by Laura Grillo). Columbia: University of South Carolina Press.

Turner, Victor. 1975. *Revelation and Divination in Ndembu Ritual*. Ithaca, NY: Cornell University Press.

*Wiredu, Kwasi. 1998. "Toward Decolonizing African Philosophy and Religion", *African Studies Quarterly* 47/1, 17–46.

Yoshida, Kenji. 1993. "Masks and Secrecy among the Chewa", *African Arts* 26/2, 34–92.

2   Christianity in Africa

Is Christianity an African religion?

Christianity is often considered a Western religion. This is understandable from the historical trajectory in which Christianity, early in Christian history, settled in Europe and from there begun to spread to other parts of the world, including Africa, in the modern era. However, this is only one trajectory in the history of Christianity. In fact, Christianity both historically and to date is much more diverse and cannot be reduced to the label of being a Western religion. This chapter argues that there are good reasons to think about Christianity as an African religion. There are several arguments for this: first, the history of Christianity in Europe is intricately connected to the African continent, especially Egypt and North Africa; second, since early Christian history there have been Christian traditions on the African continent that existed more or less independently from the West, and some of these thrive until today; third, those strands of Christianity that were introduced to Africa by the West have found a home on the continent and in different ways have "Africanized", that is, they have integrated African views and practices; fourth, there are significant African initiatives in Christianity. The present chapter provides the necessary historical background to Chapter 5, which has a focus on contemporary forms of Christianity in Africa. Together, both chapters provide insight into the diverse and unique manifestations of Christianity on the continent.

Early roots of Christianity in Africa

Since the 1st century of the Christian calendar, there has been a continuous presence of Christianity on the African continent (Isichei 1995). The history of Christianity in Africa begins in Egypt – the country where Jesus himself, when still an infant, together with his parents sought refuge while King Herod was slaughtering the innocents in Bethlehem (according to the biblical account in Matthew 2: 13–23). A couple of decades later, a group of Jewish converts to Christianity with direct links to the apostles formed the first church on the continent, in the coastal city of Alexandria in Egypt.

According to some historians, the first bishop of Alexandria was ordained in the year 62 by the apostle Mark. Alexandria was an important cultural and intellectual centre in the Greek-speaking (Hellenistic) world of the time, and in the 2nd century it developed into the most important centre of Christian theology with legendary figures such as Clement (150–215), Origen (184–254) and Athanasius (296–373). From Alexandria, the Christian faith spread further into Egypt, where the non-Hellenized, Coptic-speaking population started to convert, and to North Africa, where the Latin-speaking cities of Carthage (in what is known today as Tunisia) and Hippo (in contemporary Algeria) also became important Christian centres. Each of these three cities was part of the Roman Empire which dominated the whole Mediterranean region, and where Christianity under the reign of Constantine the Great in the early 4th century became the dominant religion. In other words, the Christian centres in Egypt and North Africa played a leading role in the universal church at the time. Its leading figures – not the least of whom is Augustine (354–430) who served as Bishop of Hippo – greatly influenced the development of Christian thought, to such an extent that they are now seen as important church fathers of Western Christianity. However, on the basis of their geographical location they were Africans and therefore have been claimed to be the first African theologians, in the same way as ancient North African Christianity has been claimed to be a crucial part of the narrative of African Christianity. David Ngong (2017, 2) reminds us that the division of the continent into North and sub-Saharan Africa, and leaving out the former in the history of Christianity on the continent, reflects an "ideological separation of a geographically and historically unified continent that share much in common". Clearly, we touch here on the question of the definition of "African". What matters at this point, however, is that the history of Western Christianity is intricately connected to the African continent.

For six centuries the church flourished in North Africa and Egypt (Youssef 2016). In the latter country, the church had become more and more Coptic-speaking – that is, the liturgy was celebrated, and the Bible was translated, in an indigenous African language. The Coptic Church also developed a strong monastic tradition of committed Christians choosing to live in isolation, or in small communities, to lead a life of prayer and contemplation. This monastic model is sometimes seen as the greatest contribution ancient African Christianity has made to the universal church. Importantly, missionaries from Egypt also started to spread the Christian faith deeper into Africa, in the region then known as Nubia (contemporary Sudan) and Ethiopia. The resulting churches in these countries held close links to the Coptic Church in Egypt, as they fell under the authority of the Patriarch of Alexandria.

The ancient traditions of African Christianity were heavily affected by the advent of Islam through Arabic invasion from about the year 640 (see Chapter 3). In most countries in North Africa Christianity disappeared completely, one reason being that the church there had failed to indigenize as it was Latin speaking and Greco-Roman in its cultural orientation. In Egypt the church was reduced to a minority, and has remained so until today. Nubian Christianity flourished much longer, with a Christian kingdom being firmly established between 700 and 1200, but it was then weakened by Arab settlement and Islamization until the church finally collapsed in the early 16th century. Ethiopia, too, was affected by the advent of Islam, but Christianity there was strongly rooted in the psyche of the people, and to date the Orthodox Church has remained strong. Both the Egyptian and the Ethiopian church have historically been relatively isolated from Christianity in the Western world, and their ongoing existence means that there have always been living Christian traditions on the African continent independent from the West.

Feature: Ethiopian Orthodox Christianity

Ethiopia, a country in the Horn of Africa, is the home of an ancient but still thriving Christian tradition. Fascinatingly, Ethiopian Christianity even claims to have pre-Christian roots. Legend has it that the Queen of Sheba, who according to the Hebrew Scriptures (what Christians call the Old Testament) visited King Solomon in Jerusalem, was from Aksum, and that the son born out of their encounter brought the Ark of the Covenant to this Ethiopian city, where it is preserved in a church to date. This son, Menelik I, was the first king in the Solomonic dynasty that ruled over Ethiopia, with some interruptions, until Emperor Haile Selassie (1892–1975). Whatever the truth of this legend, Ethiopian Christianity observes several Hebrew customs. The advent of Christianity in Ethiopia is also claimed to have biblical roots: the eunuch who according to the New Testament was baptized by the apostle Philip is believed to be from Ethiopia and to have brought the Christian faith to his home country. Indeed there is evidence that a Christian community was established in Aksum very early in Christian history. From around the year 500 the country as a whole became evangelized by monks from Egypt. Since then, the Ethiopian Orthodox Church has held strong ties with the Coptic Church in Egypt and came under the authority of the Patriarch of Alexandria. Only in 1959 did the Church in Ethiopia gain full autonomy. Theologically, both the Ethiopian and the Coptic Church belong to the monophysite tradition, holding the belief that Christ has only one (combined divine and human) nature.

In addition to Aksum, the town of Lalibela – with its world-famous 12th century rock-hewn churches built to create a second Jerusalem – is a key historical site of Ethiopian Orthodoxy and an important centre of pilgrimage to date. Thanks to its long history, Christianity is deeply intertwined with Ethiopian culture and identity. Throughout the ages the Church played a pivotal role in building and unifying Ethiopia "by providing the evolving Christian nation with powerful symbolic and ideological frames" (Ancel and Ficquet 2015, 63). This was particularly important as the country became increasingly surrounded by Islamic neighbours. Its strong ties to the monarchy rendered the Church vulnerable to political upheaval, especially in the

20th century when Ethiopia went through a revolution and became a secular republic. Alongside a significant Muslim minority, the country nowadays also accommodates a growing group of Protestant and Pentecostal Christians. Although the Orthodox Church has lost its religious monopoly, about half of the population – that is, an estimated 45 million Ethiopians – are Orthodox and the Church is still firmly established in society.

Ethiopian Christianity is fascinating because it presents a unique, age-old African form of Christian faith. Indigenous musical instruments such as drums are used in worship to accompany liturgical dances. Exorcism is a common ritual practice, reflecting a worldview in which evil spirits or demons are believed to have real power (similar to contemporary Pentecostal-Charismatic forms of Christianity, see Chapter 5). Traces of indigenous religion remain visible, such as in the animal sacrifices at the dedication of a new church. Ethiopian painted and carved icons of the Trinity, Christ and Mary often depict these divine figures as black, thus presenting an African artistic representation of the Christian faith.

In the colonial and post-colonial era, Ethiopia as a country that was never colonized (although occupied by Italy from 1936 to 1941) became an important symbol of African pride for the rest of the continent suffering from European imperialism. Likewise, the Ethiopian Church as an age-old, indigenous and independent form of Christianity became an important symbol for the African independent churches that broke away from the European-established mission churches on the continent. Clearly, Ethiopian Orthodoxy presents a unique and fascinating tradition of African Christianity. (See Figure 2.1.)

Figure 2.1 Ethiopian Orthodox priests in Lalibela (Adriaan van Klinken, 2016)

Missionary Christianity

After discussing the first, ancient phase of Christianity in Africa, it is tempting to move directly to the phase of modern Christianity that was introduced in much of sub-Saharan Africa in the 19th century era of European exploration and colonization. However, it is worth mentioning that in between these two phases there has been yet another Christian movement: the early introduction of European Christianity in settlements on the coast of the continent, from the 15th to the 17th century. In this period, Europeans, in particular the Portuguese, discovered the "new world", not only the Americas but also Africa. Small settlements for trade were set up on the west coast in regions now known as Mauritania, the Gambia, Benin and Ghana, and later also in south-western Africa, in what is now Angola and the Democratic Republic of the Congo, and south-eastern Africa, in what is now Mozambique and Tanzania. In this phase, the Christian faith hardly penetrated the heartlands of the continent, and even at the coast it did not take strong roots. The major exception is the Kingdom of Kongo, which was Christianized in the 16th century after the Portuguese managed to convert the king. This presents an early example of "authentic and indigenized African Christian engagement", not least because the Portuguese and the Kongolese shared similar cosmologies, concerned with the effect of the supernatural world on matters of daily life (Fretheim 2016, 97). Evangelism was part of the motive for the "African expeditions", which were officially supported by the Catholic Church, although this motive was later obscured (not least by the growing involvement in the Atlantic slave trade). One of the visible remnants of this era is the Elmina slave castle on the Ghanaian coast, built by the Portuguese and later run by the Dutch and, subsequently, the British. The castle has a church built right on top of the dungeon where the captured slaves were imprisoned.

In the 18th century, European societies such as Britain, Germany and France not only witnessed industrialization and rapid socio-economic change, but also a significant religious transformation in the form of emergent evangelical movements in the Protestant churches. These movements were characterized by a strong emphasis on personal faith, a committed Christian life and a great missionary zeal. Especially in Britain, they also adopted a strong abolitionist stance, that is, they actively opposed slavery. This Protestant revival led to the establishment of various missionary societies that from the turn of the 19th century started working in Africa, such as the Baptist Missionary Society (founded in 1792), the London Missionary Society (1795), the Basel Mission (1815) and the Paris Mission (1822). A few decades later, from the 1840s, Catholics also became active in Africa, through a range of missionary congregations established in France and to a lesser extent Italy, Belgium and Germany, as well as in Britain (e.g. the Mill Hill Missionary Society, established in London in 1866). One prominent Catholic group was the White Fathers, also known as the Missionaries of Africa, founded in 1868 in Algiers, Algeria, and active on the continent to date. Because different missionary societies and congregations became active in different parts of Africa, the denominational diversity (or fragmentation) characterizing European Christianity was exported to Africa. Often this gave rise to competition, especially when in the course of the 19th century the mission fields became more densely populated.

It is often suggested that European mission in Africa was part and parcel of colonialism, yet in fact the missionary movement emerged before the colonial occupation of the continent began. In the 19th century, at the beginning of which Africa was still largely unknown territory for Europeans, missionaries benefited from the geographical explorations through which the heartlands of the continent were entered. Some missionaries became explorers themselves, such as the famous David Livingstone (1813–1873) who in the 1850s was the first European to make a transcontinental journey through southern and central Africa. When in the late 19th and early 20th centuries the colonial "Scramble for Africa" took place, with European powers dividing and occupying most of the continent and subjecting it to their rule, the missionary enterprise was already well under way. However, it is certainly true that the success of the various missions, and the establishment of Christian churches, benefited from colonial infrastructure of roads and railways, military control, the imposition of a uniform administration, as well as colonial systems of education and health-care. The missionary enterprise thrived throughout the colonial period, till the 1960s/70s when most African countries gained independence. Moreover, colonial attitudes – such as a sense of white European superiority vis-à-vis black African "natives" – were certainly not alien to the missionaries. Like the cultural politics of colonialism generally, missionary Christianity disparaged African customs, such as polygamy, and indigenous religious practices such as the veneration of ancestors. Missionaries instilled in Africans the idea that becoming Christian meant to become "civilized" (that is, Europeanized). Moreover, conversion gave access to education and employment opportunities under the colonial system.

So far, our account has been rather Eurocentric, as if the introduction of modern Christianity in Africa was dominated by European (and later also Euro-American) initiatives, and as if Africans themselves were largely passive receivers of the Christian faith. Such an account can be rightly critiqued for being one-sided and reductionist. Two dimensions need to be foregrounded to counter-balance the picture and to acknowledge what is called African agency in the story of modern African Christianity:

- First, Africans who converted to Christianity often became actively involved in missionary activities – as teachers in mission schools, as evangelists and lay preachers. Having the advantage of speaking the local languages and understanding the culture, they often were rather successful in making new converts. At the same time, they frequently found themselves in a delicate position, caught between the communities they came from, and the European missions they were associated with. They had to navigate the social and cultural tensions inherent to the mission field, and to negotiate their loyalties and identities.

• Second, in some parts of Africa, mission activities were in fact initiated by Christians from African descent. The liberated slaves from Britain, America and Jamaica, who from the late 18th century settled in Sierra Leone and Liberia, founded their own churches and started missionary work. This added an important black element to the story of the spread of Christianity in Africa. The colour of their skin did not always prevent these black ex-slaves from sharing the negative perceptions of African indigenous cultures and religions common among white missionaries, and they typically subscribed to the notion of mission as a form of Western civilization. At the same time, the presence of a black missionary movement was also empowering to African Christians, as it provided them with a basis for resisting white domination and developing a sense of black African identity (in a movement that became known as "Ethiopianism", claiming Ethiopia as a symbol of African pride and Christian identity).

Later in this chapter we discuss how missionary Christianity in the 20th century has been "Africanized", but first we attend to another phenomenon.

African initiated Christianity

From around the turn of the 20th century, a major development took place in the African appropriation of the Christian faith as introduced by the missionaries: the emergence of indigenous revival movements and churches. Various terms have been used to describe this phenomenon, the most common being "African independent churches", emphasizing their independence from the European missionary founded churches, "African indigenous churches", foregrounding their attempt to indigenize Christianity, or "African initiated churches", emphasizing African agency and initiative. The latter has become most widely accepted, but helpfully the acronym AIC can refer to each of these terms. The AICs form a fascinating and important part of the recent history of Christianity in Africa. Allan Anderson (2001), has referred to their emergence as an "African Reformation", of comparable significance as the Protestant Reformation in Europe four centuries earlier. What, then, are these AICs, and why are they so important?

Anderson, in his important study on African initiated Christianity in the 20th century, distinguishes three different types of AICs (while at the same time acknowledging that any typology is always a simplification, as the AICs are enormously diverse and dynamic).

• The first group, referred to as African or Ethiopian churches, emerged from the late 19th century. These churches "arose primarily as political and administrative reactions to European mission-founded churches" while at the same time they were "very similar to the churches from which they emerged" (Anderson 2001, 15). This may sound paradoxical. They had seceded from the white missionary-led churches in part because black

African Christians were often barred from fully ordained leadership; however, the founders of this type of AICs had usually received their training in the mission churches, where they had served as preachers, evangelists and elders. Once they had established their own churches, they continued much of the theology, liturgy and practices of the missionary Christianity with which they were familiar. Therefore, the most distinctive characteristic of these churches was the racial profile of their leadership and pro-African political stance, which is why they have been called, and sometimes called themselves, "African" or "Ethiopian" churches. Their anti-colonial and anti-missionary focus made them less relevant in the second half of the 20th century, when they were largely overshadowed by another group of AICs that presented a more radical transformation of African Christianity.

- The second group, referred to as Prophet-Healing or Spiritual Churches, emerged from the early 20th century. This is the largest and most significant group of AICs. They are characterized by a strong emphasis on spiritual power, that is, the workings of the Holy Spirit, such as healing and prophecy – an emphasis that is in line with indigenous religious cosmologies, although these are reframed here in a Christian idiom. Although the spiritual churches tend to reject certain traditional religious practices such as ancestor rituals and divination, "these churches have possibly adapted themselves to and addressed the popular African worldview more substantially than other types of churches have, and that is their unique contribution towards understanding Christianity in Africa" (Anderson 2001, 18). This is because they take seriously the spiritual concerns and anxieties that many Africans have – such as fears about witchcraft and spirit possession – and provide a Christian "solution" through the Holy Spirit. There is a lot of diversity within this group of AICs, but many of them use uniforms for their members, typically white robes; in their healing practices, they often use symbolic objects such as ash, fruits, blessed water, staffs, ropes and papers; they often prohibit their members from consuming alcohol, tobacco and pork, in line with the Hebrew Bible's prescriptions, while in keeping with those same scriptural teachings they sometimes allow polygamy; a good number prefer to pray and worship in the wilderness rather than in church buildings. Where the mission churches are usually defined by a concern with *orthodoxy* (Christian doctrine/dogma), these churches are characterized by a concern with *orthopraxis* (practice and experience of the Christian faith). Well-known examples of this type of AICs are the Kimbanguist Church in the Democratic Republic of the Congo, the Celestial Church of Christ in Benin and Nigeria, and the Zion Christian Church in South Africa, which were founded by charismatic leaders and are thriving denominations to date. However, in the course of the 20th century, they experienced increasing competition with another group of churches.

- The third group of AICs distinguished by Anderson are Pentecostal-Charismatic churches. Sometimes the prophet-healing churches are also referred to as Pentecostal, but where those are indigenous to Africa, the churches categorized in the third group have their roots in the Pentecostal movement that emerged in the early 20th century in North America and from there spread globally. While both types of AICs share an emphasis on spiritual power, as well as on charismatic practices such as prophecy and healing, the Pentecostal-Charismatic churches have a more Western, especially North American influence, and a global orientation. This is visible in their style of worship, their leadership patterns, and their connections to global Pentecostal movements. According to Anderson, with their modern Western outlook, "these churches tend to be more sharply opposed to several traditional practices than is the case with prophet-healing churches, and they often ban alcohol, tobacco, the use of symbolic healing objects, and the wearing of uniforms. ... They are often seen, particularly by the older AICs, as mounting a sustained attack on traditional African values (Anderson 2001, 19)"

- Especially since the last decades of the 20th century, Pentecostal-Charismatic movements have grown dramatically and have come to define the face of contemporary African Christianity (see Chapter 5).

Feature: The Lumpa Church in Zambia

The Lumpa Church is one of Zambia's most well-known African independent churches. Its history begins with an extraordinary story about a woman from Bemba land, in the north-eastern part of the country: Mulenga Lubusha Ngandu (born around 1920). In 1953 she got sick and – the story goes – died, after which she met Jesus who sent her back to life with a mission to save her people from sin by abolishing witchcraft. Until then, Mulenga had attended the Lubwa Mission led by Scottish Presbyterian missionaries. After her vision, she went there to tell them about her calling. Conflicts soon emerged as she was not allowed to preach and baptise. In 1955 Mulenga – referred to by her followers as the Queen, or "Lenshina" in Bemba – founded her own church, which she called Lumpa ("better than all others"). Its headquarters were in Kasomo village, which was renamed Zion. According to David Gordon,

> Stories of Lenshina's resurrection and her communications with God spread across the Bemba heartland, eastward to Malawi, and south and west to the Copperbelt. Upon hearing the good news, many made the pilgrimage to the striking church that Lenshina's followers were building at Zion.
>
> (Gordon 2012, 91)

This building, of an impressive size and design, was opened in 1958. Over 100 branches were established in the wide region. Estimations of the church's membership by that time range between 60,000 and 150,000 – larger than that of the Protestant and Catholic missions combined.

Its success depended on a number of factors. First, the hymns of the church, often written by Lenshina herself, were appealing because of the themes and their style, which resembled Bemba traditional music. Second, the church attracted women, not just because it had a female leader, but also because its moral teachings supported women and contributed to marital and family stability. Third, the concern with protection from witchcraft appealed to many people for whom the belief in this form of evil and its active agents was part of their spiritual worldview (see Chapter 7). Fourth, the church also offered economic security as it promoted agriculture and developed business activities. Thus, Lenshina presented a form of Christianity that was relevant to the social and spiritual concerns of ordinary people, in a way somewhat similar to Pentecostal-Charismatic churches today (see Chapter 5).

In addition, according to Gordon her church became more and more "a revolutionary and uncompromising political intervention" (Gordon 2012, 108). This refers to the fact that Lenshina, with her spiritual authority, challenged not only the power of the Bemba chiefs, the missionary churches and colonial authorities, but also that of the emerging Zambian nationalist movement. As such, the church presents a historical example of the fact that religion in Africa provides women with a site to (re)claim political agency (see Chapter 13).

Lenshina increasingly adopted a vision in which the church had to withdraw from "the world" and not engage in formal politics. In the early 1960s this led to tensions with the United National Independence Party (UNIP). Around the time of Zambian independence (1964) the conflict became violent, with UNIP leader (and the first Zambian President) Kenneth Kaunda sending military forces to Bemba land. About 1,000 Lumpa followers died, the church was banned, and Lenshina was imprisoned. She died in 1978 while under house arrest. Even today there are Christians and independent churches in Zambia claiming to continue her legacy. According to Allan Anderson (2001, 139), the Lumpa Church "was more radical than most AICs in its total rejection of the outside world, whether traditional, colonial or post-independence. ... It mounted a sustained attack of African religion as well, going further than the European missions had done."

Africanization of missionary Christianity

African independent churches have made a tremendous contribution to the appropriation and indigenization of Christianity in African contexts. However, it would be simplistic to suggest that the AICs are "authentically African" while the churches that have their roots in the European mission activity are "Western". In fact, through a number of developments in the 20th century, the latter churches have been "Africanized", too.

- First, while the mission churches were initially under the leadership of European missionaries, gradually Africans took over. This was helped by World War I and II, during which many missionaries returned home. Between 1920 and 1960, the number of African priests in the Catholic Church grew from 50 to around 2,000 (still only constituting a sixth of the whole clergy); the first two African Catholic bishops were ordained in 1939.

- Second, while the mission churches were originally directly connected to their "mother churches" in Europe, they increasingly gained autonomy and became independent (although usually maintaining some form of relationships). This development was accelerated by the political process of decolonization following World War II, through which African countries gained independence from the colonizing powers. In the words of Ogbu Kalu, decolonization "had a domino effect on the religious landscape" (Kalu 2005, 347).

- Third, while the missionaries introduced a European form of Christianity to Africa, the theology and liturgy in most churches has somehow been Africanized, by incorporating African cultural elements including language, music and styles of worship (not least because of the competition with the AICs). Especially in the Catholic Church, this has been a deliberate policy encouraged by the church hierarchy. In 1969, during a visit to Uganda, Pope Paul VI (1963–1978) famously told his audience: "You must have an African Christianity. Indeed, you possess human values and characteristic forms of culture which can rise up to be capable of a richness of expression of its own, and genuinely African" (quoted in Kalu 2005, 333). This was very different from the dismissive stance towards African cultures that had earlier characterized missionary efforts. His successor, Pope John Paul II (1978–2005), continued in this line by promoting "inculturation": the development of Christian expressions that are relevant in local African contexts. This led to liturgical renewal, with African styles of music and dance introduced in worship. It also led to theological renewal, with African arts, symbols and beliefs being used to rethink and express the meaning of the Christian faith. For example, the Catholic theologian Charles Nyamiti from Tanzania developed the theology of Jesus Christ as the great ancestor of humankind (Nyamiti 2006). In Protestant circles similar developments took place, encouraged by the World Council of Churches and the Ecumenical Association of Third World Theologians. Among Catholic and Protestant theologians on the continent, a discourse of "African theology" emerged (Parratt 1995), which broadly followed two strands: one strand is primarily concerned with "culture" in line with the quest for inculturation; another strand is concerned with "context" more broadly defined, referring to the social, economic and political life situation of people. In the latter strand, issues such as poverty, conflict and disease have been addressed, as well as issues of race (especially in South African black theology) and of gender (especially in African women's theology).

African Christianity in numbers

The above discussion has focused on the Africanization of Christianity. A parallel and related development can be referred to as the Christianization of Africa. In the course of the 20th century, Christianity on the continent has grown enormously. Together with the growth of Islam, this has contributed to dramatic religious change on the continent, at the expense of primary adherence to indigenous religions (though we should keep in mind that African religious practice tends to be hybrid or syncretic). As a result of the growth of Christianity in Africa, African Christianity now makes up a significant part of global Christianity. Nowadays one out of five Christians worldwide is African.

The growth of Christianity is remarkable, both in terms of the total number of Christians, and the percentage of the population that is Christian (see Table 2.1).

Where the northern part of the continent is overwhelmingly Muslim, almost all African Christians live in sub-Saharan Africa. In some countries in that part of the continent, over 90 per cent of the population is Christian.

The five African countries with the largest Christian population (estimations for 2020) are shown in Table 2.2.

The five African countries with the highest percentage of Christians (estimations for 2020) are shown in Table 2.3. [1]

Table 2.1 Growth of Christianity in Africa

	African population	Percentage of population that is Christian	Total number of African Christians
1910	120,000,000	9%	11,000,000
1970	368,000,000	39%	143,000,000
2020	1,278,000,000	49%	631,000,000

Source: Center for the Study of Global Christianity 2013

Table 2.2 African countries with largest Christian population

Country	Total number of Christians	Percentage of population
Nigeria	95,695,000	47%
DR Congo	80,919,000	95%
Ethiopia	60,754,000	60%
Kenya	43,068,000	82%
South Africa	42,926,000	82%

Source: Center for the Study of Global Christianity 2013

Table 2.3 African countries with highest percentage of Christians

Country	Total number of Christians	Percentage of population
DR Congo	80,919,000	95%
Angola	23,174,000	94%
Burundi	9,383,000	93%
Rwanda	12,964,000	92%
Lesotho	2,204,000	92%

Source: Center for the Study of Global Christianity 2013

Conclusion

In a nutshell this chapter has presented the long, rich and diverse history of Christianity in Africa. Where this chapter has introduced different traditions and denominations from a historical perspective, in the various chapters in the second part of this book attention will be paid to the social, public and political roles of Christian communities in Africa today (also see Bongmba 2016). At this stage, let us conclude with a quotation from Andrew Walls who has stated: "African Christianity is undoubtedly African religion, as developed by Africans and shaped by their concerns and agendas of Africa; it is no pale copy of an institution existing somewhere else" (Walls 2002, 119). This is not to say that Christian churches in Africa do not have links, historically and currently, to Western Christianity, and reflect Western influences. Africa is part of a globalized world, and so is African Christianity. However, Walls' words remind us that the many different forms of Christianity in Africa have been appropriated and become relevant in African socio-cultural contexts, speak to the spiritual needs of Africans, and shape their identity in relation to the outside world.

The latter applies equally to the ancient tradition of Ethiopian Orthodoxy, to the Catholic Church and the Protestant mission churches dating back to the colonial and missionary encounter, and to the Pentecostal-Charismatic churches mushrooming all over the continent today. Like the indigenous religions discussed in the previous chapter, and often in a complex symbiosis with them, these diverse expressions of Christian faith provide adherents with an orientation in life, reveal divinity and assist them to engage spiritual power, distinguish practitioners and shape their identity, and empower them spiritually. For many Africans today, identifying as Christian is also a way of adopting a modern identity and inscribing themselves in a global religious narrative, while at the same time the way they practise their Christian faith continues to be shaped by African concerns and realities, such as the strong belief in the supernatural world. The example par excellence is the Pentecostal-Charismatic movement that has become so prominent and popular in recent decades, the various forms of which are reshaping the face of African Christianity (see Chapter 5).

Questions for discussion

- Given that ancient Christianity in North Africa was part of the Roman Empire and was largely Greco-Roman in its cultural orientation, one might contest that it is an important part of the story of African Christianity. Scholars such as Ngong (quoted above), however, have defended the geographical unity of the continent and argued that ancient North African Christianity is a crucial part of the African Christian tradition. What is your take on this question, and why do you think this issue matters?

- Given that modern Christianity in much of Africa was introduced by Western missionaries, and benefited from its link to the colonial administration, many observers expected that after independence Christianity would lose its attraction. The opposite happened, with most countries demonstrating significant growth of the Christian population. Yet some African intellectuals maintain that Christianity is inherently colonial, and that the decolonization of Africa should imply a de-Christianization. What are the pros and cons of this argument?

- Highlighting the enormous diversity of Christian traditions in Africa, some scholars argue for adopting the plural "African Christianities". This is to "emphasize these different strands or traditions that may or may not be compatible one to another" (Ukah 2007, 2). From your reading about the different forms of Christianity discussed in this chapter, what do they have in common, and what are their differences? How do you understand their mutual compatibility?

Note

1 Not included are the small islands surrounding the main African continent, many of which have an extremely high percentage of the population that is Christian.

References (*indicates recommended reading)

Ancel, Stephane, and Eloi Ficquet. 2015. "The Ethiopian Orthodox Tewahedo Church (EOTC) and the Challenges of Modernity." In *Understanding Contemporary Ethiopia: Monarchy, Revolution and the Legacy of Meles Zenawi*, edited by Gerard Prunier and Eloi Ficquet, 63–92. London: Hurst & Co.

*Anderson, Allan. 2001. *African Reformation: African Initiated Christianity in the 20th Century*. Trenton: Africa World Press.

*Bongmba, Elias, editor. 2016. *The Routledge Companion to Christianity in Africa*. Abingdon: Routledge.

Center for the Study of Global Christianity. 2013. "Christianity in Its Global Context, 1970–2020: Society, Religion, and Mission." http://wwwgordonconwell.com/netcomm unity/CSGCResources/ChristianityinitsGlobalContext.pdf.

Fretheim, Sara. 2016. "Early Central African Christian History: Prophets, Priests and Kings." In *The Routledge Companion to Christianity in Africa*, edited by Elias Bongmba, 92–107. Abingdon: Routledge.

Gordon, David. 2012. *Invisible Agents: Spirits in a Central African History*. Athens, Ohio: Ohio University Press.

*Isichei, Elizabeth. 1995. *A History of Christianity in Africa: From Antiquity to the Present*. Grand Rapids: Eerdmans.

Kalu, Ogbu. 2005. "African Christianity: From the World Wars to Decolonization." In *African Christianity: An African Story*, edited by Ogbu Kalu, 333–360. Pretoria: Department of Church History, University of Pretoria.

Ngong, David Tonghou. 2017. "Introduction." In *A New History of African Christian Thought: From Cape to Cairo*, edited by David Ngong, 1–25. New York: Routledge.

Nyamiti, Charles. 2006. *Jesus Christ, the Ancestor of Humankind: An Essay on African Christology*. Nairobi: Catholic University of Eastern Africa.

Parratt, John. 1995. *Reinventing Christianity: African Theology Today*. Trenton, NJ: Africa World Press.

Ukah, Asonzeh. 2007. "African Christianities: Features, Promises and Problems (Working Papers Nr. 79)." Mainz: Institut für Ethnologie und Afrikastudien, Johannes Gutenberg-Universität. http://edoc.bibliothek.uni-halle.de/servlets/MCRFileNodeServ let/HALCoRe_derivate_00002033/AfricanChristianities.pdf.

Youssef, Youhanna Nessim. 2016. "Christianity in Egypt: The Coptic Church." In *The Routledge Companion to Christianity in Africa*, edited by Elias K. Bongmba, 45–60. Abingdon: Routledge.

Walls, Andrew. 2002. *The Cross-Cultural Process in Christian History: Studies in the Transmission and Appropriation of Faith*. Maryknoll, NY: Orbis.

3   Islam in Africa

Is Islam an African religion?

The question raised in the previous chapter in relation to Christianity can also be asked in relation to Islam: can it be considered an "African religion"? Some scholars (e.g. Idowu 1973; Mbiti 1991) have argued that the term "African religion" should strictly be reserved for those religious traditions that are indigenous to Africa. This definition centres on the *origins* of the religion concerned. Other scholars have adopted a broader definition, centring on the *practice* of the religion. On the basis of the first definition, one could easily argue that Islam is not African, as it did not originate from African soil and its historical prophets are not of African origin. However, today almost half of the population on the African continent does identify as Muslim, and African Muslims make up almost a quarter of the global Muslim population. Thus to argue that Islam is not African raises the question what we actually mean by that simple term, "African".

The presence of Islam on the continent varies by region, and can be characterized by whether Muslims represent majority or minority groups in particular societies. Islam is most strongly represented in North Africa, with significant adherence within West Africa and East Africa, including the horn of Africa. When one turns to the middle of the continent, Islam has a relatively weak religious presence and in Southern Africa adherence is very thin (with the exception of Malawi, which has a relatively substantial Muslim minority). Northern African countries like Egypt, Libya, Tunisia, Algeria and Morocco have been heavily influenced by the Arabic culture from the Arabian Peninsula including Arab language. Whereas countries like Senegal, Mali, Guinea and Niger (in West Africa) and Somalia (in East Africa) are less informed by Arab culture, the majority of their populations are Muslims. There are also countries with Muslim pluralities (where Muslims are the largest single group, but not necessarily the majority), which include Sierra Leone, Chad and perhaps Liberia. Apart from this category, one could also find African countries with approximately as many Muslims as Christians, of which Nigeria is the most prominent example.

Due to various processes of Islamization and taking into account that indigenous religions are still practised even among Muslims, the Muslim population in Africa today is estimated as indicated in Table 3.1 below.

In the following sections, the chapter will explore the place of "black Africa" within the Islamic religious tradition. According to John Hanson (2017np), there is no doubt that:

> Islam in Africa has its roots in the origins of the faith, as Ethiopia was a refuge for Muslims who fled Arabia during the time of Prophet Muhammad (*c*. 570–632 CE), and then Muslim Arab conquests in the decades after Muhammad's death brought northern Africa into a Muslim imperial domain that came to encompass south-western Asia and the Mediterranean world.

Arrival and expansion of Islam in Africa

According to scholars the history of Islam in Africa is virtually as old as the history of the religion itself. Islam first arrived in Ethiopia (615–616) at a very early stage, through Arab Muslim converts seeking asylum. In other words, Islam first arrived on African soil as a refugee religion in search of protection. According to Islamic history, when life became unbearable for a certain section of the earliest Muslims due to persecution by non-Muslim Meccan elites, the Prophet arranged for a small group of Muslims to seek refuge in the Christian kingdom of Aksum (present day Ethiopia). Due to the king's benevolence towards the Muslim refugees, they were allegedly allowed to practise their faith without interference from the state (Ahmed 1993). Arguably, this 7th century episode suggests that the first encounter between Christianity and Islam on African soil was one of a peaceful nature. Despite this seemingly historical peaceful encounter, subsequent relations between Muslims and Christians in sub-Saharan Africa have been characterized by higher levels of suspicions, tensions, conflict and hatred.

There are several modes that are associated with the spread of Islam in Africa. Due to the diversity of the African continent, and the multiplicity of factors contributing to processes of conversion, we will present separately North Africa, West Africa, and East Africa as the three key regions that experienced different historical processes. However, the historical narrative will

Table 3.1 Muslim population in Africa

Geo-political region	Population	Percentage
North Africa	180,080,076	87%
West Africa	133,994,675	50%
East Africa	66,381,242	34%
Central Africa	12,582,592	15%
Southern Africa	8,935,043	7%

Source: Bangura 2015, 110.

not have a continuous flow because there is scattered and incomplete knowledge of this early period.

North Africa

Though the introductory chapter stated that the North African region was not going to feature prominently in this book, it is necessary to briefly discuss the spread of Islam in this area to put into perspective its diffusion in some parts of sub-Saharan Africa. The history of Islam on the continent can simply not be understood without acknowledging its early spread in North Africa. After the earliest contact between Islam and Africa, Arab-Muslim forces conquered Egypt in 639 and bought it under the control of Muslim dominion. This time around, Islam made its presence in Africa felt as a military force and victor in search of new worlds to conquer. The conquest of Egypt acted as a stepping stone, as the Muslim forces moved further west conquering much of the North African region. From Egypt, the Muslim conquest extended to Tunisia and Qayrawan in 670, and reached Morocco in 711. The 7th century conquests led to the establishment of an Arab-Muslim political dominion in Tunisia and the adoption of Islam became the basis of tribal coalition in the rest of North Africa (Levtzion and Pouwels 2000; Lapidus 1998).

With the Arab-Muslim conquest of North Africa, two processes were set in motion: the processes of "Islamization" and "Arabization". Islamization was the gradual diffusion of the Islamic religion, while Arabization was the transmission of the Arabic language (and culture) among the North African populations who over the centuries became predominantly Arabic speaking. In addition to conquest, the rapid Islamization and Arabization evident in the North Africa region were also achieved through migration and settlement of Arab Muslims from the Arabian Peninsula. The Arab-Muslim occupation increasingly gave North Africa an Arab identity due to successive waves of Arab migration and dominance. Consequently, in the 20th century, Arabic language and culture became a mark of identity of the societies in this region (Levtzion and Pouwels 2000; Lapidus 1998). Arguably, this explains why the North African region has often been considered as part of the Middle East rather than Africa.

West Africa

Whereas Islamic societies in North Africa were established by Arab-Muslim conquest, Islam in sub-Saharan West Africa was diffused by migration of Muslim merchants, teachers and settlers linked together by trading networks, family connections, teacher-student and Sufi fellowship. The Arab-Muslim conquest of North Africa increased interest in the Saharan trade routes, facilitating numerous interactions among Arab, Berber and West African people. The trans-Saharan trade facilitated the diffusion of Islam from North Africa to West Africa. From the 10th century trade developed between the ancient dynasties of West Africa, such as Goa, Ghana and Mali, and Arab Muslims of North Africa. Countries like Guinea, Mali, Senegal and Niger are, today, overwhelmingly Muslim in population owing to the trans-Saharan trade. According to David Robinson (2004, 28), this happened in three phases: from "minority Islam", with North African traders and entrepreneurs settling in small communities in West Africa, to "court Islam", with members of the ruling classes in those societies gradually converting to Islam, to "majority Islam", where the majority of people (beyond merchants and rulers) in a given society would embrace the Islamic faith.

Due to administrative support and commercial contacts, the local rulers accepted Islam in the late 10th and 11th centuries. In most cases, the local rulers became the major recipients of Islam, indicating the importance of politics and states in the process of Islamization. Conversion to Islam became indispensable for those who wanted to be incorporated into the trade connections as it created mutual assurance among merchants when dealing with their co-religionists. But there were also other instances, when Muslims lived under the hospitality of non-Muslim rulers whom they praised for their goodwill toward the believers. This was evident in the 11th century Empire of Ghana (located in what is now south-eastern Mauritania) and in 19th century Asante territory in the contemporary country of Ghana on the Gulf of Guinea. The process of Islamization increased when Muslim clerics assisted African rulers to overcome droughts, as in the case of 11th century Malal (in contemporary Mali), or to secure victory, as in the 14th century Kingdom of Kano (in contemporary Nigeria) and in the 16th century Kingdom of Gonja (in contemporary Ghana). Since only the ruler and his immediate associates came under the influence of Islam, it was through their courts that Islamic beliefs slowly penetrated to the general society. Muslim clerics who provided religious services to converted local rulers were incorporated into the socio-political system of the state, playing similar functions to those held by traditional priests. Due to their neutrality in political matters, the Muslim clerics would at times be used to resolve conflicts (Levtzion and Pouwels 2000; Lapidus 1998).

From the 11th to the 16th century several kingdoms, in different geographical locations, succeeded each other as major centres of political power, trade and Islamization. Takrur, which was strongly committed to jihad against its non-Muslim neighbours, came under Mali's dominion in the 13th century. From the 13th century to the end of the 16th century, Mali (through the Keita dynasty) became the dominant political power and major centre of Islam in West Africa. (See Figure 3.1.) The Keita dynasty, which had its origin among the Malinke peoples living between the Senegal and Niger rivers, emerged as a typical West African Islamic empire (Lapidus 1998). The rulers of the Keita dynasty brought Muslim scholars from Cairo and Fez to help establish a West African tradition of Islamic learning. The most famous of its rulers, Mansa Musa (1307–32), made a pilgrimage to Cairo in 1324, and returned to Mali with Arab and Berber Muslims who served in his administration. He built new mosques and introduced Arabic style poetry to his court. Under Mansa Musa's and his

Figure 3.1 Annual repair of the world's largest mud brick building: the Great Mosque of
Djenné in Mali (courtesy of Ralph Steinberger, 2009)

descendants' leadership, Timbuktu (popularly known as the city of God) developed into a city of Islamic scholarship credited to black African scholars in
establishing its high reputation (Ware 2014). A similar role of the state in the
Islamization of the West African societies was evident with the appearance of the
Songhay dynasty (located in the middle Niger and western Sudan region) following the breakup of the Keita dynasty. One of its rulers, Askiya Muhammad
Toure (1493–1528) made Islam the official religion and continued with the tradition of inviting Muslim scholars, including the famous al-Maghili (d. 1504).
Due to his commitment to Islam, he was given the title of the Caliph of the lands
in Takrur by the Sharif of Mecca (Levtzion and Pouwels 2000; Lapidus 1998).

East Africa

On the coasts of the Indian Ocean and the horn of Africa another form of Islamic
civilization emerged due to the influence of Muslim traders and settlers upon the
local African communities. This is especially the case of migrant Arabs from
Yemen and Oman who settled in East Africa along the coast all the way from the
Somali coast to Kilwa (in present-day Tanzania). On the Ethiopian coast of the
Red Sea, Muslims settled as early as the 8th century. The town of Harar in present day Ethiopia developed as the most important centre for trade and Islamic
learning. The local communities grew to become Muslim principalities that
challenged the hegemony of the Christian Ethiopian state. Though Islam had
made contact with the east coast as early as 780, it became the religion of the

majority of the Swahili-speaking people between 1200 and 1500. By the 13th century several city states that were Islamic in character emerged along the East African coast, the most important of which were Malindi, Mombasa, Zanzibar and Sofala (Levtzion and Pouwels 2000; Lapidus 1998).

The interaction that ensued between the migrant Arab-Muslims and the local people living along the coast of Kenya and Tanzania led to the expansion of Kiswahili, which became the common language of trade in these areas. Some of the Muslim migrants intermarried with the indigenous communities, facilitating the local peoples to embrace Islam, and developed an Arabic-African culture in language, architecture and dress. Though earlier studies considered the resultant Swahili language and culture a product of assimilation of Africans into the Arab-Muslim society, other scholars have insisted on the indigenous African basis of Swahili civilization (Mutembei 2014; Mazrui and Mazrui 1995). From this viewpoint, Kiswahili is essentially a Bantu language, albeit with Arabic influence as well as some Portuguese and English vocabulary. By the 19th century the East African coast was the home of a Swahili Muslim civilization. The principal centre of Islamic identity was Zanzibar, which was the capital of the Omani sultanate in the region established by Sayyid Said b. Sultan (1804–56). The period witnessed the appearance of a new class of merchants and landowners with wealth from plantations and trade, contributing to the expansion of Islam on the East African coast. This group of elite and wealthy Muslims was responsible for the increase in the number of mosques and schools in this area (Levtzion and Pouwels 2000; Lapidus 1998).

Later in the 19th century Arabs together with Swahili traders in the East African coast indirectly played a significant role in spreading Islam into the hinterland along two major trade routes. One of the routes connected the coastal town of Kilwa and Malindi with the Lake Malawi region, while the second one linked Zanzibar and the coastal town of Dar es Salaam with the Manyema and Buganda regions. Through contacts with the Muslim traders, a local king in Buganda, Kabaka Mutesa I (ca. 1838–1884) adopted Islam and played a significant role in the Islamization process comparable to those of monarchies in West Africa. The ruler Islamized his regime by observing Ramadhan, building mosques, and ensuring that Muslims occupied significant positions in the state. Despite merchants establishing commercial routes that exposed African societies to external influences, they did not themselves actively engage in the proselytization of Islam. Rather, those who converted to the new faith were mostly immediate members of the Muslim traders: spouses and their relatives, porters and other employees of the merchants (Levtzion and Pouwels 2000; Lapidus 1998).

Islam and the place of black Africans

The Arab subjugation of black Africans as slaves and participation in the Atlantic slave trade as well as the Red Sea and Indian Ocean slave trade is a matter of historical record. Nevertheless, there are divergent views with regard to the problem of slavery in Islam. While some sources consider "slavery as an indelible institution within Islam", others maintain that "slavery was best understood as an economic rather than religious institution" (Ware 2014, 112). Due to Arab chauvinism that increased with the conquests of the first Muslim century, according to Rudolph Ware (2014, 29), "Blackness and slavery, slavery and unbelief were now all collapsed together in unprecedented ways. This development had important implications for Muslims' perceptions of religiosity of blacks – or at least religious inferiority – was increasingly read onto black bodies". Despite this problematic history, many black Africans have come to identify as Muslim and have embraced Islam.

In a global perspective, Islam is a religion with a significant number of adherents in Africa. As indicated above, Muslims in Africa cut across geographical and ethnic boundaries. In sub-Saharan Africa they include the Hausa, Fulani and Wolof of West Africa, Sudanese and Swahili-speaking East Africans, as well as other minorities in southern African regions. All these ethnic groups represent innumerable variations of human experience but are united by Islam. The Islamic faith has permeated their self-conception, regulates their daily existence, provides the bonds of society and fulfils the yearning for salvation. Despite the earliest evidence of the spread and expansion of Islam in Africa, slavery in Islamic societies has contributed in doubting the religious "intellectual achievements of African Muslims" by other (non-black African) Muslims (Ware 2014, 24). This attitude runs counter to the courteous place accorded to black Africans by the Prophet Muhammad himself, according to the tradition. This is demonstrated by a hadith attributed to the Prophet: "Emulate the blacks, for among them are the three lords of the people of Paradise, Luqman the Sage, the Negus [Emperor of Abyssinia], and Bilal the Muezzin" (Ware 2014, 13). The pronouncement by Muhammad indicates that he viewed Africans in a respectful way, mentioning three of them explicitly by name. Who were these figures?

Feature: The three black Africans of paradise

Despite the Arab-Muslims' condescending and paternalistic attitude towards Africans, the Qur'an comprises a chapter, "Luqman". It takes its name from a pre-Islamic African "sage" whom the revelation symbolizes as a representation of piousness who taught the doctrine of *tawhid* (God's unity and oneness). Though some earlier interpretations had maintained that Luqman was a prophet, later interpretations insisted that he was merely a sage, in spite of his prominent and favourable illustration in the Qur'an. Perhaps because of his African descent, they would also insinuate that Luqman was a slave, even though the Qur'an does not make such a declaration (Ware 2014).

Historically, the African Christian Kingdom of Aksum (present-day Ethiopia) had occupied parts of the Arabian Peninsula, but this came to an end with the eventual expulsion from Hijaz (western Arabia) in 570 (the year of the Prophet's birth). The Prophet's mention of the King of Aksum was not, however, in reference to the power of an African king, but instead alluded to

the piousness of an African Christian ruler who saved the earliest Muslim community from the danger of possible annihilation. Though expelled from Hijaz, the
Ethiopian kingdom, nevertheless, remained a principal power player in the Red
Sea region (Ware 2014). When the initial Muslim community was vulnerable to
destruction in Mecca, Muhammad petitioned the Christian ruler, Negus Armuh,
for assistance, who responded by giving Muslims asylum. When torture and
persecution became agonizing to the nascent group of believers, the Prophet
advised around one hundred Muslim converts to seek refuge in Aksum in 615
and 616. With these events, Islam arrived to sub-Saharan Africa even before the
commencement of the Islamic calendar that began in 622. Muslim historians
have arguably maintained that, as a result of the interaction between the Negus
and the Muslim emigrants, the King of Aksum was so impressed with the faith
that he secretly converted to Islam, a view that has been rejected by Christian
historians in Ethiopia (Ahmed 1993). This divergent interpretation of a historical
event should be understood within the existing context of rivalry and competition
between Muslims and Christians in sub-Saharan Africa.

Bilal ibn Rabah (580–642), the muezzin (caller for prayer), is the final black
African representing justice and piousness in the above dictum according to
Islamic tradition. He was an emancipated slave who became one of the
closest companions to Muhammad. During the period of the Prophet, he
was also appointed to serve in the important position of the custodian of the
treasury (*bayt al mal*) (Gardell 1996). As a slave of a Meccan elite family who
were infuriated when he embraced Islam, Bilal was cruelly punished, laid out
to roast on the hot desert sand with heavy stones on his chest. When his
tormentor would come to ask if he would renounce Islam, he would repeat-
edly groan in pain the word *ahad* (reference to one God). Bilal's affirmation
of *tawhid* (oneness of God) in the face of torture appears to have moved
Prophet Muhammad to purchase the enslaved man's liberty (Ware 2014).

Later, after the Prophet received the commandment to observe the prayer,
and eventually preferred the human voice as the means of calling Muslims to
congregational worship, Bilal became the first muezzin of the Muslim community. Bilal's powerful and sweet voice is cited as the reason why he was
selected for this role. But possibly the Prophet was also convinced that Bilal's
genuine belief in God's oneness, which could not be weakened by his master's torture, made him exceptionally qualified for the task.

Of the three Lords of Paradise, Bilal's legacy presented several opportunities for African Muslims to identify with because of his close link with the
Prophet. Accordingly, records preserving Sundiata Keita's (1217–55) "legacy
as the founder of the Mali Empire during the 13th century frequently claim
an ancestral link to Bilal" (Galyon 2017, 70), despite his Ethiopian ancestry.
His role as the first muezzin was extremely vital to African Muslims because
it symbolically asserted that "it is the black man who leads humanity to
God" (Gardell 1996, 36). By awarding a black African this role, Prophet

Muhammad demonstrated the special status some African Muslims held in Islam. Allegedly, some muezzin associations in Africa have always "venerated the original practitioner of their noble profession", and generally, African Muslims "feel a special closeness and kinship to him" (Hoberman 2008, np). As an African, the story of Bilal, "remains the classic and most frequently cited demonstration" of the honour a Black Muslim held in Islam (Hoberman 2008, np).

Adopting and adapting Islam in Africa

As shown above, in sub-Saharan Africa's religious landscape, Islam is stronger in West Africa than in Eastern and Southern Africa. This raises the question: Why is the development of Islam on the continent not uniform? Part of the answer could be due to the longer history of indigenizing and Africanizing Islam in West Africa. In this region, Islam had ceased to be Arab-led and it attained African leadership earlier than in various parts of Eastern Africa. In West Africa, the great religious leaders, preachers and warriors of jihad were of African descent. In Eastern Africa, on the other hand, Islam was for a long time in the hand of Arabs, reducing the vitality of the faith in these regions, while in Southern Africa the much more recent history of Islam is mostly related to forced labour migration from India during the British colonial period.

Regional differences are evident as cultures of indigenous African societies were integrated with the practices of Islam that readily accommodated them. Islam's accommodation to African cultures has contributed to the observance of a particular form of Islam differing from one region to the other. For instance, there is evidence that clitoridectomy was a widespread practice in some local African traditions that included Somalis and Northern Sudanese (Boddy 1989). Due to the accommodating nature of Islam, it was certainly promulgated later by the mistaken belief that it was a requirement of the faith. Among some Muslim communities in Sudan and others on the East African coast, spirit possession practice has been a common traditional phenomenon among the local people (Sperling 1995; Boddy 1989). With the appearance of Islam, this practice also found its way into Muslim practice, appropriating unique Islamic symbols and ideas. The accommodation of African customs was only under the condition that the practice in question did not directly challenge the tenets of the Islamic faith.

Scholars of Islam in sub-Saharan Africa characterize it in two very different ways, as either "African Islam" or "Islam in Africa". The first describes a system of syncretism, which is the simultaneous practice of more than one tradition. It is a form of Islam that includes divination, spirit possession, and the use of written texts from the Qur'an as charms. Sufism, which is not present in certain Muslim orthodoxy, is also a feature integrated into "African Islam". While these practices are contentious for some, they were also features of Muslim societies outside Africa as well as evident in both ancient and contemporary periods. On the other hand, "Islam in Africa" is frequently regarded to be identical to Salafiyya-Wahabi (Islamic modernism/reformism) and Islamist influences, which are usually associated with

Islamic orthodoxy. It consists of "reform" that supports the establishment of modernized schools, encouraging literalist approaches to texts, values Arab cultural customs and rejects what is perceived as esotericism (e.g. divination). Muslims who subscribe to this category of Islam consider themselves to be the proponents and carriers of Islamic orthodoxy and textual legitimacy (Seesemann 2006). In this dichotomy, David Robinson (2004, 42) concluded that, "there is nothing pejorative about the Africanization of Islam", however, "there is something pejorative about the way that European and many Mediterranean-based Muslims have perceived 'African Islam' and the Africanization of Islam".

The process of "Islam in Africa" aspires to propagate an Islam that is considered to be free of African customs, but loaded with Arab culture. Today, with the wealth emanating from the oil resources of the Middle East and Gulf States, Africa is witnessing deliberate efforts to initiate Muslims to the reforming ideas (see Chapter 6) of this form of Islam by committing huge sums of money for the cause. As a result these Muslim countries are competing in establishing cultural and educational institutions in the continent, and also offer scholarships to enable African Muslims to study abroad with the hope after returning they would be the bearer of "Islam in Africa". To illustrate that Africanized Islam is exoticized by the advocators of Islamic orthodoxy, Rudolph T. Ware (2014) makes the observation that in Islamic scholarship, African religious culture + Islam = syncretism; while Arab religious culture + Islam = Islam (that is, the "true" Islam). These two distinct situations demonstrate a scenario where Arab Islam, which is considered to be different from African Islam, is presented as the rightful form of Islam.

However, according to Ruediger Seesemann (2006), the Islamization of Africa and the Africanization of Islam are not opposite, but parallel processes and closely interconnected. An interesting, though complicated, case here is Kenya. Although Seesemann later nuanced this idea, within the Kenyan context he presents African Islam as illustrated by the Swahili Islam as being traditional, particularistic and local, whereas the process of Islam in Africa as demonstrated through the Salafiyya is viewed in his analysis as modern, universalist and reformist Islam from outside. To rid the faith of practices regarded as innovations (*bid'a*), the Salafiyya brand of Islam advocates for the return to the "original" Islam of the pious predecessors (salaf), a theme that will be examined in Chapter 6. But despite Salafiyya being considered as alien (read Arab Islam), in Kenya its proponents have in fact encouraged the usage of Kiswahili, at least in contexts other than the formal recitation of the Qur'an and ritual prayer. The supposed representatives of Swahili Islam, on the other hand, regard Arabic as the authentic medium for Islamic rituals. This contradicting scenario demonstrates that the binary scheme for explaining the development of Islam in African societies is not satisfactory. Such an approach is based on the teleological assumption that Islamization follows a linear path, which is disputed with the evidence from Kenya. It is yet to be seen if the Islam in Africa approach will be stronger than the Africanization of Islam in future. It is pertinent to understand the complex construction of Islamic practice in Africa, which often is *glocal* – that is, simultaneously local and global – navigating global Islamic identity and politics with local expressions and forms in multiple ways. (See Figure 3.2.)

Figure 3.2 Muslim prayer on the streets in Kariakoo, Dar es Salaam (Adriaan van Klinken, 2015)

Feature: Islam noir/Black Islam: a political tool

The notion of "Black Islam" (or *Islam noir*, in French) is a problematic one because it has a political meaning, as examined by Jean-Louis Triaud (2000). It was first used by the French administrators in the colonial governments to present the idea that there is a black African form of Islam, which is different from Arab Islam. Generally, the French colonial policy towards Islam has always carried anti-Islamic dimensions. As they encountered Islam in the new Muslim colonies, French administrators considered Islamic institutions to be intolerable and obstacles to progress.

In their bias the French authority saw Islam as midway between barbarism and progress given that it possessed a written culture. Though Islam was seen as a sign of backwardness compared to European Christian societies, in the context of Africa it occupied a different and complex place. Islamic culture was judged, on the one hand, to lag behind Western civilization; but on the other, it was seen as a force that could potentially advance sub-Saharan societies designated as "fetishist". These French perspectives were racist and misguided evolutionist views of society that have been rebuked and abandoned today. In their effort to control Muslims in sub-Saharan Africa (especially West Africa) and possibly erode the notion of global Islamic unity, the French developed the notion of Black Islam as a political tool. They believed that by encouraging the establishment of Black Islam, Islam would be ethnicized, thereby weakening its capability of participating in the global Muslim community, which could threaten the French colonial administration in the region. Consequently, the administration initiated mutual working relations with the local Sufi orders, which was viewed as a new religion born out of Islam (Triaud 2000). Undoubtedly, the developed theory of Black Islam was intended to undermine any political opposition that would be formulated through the Islamic symbolism of unity.

To some extent Muslim elites and French administrators established mutually cordial, though still mistrustful, relationships. For instance, there were cases in which some administrators attended certain Muslim festivals, subsidized Islamic institutions and so on. Even though the French colonial policy was to a certain extent successful in terms of cooperation with some Muslim leaders, it did not stop viewing Islam as a danger to their rule. In response any Islamic leadership that was viewed to be rebelling was severely repressed. Later in the 1950s, reformers in the form of Wahhabism emerged and presented a threat to the colonial administration. The reformers were seen as a sign of a conspiracy emanating from the Muslim world (see Chapter 6) (Triaud 2000).

Conclusion

The history of Islam in Africa is rich and complex, varying in relation to the various regions and ethnic groups of the continent. Although there is a long and strong presence of Islam on the African continent, Muslim history tends to be viewed in the prism of accomplishment around the Middle East and the Arab world, to the exclusion of Africans. Yet African Muslims have made and continue to make a significant contribution to Islam as reformers, teachers, scholars and jihadists, thereby qualifying Islam as an African religion. By the end of the 18th century, Islam was deeply rooted in the daily life of certain ethnic groups in Africa. But even among these communities of African Muslims, pre-Islamic elements persisted through hybrid or syncretistic religious practice, a process described in this chapter as African Islam. This scenario created a conducive environment and a justification for the appearance of reformers to bring about the desired break accompanied with a more literate form of Islam, a theme that is explored in Chapter 6.

Questions for discussion

- To what extent are marabouts a representation of authoritative Islam? And how would you respond to the claim that the marabout or the wearing of Qur'anic amulets do not represent a "pure" form of Islam?
- "African Islam" versus "Islam in Africa" may be a somewhat simplistic generalization. Do you think they can still be helpful categories to think about the different ways in which Islamic practice is shaped in African contexts? If so, what would be essential terms in reference to the two processes?
- Given that the history of Islam in Africa is associated with conquest and slavery, how can we reconcile the positive interpretation of the hadith on the three lords of paradise? And how can we explain the appeal of Islam to Africans in such great numbers?

References (*indicates recommended reading)

Ahmed, Hussein. 1993. "Trends and Issues in the History of Islam in Ethiopia". In *Islam in Africa*, edited by Nura Alkali, 205–220. Ibadan: Spectrum Books.

Bangura, Abdul Karim. 2015. "The African Roots and Transnational Nature of Islam", *Journal of Islamic Studies and Culture* 3/2, 108–132.

Boddy, Janice. 1989. *Wombs and Alien Spirits: Women, Men, and the Zar Cult in Northern Sudan*. Madison: University of Wisconsin Press.

Galyon, Derek. 2017. "The End of a Nation: Warithuddin Muhammad and Muslim Identity in the Nation of Islam", *Pursuit* 8/1, 68–78.

Gardell, Mattias. 1996. *In the Name of Elijah Muhammad: Louis Farrakhan and the Nation of Islam*. Durham: Duke University Press.

Hanson, John. 2017. "Islam in Africa", *Oxford Bibliographies*. http://www.oxfordbiblio
graphies.com/view/document/obo-9780199846733/obo-9780199846733-0007.xml (accessed 14 June 2018).

Hoberman, Barry. 2008. "The First Muezzin – Bilal ibn Rabah, an Ethiopian." An
Ethiopian Journal. https://tseday.wordpress.com/2008/11/05/the-first-muezzin-bila
l-ibn-rabah-an-ethiopian/ (accessed 15 June 2018).

Idowu, Bolaji. 1973. *African Traditional Religion: A Definition*. Maryknoll: Orbis Books.

Lapidus, Ira. 1998. *A History of Islamic Societies*. Cambridge: Cambridge University Press.

Levtzion, Nehemia and Randall Pouwels, editors. 2000. *History of Islam in Africa*.
Athens: Ohio University Press.

Mazrui, Ali Al'Amin and Mazrui, Alamin M. 1995. *Swahili State and Society: The
Political Economy of an African Language*. Nairobi: East African Publisher.

Mbiti, John. 1991. *Introduction to African Religion*. London: Heinemann Educational
Books.

Mutembei, Aldin. 2014. "African Languages as a Gateway to Sustainable Development,
Democracy and Freedom: The Example of Swahili", *Alternation* 3, 326–351.

Robinson, David. 2004. *Muslim Societies in African History*. Cambridge: Cambridge
University Press.

Seesemann, Ruediger. 2006. "African Islam or Islam in Africa? Evidence from Kenya." In
*The Global Worlds of the Swahili: Interfaces of Islam, Identity and Space in the 19th
and 20th Century East Africa*, edited by Roman Loimeier and Ruediger Seesemann,
229–250. Berlin: Lit Verlag.

Sperling, David. 1995. "The Frontiers of Prophecy: Healing, the Cosmos and Islam in the
East African Coast in the Nineteenth Century." In *Revealing Prophets: Prophecy in
Eastern African History*, edited by David Anderson and Douglas Johnson, 83–97.
London: James Currey.

Triaud, Jean-Louis. 2000. "Islam in Africa under French Colonial Rule." In *The History
of Islam in Africa*, edited by Nehemia Levtzion and Randal Pouwels, 169–182.
Oxford: James Currey.

Ware, Rudolph. 2014. *The Walking Quran: Islamic Education, Embodied Knowledge
and History of West Africa*. Chapel Hill: University of Carolina Press.

4 Neo-traditional religious movements in Africa

Introduction

The long history of encounters, clashes and entanglements between practitioners of African indigenous religions, Christianity and Islam in sub-Saharan Africa caused radical shifts in the forms and purpose of African religious practice. Colonialism and the Christian missions further undermined indigenous religious authority and suppressed traditions. Since the 1960s, the era of African independence, the pressures of modernity and the promise of globalization have further eroded the appeal of indigenous religious practice. But today an even greater challenge to the vitality of African indigenous religious values and practices arises from the new fervour among African converts to Christian Pentecostalism (Chapter 6) and the Muslim reform movements (Chapter 7). The category "neo-traditional religious movements" (NTRMs) refers to widely divergent types of religious movements that were organized in conscious response to these many challenges.

A great variety of religious movements with indigenous roots have regularly appeared on the ever-changing social landscape. Harold Turner (1966, 281) vividly captured their omnipresence in the early days of Africa's political independence, but the phenomenon is no less visible or animated today:

> Even the most casual observer driving through a large African town cannot fail to notice the succession of exotic names on sign boards or to meet a white-robed religious procession, and if he tries to trace the bell-ringing, drumming, and chanting that fill the night air for hours on end the chances are that he will be led to one of these sign boards and to some humble structure filled with tireless worshippers.

The range of phenomena that could be classified as NTRMs is quite diverse, and their types overlap. Many prophetic movements creatively combine biblical teachings with African beliefs. African Initiated Churches are examples of such fusions. They foreground distinctively African aspects of worship (like spirit possession) and focus on traditional concerns (like healing), but they remain fundamentally Christian (see Chapter 2). Certain groups that fused indigenous African concepts and practices with Islam can also be classified among NTRMs. Among them is the Dozo (Côte d'Ivoire, Burkina Faso, and Mali) a secret society of traditional hunters that blends indigenous sorcery with Muslim veneration of saints. During the recent civil wars in Côte d'Ivoire the Dozo transmuted into a sacred militia backing Muslim rebel fighters, a movement called Benkadi (which in the local Mande language means "Agreement is sweet") (Hellweg 2011, 4; see fuller discussion below).

Other NTRMs, by contrast, are strategic efforts to pose a critical alternative to Islam or Christianity, even when their expressions have African inflections. This type of movement aims to rehabilitate indigenous traditions in their own right, defend their dignity and restore cultural pride for new generations. Often such revitalization movements have also served to energize struggles for national liberation from colonial domination and neo-colonial abuses. Their promotion of indigenous principles and practices should not be seen as a nostalgic turn backward, but as an assertion of the value of African traditions and their ability to address contemporary crises. This chapter will present select cases representing different types of NTRMs that arose over the past century, situate them in the historic contexts, and consider how globalization is causing them to shift their shape and purpose.

When does "tradition" become "neo-traditional"?

Tradition is never a fixed matter, but is always a synthesis of past practices, living memory, and accommodation to present circumstances. The religious traditions of indigenous Africa are no different. This, however, raises the troubling question of "where traditional religion ends and neo-traditional religion begins" (Hackett 1991, 136). Rosalind Hackett helpfully notes that when changes happen within a tradition it is not the entirety of a religious system that is revamped, nor are transformations immediate. Instead, only certain features – concepts, practices or symbols – shift, and they do so gradually while the institutional framework remains largely intact. Neo-traditional religious movements, by contrast, can be defined by either a decisive break or significant refashioning of their originating institutions.

According to some observers, as African indigenous religions met with the supposed monotheism of world religions, they shifted emphasis from local divinities to the worship of a supreme being. An example is "The Church of Orunmila", an adaptation of the traditional Yoruba cult to the divinity (*orisha*) who created the human form. Orunmila is considered to have been present when Olodumare created the universe, and the one who moulded the human form. As the spirit of divine wisdom, Orunmila presides over destiny and brought it to earth in the form of Ifa divination. In 1943, the Church proclaimed that Ifa was the revelation of "the God of Africa" (Hackett 1991, 139). Other analysts maintain that although the collective aspects of religion may weaken, the more individualistic practices endure or even increase in the face of new challenges. For example calendrical rites may become rare while those with a personal religious focus such as healing rites, and the use of charms, talisman or spells for protection remain popular and such traditional forms are even on the increase. This phenomenon is visible in the proliferation of divination not only on the streets of African urban metropolises, but also across the African diaspora via websites that transmit religious knowledge and offer divinatory readings via the internet (see Chapter 15). However, neither kind of shift radically alters the fundamental vision of their indigenous religious sources.

What most warrants a change in classification from traditional to neo-traditional is *the self-conscious and systematic refashioning* of fundamental forms and concepts *in light of competing ideas*. NTRMs are therefore more than "survivals" of traditional religious ways. They are *new imaginative reconstructions* of "a world as an integral whole out of the remains of their past, the cultural ambiguities of their present, and the bits of their perception of Christian and other alien traditions" (Werbner 1985, 115). Neo-traditionalism remains grounded in distinctively African sources of knowledge and empowerment but goes beyond mere revitalization. It involves a *comprehensive reinterpretation* of indigenous traditions to serve new ends in the contemporary moment.

Schism and power

Many NTRMs were inaugurated as break-away initiatives (schisms). The new factions defined themselves in contradistinction to the founding religious entity even while maintaining some of its outward features. The adoption of the term "Church" to refer to a movement's organization and leadership is one example. Reference to leaders of neo-traditional African indigenous religious movements as "prophets" betrays the influence of Christianity and Islam. The religious content varies considerably among them, however, ranging from those that are essentially revivals of indigenous practices (like healing) in new guises to those with commitments that are more closely aligned with the Christian parent body (like prophecy). However, a central concern of all such schismatic groups is power.

Many African Independent (or Initiated) Churches (AICs) broke with the older mainline missions in order to assert their own leadership (see Chapter 2). More importantly, the neo-traditional movements have been consistently invested in self-empowerment through the assertion of the dignity and worth of African indigenous worldviews and customs. Their preoccupation with power and self-determination is also reflected in the relation between the indigenous religious movements and the emergence of nation-states. Some NTRMs inspired revolts against colonial domination which were fought as "holy wars" under divinely sanctioned leaders; the revolt of the Religion of the Ancestral Spirits (*Dini ya Msambwa*) in Kenya in 1948–50 as well as the Mau Mau rebellion against British imperialism there in the 1950s are well known examples (Turner 1980, 44).

Colonial authorities recognized the subversive potential of NTRMs, but in some cases their suppression only spurred them on. Kimbanguism is an example. Founded in 1921 by the preacher/healer named Simon Kimbangu (1887–1951) in what was then called the Belgian Congo (now the Democratic Republic of the Congo), the movement began as a healing ministry. But Kimbangu attracted such a following that colonials saw him as a threat. They persecuted and imprisoned him for undermining security, holding him until his death. His martyrdom turned

Kimbangu into a messianic figure around which followers rallied, and his underground Church spread. "Kimbangu was given the title of *ntoma*, meaning the 'One Sent', or the messenger, equating him to John [the Baptist]" (Ayegboyin and Ishola 1997, np). The movement's resistance yielded nationalist pride and Kimbanguists rallied to struggle against colonialism. In contemporary DRC the state has used Kimbanguism to promote a sense of national identity. As a result of migration, the church in recent decades has spread beyond national borders, becoming a global phenomenon. While Kimbanguism can be classified as a neo-traditionalist movement, its strict code of biblical conduct requires that African practices like polygamy, "fetishes" and witchcraft belief be abandoned. This illustrates the ambiguity and complexity of movements in the category of NTRMs.

Some schismatic groups sprang up under charismatic leaders but were ephemeral initiatives, perhaps too much a reaction to immediate and local disturbances to survive. But some NTRMs that arose at the beginning of the 20th century still flourish today, even transcending national and ethnic boundaries. One example is the Celestial Church of Christ that originated in Benin in 1947, but which soon spread to Nigeria and other parts of West Africa, and more recently worldwide (Figure 4.1). The Celestial Church is part of a wider group of so-called Aladura ("prayer") churches that reject Western medicine on the basis of the African understanding that disease also results from spiritual vulnerability including witchcraft, and which therefore emphasizes faith healing (see Chapter 12).

Figure 4.1 Women's section in the Celestial Church of Christ, Makoko Parish, Lagos, Nigeria (courtesy of Nienke Pruiksma, 2009)

The Harrist movement is another enduring NTRM. Harrism is distinctive because it was independently founded by an African leader "and not originating out of a separation from a mission church" (Shank 1985, 73). While it was eventually consolidated as a "Church", Harrism reflects an abiding respect for fundamental African values and customs. Today it is one of the largest denominations in Côte d'Ivoire.

Feature: The Harrist Prophetic Movement and Church

In 1913 a prophetic evangelist named William Wadé Harris, donned a white robe and turban, and travelled by foot from Liberia through Côte d'Ivoire proclaiming the rejection of paganism and the coming of the Christian missions, the "Whites with the Bible" (Shank 1985, 70). He preached simple biblical messages of baptism and forgiveness of sins, but maintained the value of African customs like polygamy. Formerly a rebel in political uprisings in Liberia, "Harris perceived himself to be the eschatological Elijah", preaching in the end-time before the coming of the Kingdom (Shank 1985, 72). Harris converted followers at an astonishing rate. His following amounted to the largest religious mass movement of the century in West Africa (Turner 1966, 294). Panicked French colonial authorities ejected Harris from the country in 1914, temporarily suspending the movement's momentum. The Harrist movement returned in the newly self-conscious form of the Harrist Church, established in 1928 under the leadership of Harris' authorized successor John Ahui.

Harris himself had expected new believers to be subsumed under the direction of the Christian missions once they were established there. Indeed, by the time the Harrist Church was founded, its members were Protestant separatists reacting against the missions' dogmatic rejection of African traditions, refusing them participation in even non-religious local festivities. The Ivoirian Harrist Church not only embraced polygamy, it also distinguished itself theologically by elevating Harris and reducing Christ to a similar prophetic role (Shank 1985, 74).

Both Harris and Kimbangu had brief but astonishingly effective ministries. Threatened colonial authorities interrupted both of their missions. The legacy of both prophet/healers has endured and spread geographically, a testimony to their empowering contributions to the neo-traditional religious landscape.

Imaginative reconstructions

Other NTRMs are more loosely aligned with Christianity, greatly modifying its tenets or rituals in the service of the promotion of African indigenous religions under new historical circumstances. These represent imaginative reconstructions of indigenous religions that preserve their essential features in novel form. One of the oldest, most widespread of these types is Bwiti, a neo-traditional revitalization movement among Fang and others in Gabon and Equatorial Guinea.

Feature: Bwiti

In his magisterial study, James W. Fernández (1982) warns against calling Bwiti a separatist sect or independent form of Christianity. Bwiti is not Christocentric. It presents the crucifixion as a curse upon humanity not a means to its salvation. Moreover, Jesus is not worshipped as a saviour but is modelled on the *nganga*, the clairvoyant healer/diviner whose insight leads clients into unseen worlds (Fernández 1982, 406). Christ is called "He Who Sees God", and in ritual enactment is made to engage "in activities associated with the old Fang religion, including invoking the ancestors and leading a witch hunt" (Schoffeleers 1986, 355). By contrast, the Virgin Mary is elevated in status and bears the name of the female Goddess.

The Bwiti ritual leader is an nganga who leads the group on a ritual path, traced with the aid of a hallucinogen. The trajectory of the path recalls the Fang's historical-legendary southwestern migration from the sea. The final destination on the spiritual path is never completed, but the focus is instead on the ritual progression (Fernández 1986, 355). It aims to move members from the suffering, confusion and despair that arose with cultural disintegration, to the state of tranquillity that comes when one is re-established in a centred social and physical cosmos. The movement restores the flow of power and fertility bestowed by the ancestors, as well as God in the twinned form of *Zame* and his sister *Nyingwan Mebege*, "the 'universal matrix and source of knowledge'" (Werbner 1985, 116).

Fernández argues that Bwiti rebuilds the Fang social space that was disrupted by colonials, reconfiguring in ritual arenas and religious practices the spatial arrangement of the traditional Fang village and the social dynamics that were inscribed in it. Both the traditional Fang domestic spaces and Bwiti ritual are arranged in binary oppositions: village and forest, male and female domains, men's council houses and women's sleeping and cooking huts, for example (Fernández 1986, 356). The village itself however had no central focal point such as a palace or plaza. Bwiti ceremonies therefore orchestrate movement back and forth between poles and quadrants, reproducing the movement in traditional social space as well as traditional rites, like marriage, in which the Fang bride is escorted from the courtyard of her father's kin to the groom's domain before being returned to the women's arena.

The Fang were originally semi-nomadic, and revitalized their villages by relocating them every ten to twelve years. The colonial administrations, however, forced the Fang out of the forest to establish new permanent dwellings along commercial routes. This upheaval was not a renovation but a destabilizing dislocation. The sacred spaces constructed by Bwiti through ritual compensate for that dislocation. A midnight candlelight processional enters the forest to seek out ancestors who may be lost, returning them to

> the cult house. There the line of participants winds into a circle and links
> their flames overhead to form one light symbolizing the achievement of "one
> heartedness" (Fernández 1986, 364). Bwiti also traces a progressive path
> back to "the great ocean of salvation that is identified with the sea" (ibid.).
> Participation in Bwiti ritual perambulation recapitulates the people's great
> migration, consolidates Fang collective identity, and reconstructs traditional
> moral space. In this way it forges at least a provisional Fang identity in a
> challenging time of profound social transition.

The prominent role of the nganga as diviner/healer in the Equatorial African
regions combined with the potent figure of the prophet in Christianity and
Islam has led to the emergence of a significant new religious figure around
which many, more ephemeral, NTRMs regularly coalesce. An example is a
female nganga in Cameroon who directed her energies against witchcraft in the
1990s (see Chapter 7).

> In the early 1990s a woman began a new kind of practice as healer. She had
> recently returned from Douala, where her father had spent most of his life in
> relative obscurity. She claimed to be both a "diviner" and an "exorcist" and,
> as the last term suggests, her cures were deeply influenced by Catholic ritual.
> In contrast to other nganga in the area, who are supposed to be able to protect
> against the witches because they themselves have developed their djambe
> ("witchcraft") to an extreme degree, this new healer claimed to have nothing
> to do with this djambe. A striking difference was also that her customers did
> not have to pay anything; they only had to bring a new candle. After her
> "invocations", the woman had her clients drink blessed water, rubbed them
> with oil, and then gave them her benediction. Probably because of the novel
> character of her treatment – and maybe also because it was free – she became
> a great success; sometimes she received more than eighty persons a day.
>
> (Geschiere and Nyamnjoh 1998, 83)

Like Bwiti, this case demonstrates the significant imaginative achievement
that is typical of NTRMs. It is unusual in that its founder was female, however,
despite her success she remains anonymous.

Post-independence NTRMs and the promotion of pan-Africanism

African intellectuals were at the forefront of self-consciously organized NTRMs
seeking to rehabilitate the reputation and standing of African traditions that had
been so demeaned throughout the colonial era. They were especially interested in
articulating a coherent system of African religious philosophy that could rival that
of the so-called world religions.

An early example of the wholesale reformulation of African indigenous religion is Godianism, a movement that emerged in Nigeria in 1948. Its founder and High Chief Priest, Chief K.O.K. Onyioha, aimed to articulate traditional ideas in terms of a unified philosophy. His book, *African Godianism: A Revolutionary Religion for Mankind through Direct Communication with God* (Onyioha 1980), underscored the revelatory nature of the ancestors' traditional practices, and defended against the common charge that this unmediated heritage amounted to paganism. Onyioha's treatise on the Godian creed aimed to demonstrate that Africa was not a philosophical void but offered a universal religion that can transcend ethnic and national boundaries.

A similar, more recent example of this intellectual nationalist NTRM is the Afrikania Mission in Ghana.

Feature: The Afrikania Mission

Afrikania was founded in 1982 by Kwabena Damuah, a former Roman Catholic priest who earned a Ph.D. in theology in the 1970s in the United States. There he was inspired by the Black Power movement, which instilled pride in African-American identity. Back in Ghana Damuah earned a reputation as a rebel when he tried to introduce local drumming into the Catholic Mass. He served briefly in the revolutionary government of Jerry Rawlings, but withdrew to dedicate his efforts to "the cultural, religious and moral aspects of nation building" as a necessary underpinning for effective independent governance (de Witte 2012, 176, 177).

Damuah first established Afrikania as a national cultural centre to affirm the universal value of African traditional religion. He and his followers established a systematic doctrine on the basis of select indigenous African beliefs and practices, including those of ancient Egypt. Later he led a nationwide crusade to spread this Afrikania message and attempt to found a modern pan-African religion that would transcend ethnic differences. During this period the Afrikania Mission was briefly affiliated to Godianism. Even after Damuah's death and succession the movement thrived. By 2000 the Afrikania Mission had convened several conventions of traditional practitioners, built headquarters, established the Afrikania Priesthood Training School and launched an international programme of "evangelization" (de Witte 2012, 177).

From its inception Afrikania deftly made use of media to spread its message, first through weekly radio broadcasts supported by the Rawlings government, and later through representation on TV talk shows and press coverage of Afrikania events. Ironically, the widespread coverage alienated some shrine priests and devotees whose traditions are protected by secrecy and restricted access to spiritual knowledge (see Chapter 15). Its public defence of traditions also seemed at odds with Afrikania's concern to present a seemingly more palatable image of them by the "elimination or concealment of practices considered ugly or dirty, such as bloody animal sacrifices" or "frenzied spirit possession" (de Witte 2012, 181).

Although Damuah was initially supportive of the Ghanaian state, Afrikania increasingly criticized the government for its disproportionate numbers of born-again Christians and their imposition of foreign values through Christian indoctrination in schools (de Witte 2012, 178).

NTRMs and the post-colonial African state in crisis

The history between NTRMs and contemporary African states is entangled and their relationship is ambivalent. In the colonial era, NTRM movements arose in response to political domination and injustice. As natural wellsprings of nationalist sentiment and resistance, they were viewed as subversive by imperialist forces and mainline mission Churches alike. After independence, certain African Initiated Churches and NTRMs were eager to register with the state and enjoy the sanction of their new governments. In other cases, the state coerced the NTRMs' cooperation with their modernist agendas, which sometimes ran counter to practices that the NTRMs aimed to revivify.

The goals of many new African states and their leaders seemed more in keeping with the orientation of Pentecostal and charismatic forms of Christianity that promoted prosperity and modern lifestyles, while the apolitical stance and otherworldly focus that they preached posed less of a threat than the NTRMs (see Chapters 5 and 8). The heads of state in Benin, Côte d'Ivoire, Nigeria, Kenya and Zambia all at one time during their rule proclaimed themselves "born-again" Christians. However, in the wake of the economic collapse of many African economies, new NTRMs emerged to meet the pressing needs of a suffering populace. While some presented inspiring visions of religious renewal and community support, they often also fed on inter-ethnic conflict and fostered violence and destabilization. Their relation to the post-colonial state has been so volatile that many governments harassed or banned them. The Lord's Resistance Army that recruited child soldiers to fight the Ugandan regime in the late 1980s is a prime example of the militant threat that an NTRM may pose. Kenya's Mungiki movement is another.

Feature: Mungiki, revival of Kikuyu religion or violent militia?

Mungiki, a Kikuyu word meaning "masses", or "multitude", started as a religious movement in 1987 when Maina Njenga had a vision in which God commanded him to lead his people out of the bondage of poverty and a corrupt political order (Mageria 2002, np).

Comprised of disenfranchised urban youth, Mungiki's large following operates in the Nairobi slums and the Central Province and Rift Valley. Most are Kikuyu, Kenya's largest ethnic group, and draw inspiration from the history and ideology of the famous nationalist movement, Mau Mau, which fought for liberation from British colonialism. During clashes preceding elections in 1992, Mungiki called poor, jobless, and landless Kenyans to unite "to fight against the yoke of mental slavery" under a largely Christian political elite (Wamue 2001, 453). It enjoined them to re-convert to their African indigenous beliefs, practices, and ancestral values purged of foreign religion. Youths embraced Kikuyu practices such as taking snuff, male ear piercing and initiation of dreadlocked youths (Mageria 2002, np).

Since African identity is inextricably bound up in ethnicity, Mungiki envisions every ethnic community renewing its own religion. A new collective government, comprised of a council of elders representing each of the newly restored ethnic kingdoms, would rule. Preparations require a "cleansing ritual known as *guthera*" (Wamue 2001, 461). This stage of purification has taken a coercive, violent turn.

Some glorify Mungiki as the heirs of the righteous Mau Mau mantle. Indeed, Mungiki facilitated the return of displaced persons fleeing ethnic violence and rebuilt wrecked communities, but the quasi-religious gang also engages in "mafia-like" economic and political activities to protect their Kikuyu stronghold. According to the international agency Human Rights Watch, those who do not submit to their rackets have been "kidnapped, tortured, and, in several notorious cases, beheaded" (UNHCR 2008, np). Mungiki was also accused of forced clitoridectomy of all females residing in their turf or associating with members. Church leaders decried the group as "morally impaired" (Wamue 2001, 460). The state condemned Mungiki for administering illegal oaths, ostensibly to overthrow the government (Kagwanja 2003, 40).

The government had historical reasons to fear Mungiki as a clandestine political adversary. Mungiki was formed as an offshoot of an older group, the *Tent of the Living God*, a prophet-led movement which advocated the return to African religious heritage. However, "the Tent" was ultimately banned for organizing political rallies and its leader, Ngonyawa Gakonya, was arrested and imprisoned for his fervent public campaigns against Kenya's single party political system. Moreover, Mungiki youth openly advocate a return to "the Kikuyu religio-cultural and political system" in which governing power is handed over to a new generation, a process they felt was long overdue (Wamue 2001, 463). In 1998, on the anniversary of Kenyan independence (*Jamhuri* Day), Mungiki organized a congress at a Kikuyu ancestral shrine where they chanted Mau Mau war songs. Significantly the shrine had just been made a National Monument by the Minister of Home Affairs and National Heritage (Wamue 2001, 465). The symbolic contest of authority over sacred territory was a clear political challenge.

In 2000 Mungiki's leader converted to Islam, with hundreds of its members following suit. Ndura Waruinge (renamed Ibrahim) proclaimed that it would "hasten the realization of the movement's goal of fighting against corruption, bad governance, poverty, immorality and diseases such as AIDS among Kenyans" (Kagwanja 2003, 39). Critics charged that Mungiki was using Islam to shield its members from police harassment. Indeed, Muslim Imams warned that government interference with Mungiki activities "would now be seen as an insult to Muslims worldwide" (Kagwanja, 2003, 39).

The Mungiki case is far from unique in an increasingly volatile world. Joseph Hellweg (2011) presents the case of the Dozo of northern Côte d'Ivoire, Burkina Faso and Mali, an indigenous society of hunters that reconciles their traditional beliefs and practices with Islam. Initiates make sacrifices to their tutelary spirit, Manimory, who is an all-powerful presence in the forest but whom they also claim as a Muslim saint. They revere Manimory as Muslims do the Sufi saints, honouring him at the site where, according to Dozo mytho-history, he sacrificed his wife and son and where he disappeared. Although the killing of game does not conform to Muslim prescriptions for the proper butchering of meat (halal), hunting poses no problem for Dozo because Manimory sanctifies it. Dozos use sorcery to blend with the forest, like their omnipresent spiritual guardian, and make themselves invisible to their prey. But in the morning when they make their Muslim prayers they remove their "amulet-laden shirts" (Hellweg 2011, 11). This imaginative co-joining of pre-Islamic indigenous belief and practice with Islam shows Dozo to be neo-traditionalists. However this NTRM was further transformed into an armed force that, like Mungiki, threatened and helped overturn the Ivoirian state.

During Côte d'Ivoire's civil wars in 2002 and 2011 and the period of national insecurity in between, the Dozo organized a movement called Benkadi to fight and protect the community of northern Muslims. Drawing on their sorcery to track criminals, they hunted the enemy. The Benkadi shifted the secret and sacred Dozo initiatory society into a ritual-based police patrol, and it in turn transmuted into a morally questionable militia. Tens of thousands joined Benkadi to fight in the civil war in support of the Muslim rebel faction. As soldiers, "dozos committed atrocities against the same people they were ostensibly trying to protect ... women, the poor, immigrants, Ivoirian citizens, and police" (Hellweg 2011, 17).

The NTRMs' transformation into violent militia may be understood as a response to globalization, characterized by "growth without emancipation" and the combination of "a widening gulf between the richest and the poorest" (Atieno 2007, 530). The perhaps inevitable result is a crusade for the rights of the multitude that "feels acutely deprived and marginalized in a rapidly globalizing world" (Kagwanja 2003, 29). If the state cannot meet the needs of its people, the people turn to their time-honoured sources of inspiration to rally on their own terms.

Questions for discussion

- Given that African indigenous religions are always adjusting to new conditions, and the fact that certain communities such as African Indigenous/ Independent Churches might well be categorized as Neo-traditional Religious Movements as well, how useful is the term "NTRM" as a category of analysis? Are the overlaps instructive or merely confusing?
- What do you imagine would cause some youth movements to seek out globalized religious identity (e.g. Pentecostal) and others to embrace African ethnic identity through NTRMs?
- At what point/under what circumstances does a movement cease to be religious in nature and become a largely political mobilization?
- Why would some postcolonial states be supportive of NTRMs and under what circumstances might they suppress or oppose them?

References (*indicates recommended reading)

Atieno, Awinda. 2007. "Mungiki, 'Neo-Mau Mau' and the Prospects for Democracy in Kenya", *Review of African Political Economy* 34/113, 526–531.

Ayegboyin, Deji, and S. Ademola Ishola. 1997. "African Indigenous Churches — Chapter Fifteen". Institute for Religious Research (IRR). http://irr.org/african-indigen ous-churches-chapter-fifteen.

*De Witte, Marleen. 2012. "Neo-Traditional Religions." In *The Wiley-Blackwell Companion to African Religions*, edited by Elias Bongmba, 173–183. Malden: Wiley-Blackwell.

Fernández, James. 1982. *Bwiti: An Ethnography of the Religious Imagination in Africa*. Princeton: Princeton University Press.

Fernández, James. 1986. "Location and Direction in African Religious Movements: Some Deictic Contours of Religious Conversion", *History of Religions* 25/4, 352–367.

Geschiere, Peter, and Francis Nyamnjoh. 1998. "Witchcraft as an Issue in the 'Politics of Belonging': Democratization and Urban Migrants' Involvement with the Home Village", *African Studies Review* 41/3, 69–91.

*Hackett, Rosalind. 1991. "Revitalization in African Traditional Religion." In *African Traditional Religions in Contemporary Society*, edited by Jacob Olupona, 135–149. St. Paul, MN: Paragon House.

Hellweg, Joseph. 2011. *Hunting the Ethical State: The Benkadi Movement of Côte d'Ivoire*. Chicago: University of Chicago Press.

Kagwanja, Peter Mwangi. 2003. "Facing Mount Kenya or Facing Mecca? The Mungiki, Ethnic Violence and the Politics of the Moi Succession in Kenya, 1987–2002", *African Affairs* 102/406, 25–49.

Mageria, David. 2002. "Banned Kenyan Sect Has Keen Following", 8 May 2002, Reuters News Agency. *The Globe and Mail*. https://www.theglobeandmail.com/news/national/ banned-kenyan-sect-has-keen-following/article4134777/.

Onyioha, Chief K.O.K. 1980. *African Godianism: A Revolutionary Religion for Mankind through Direct Communication with God*. Buffalo, NY: Conch Magazine.

Schoffeleers, Matthew. 1986. "Bwiti (Book Review)", *Africa* 56/3, 352.

Shank, David A. 1985. "The Harrist Church in the Ivory Coast: Review Article", *Journal of Religion in Africa* 15/1, 67–75.

Turner, H.W. 1966. "A Methodology for Modern African Religious Movements", *Comparative Studies in Society and History* 8/3, 281–294.

Turner, H.W. 1980. "The Place of Independent Religious Movements in the Modernization of Africa", *Journal of Religion in Africa* 11/1, 43–63.

UNHCR (United Nations High Commissioner for Refugees). 2008. "World Report 2008 – Kenya". Refworld. Accessed 6 May 2018. http://www.refworld.org/docid/47a 87c0837.html.

Wamue, Grace Nyatugah. 2001. "Revisiting Our Indigenous Shrines through Mungiki", *African Affairs* 100/400, 453–467.

Werbner, Richard P. 1985. "Review of James W. Fernandez, *Bwiti: An Ethnography of the Religious Imagination in Africa* (Princeton, New Jersey, Princeton University Press 1982)", *NUMEN* 32/1, 115–117.

5 Pentecostal-Charismatic movements in Africa

The nature of contemporary Christianity in Africa

The statistics in Chapter 2 gave an idea of the remarkable growth of Christianity on the African continent in the 20th and early 21st centuries. The chapter also gave an impression of the enormous diversity of denominations and traditions represented by the approximately 600 million African Christians to date. The present chapter aims to provide a more in-depth account of the nature of contemporary Christianity in Africa, specifically its Pentecostal-Charismatic orientation. In general, Protestant Christianity in Africa tends to have a strong evangelical character, that is, an emphasis on born-again conversion, a personal relationship with Jesus Christ and God, the authority of the Bible and on evangelization. Pentecostal-Charismatic movements share this evangelical orientation, yet add a new and very prominent element to it: the emphasis on the experience and power of the Holy Spirit. In this chapter, we use "Pentecostal-Charismatic Christianity" as a broad umbrella term, referring to a wide range of movements that can be classified as Pentecostal and/or Charismatic. The word "Pentecostal" originates from the biblical story about Pentecost (Book of Acts), according to which the Holy Spirit was poured out over the followers of Jesus after his ascension. In the 20th century, the word was used as the name of a new strand of Christianity emphasizing the ongoing relevance of the biblical Pentecost experience. The word "charismatic" has its origins in the Greek word *charismata*, which is used in the New Testament for the gifts of the Holy Spirit, such as prophecy, speaking in tongues and healing. In broader sociological parlance, "charismatic" often refers to a particular form of religious (but also political) leadership and authority, and to particular forms of religious experience that tend to be ecstatic, embodied and energetic.

As much as there is a great diversity of Christian traditions on the continent, since the last decades of the 20th century Pentecostal-Charismatic movements have grown dramatically and have come to define to a considerable extent the face of African Christianity. As Allan Anderson (2015, 54) points out, "African Christianity as a whole – Catholic, Anglican, Protestant and independent – has moved considerably in a 'Pentecostal' or Charismatic direction, quite apart from the enormous growth among Pentecostal churches themselves". That is, even the mainline churches have taken on the flavour of Pentecostalism, featuring impassioned, spontaneous manifestations of the presence of the Holy Spirit in the life of the believer, and focusing on spiritual purity as the source of bodily healing. The enormous popularity of Pentecostal-Charismatic movements has to be understood in relation to demographic developments, that is, the population growth of African societies and the subsequent enormous numbers of youth. Young people, in particular, are attracted to Pentecostal-Charismatic expression of the Christian faith. Therefore, an understanding of Pentecostalism is also vital to a deeper understanding of the relation between religion and youth in Africa, as well as between religion and modernity, religion and popular culture, and religion and globalization.

Histories and categories of Pentecostal-Charismatic Christianity in Africa

Pentecostal-Charismatic Christianity in Africa is an enormously diverse phenomenon. Four main categories can be broadly distinguished. First, the beginning of Pentecostalism globally is often located in Los Angeles where in 1906 the preaching of African American pastor William Seymour gave rise to the Azusa Street Revival, with people receiving the Holy Spirit and starting to speak in tongues. From there the early Pentecostal movement began to spread, within the United States but also to other parts of the world, including Africa. Several Pentecostal denominations that can be found in Africa to date, such as the Apostolic Faith Mission and the Assemblies of God, have their roots in this historical trajectory, and they are often referred to as "classical Pentecostal churches". However, it would be a misconception to explain the origins of Pentecostalism as a whole, both in Africa and worldwide, with this American-centred narrative. In the late 19th and early 20th centuries, various revival movements emerged around the world, many of them independently from Azusa Street. African scholars of Pentecostalism, such as Kwabena Asamoah-Gyadu and Ogbu Kalu, emphasize that Pentecostalism does not have a homogenous history that can be traced back to North America, but that it refers to a complex global phenomenon with multiple beginnings and diverse genealogies. Among others, they point at prophetic figures and charismatic movements that emerged in West, East and Southern Africa from around the turn of the 20th century, which caused a "pneumatic [spirit-filled] explosion" into missionary Christianity of the time (Kalu 2008, 8). Thus, second, the African Independent Churches discussed in Chapter 2, especially the AICs of the Prophet-Healing or Spiritual type such as the Zionist and Apostolic churches in Southern Africa and the Aladura churches in West Africa, are referred to by Asamoah-Gyadu as presenting a form of "Independent Indigenous Pentecostalism":

> The groups concerned are described as both "independent" and "indigenous" because there is virtually no foreign missionary element in their

origins. … They are considered Pentecostal because they consciously seek to experience and affirm the active presence of the Holy Spirit as part of normal Christian expression.

(Asamoah-Gyadu 2005, 16)

In this line of thought, what the diverse phenomenon called Pentecostalism unites is not a common history but a shared emphasis on the experience of the Holy Spirit through spiritual gifts such as prophecy, healing, speaking in tongues and other charismatic expressions. At the same time, it is important to keep in mind the significant differences between the AICs and other Pentecostal-Charismatic churches. The latter frequently dismiss the former as syncretistic (that is, as mixing two religions). They see the AICs as not truly Christian because of their use of symbolic objects and the incorporation of elements from African indigenous religions and cultures.

The discussion so far has identified two categories of Pentecostalism in Africa: the AICs, especially the Prophet-Healing churches, which present a form of indigenous African Pentecostalism, and the classical Pentecostal churches that are the result of American and British Pentecostal missionary activities. Churches in both categories demonstrated great vitality and growth in the 20th century, and in many parts of Africa they continue to thrive. They have also had a significant influence on the European mission churches in Africa, with both the Catholic, Anglican and Protestant churches in many African countries having strong charismatic movements within their denominations. The latter development is sometimes referred to as the "Pentecostalization of the mainline churches" (Omenyo 2005), and Christians within these movements are sometimes classified as a separate category, called "older [or mainline] church charismatics" (Anderson 2015, 68). Thus, third, the term "charismatic movements" is often used for these Pentecostal-influenced groups within the established denominations.

Although churches and movements in these categories still comprise a considerable number of Christians, from around the 1980s there has been a new wave in African Pentecostalism, giving rise to a fourth category. Variably called neo-Pentecostal, neo-charismatic, or Pentecostal-Charismatic churches, they have grown rapidly and have come to define the face of contemporary Pentecostal Christianity in Africa. Capturing the difference between the older AICs and these neo-Pentecostal churches (NPCs), Birgit Meyer writes:

Nothing can better evoke what is at stake than the salience of the contrast between the familiar image of African prophets from Zionist, Nazarite, or Aladura churches, dressed in white gowns, carrying crosses, and going to pray in the bush, and the flamboyant leaders of the new mega-churches, who dress in the latest (African) fashion, drive nothing less than a Mercedes Benz, participate in the global Pentecostal jetset, broadcast the message through flashy TV and radio programs, and preach the Prosperity Gospel to their deprived and hitherto-hopeless born-again followers at home and in the diaspora.

(Meyer 2004, 448)

Thus what distinguishes the NPCs is a combination of a modern style of presentation, the use of popular forms of communication, a global orientation, and a theological emphasis on prosperity. In addition, they are often associated with a concern with spiritual warfare against demonic forces and deliverance from evil (see below). Of course, different churches within this broad category may put greater or lesser emphasis on certain characteristics. Many NPCs are independent churches, but others have become pan-African or even worldwide denominations, such as the originally Nigerian Winners Chapel International. Some churches that initially belonged to the AIC category have recently restyled themselves in a neo-Pentecostal way – the originally Nigerian (but now worldwide) Redeemed Christian Church of God is a well-known example of this. Other churches that historically speaking have roots in classical Pentecostalism have incorporated neo-Pentecostal elements, such as an emphasis on prosperity and deliverance – the Zimbabwe Assemblies of God Africa serve as example here.

This short overview of histories and categories of Pentecostalism in Africa has foregrounded the complex, dynamic and fluid nature of churches and movements referred to under this umbrella. In the remainder of this chapter, the focus is on contemporary Pentecostalism, especially of the fourth category, the Pentecostal-Charismatic churches.

Contemporary neo-Pentecostal churches

The neo-Pentecostal churches that have come to define contemporary Pentecostal-Charismatic Christianity emerged from around the 1980s, often in the form of interdenominational prayer and bible study groups, Christian student movements, or Christian businessmen fellowships. Under the direction of spiritually "anointed" leaders, they gradually evolved into independent (mega) churches and transnational denominations. In most cases these leaders are male (with the pastor's wife usually playing a strong supportive role), but there are some prominent examples of female leadership, such as Rev. Dr Christie Doe Tetteh, founder of Rock Solid Chapel International in Ghana, and Bishop Margaret Wanjiru, founder of Jesus Is Alive Ministries in Kenya. Both women founded their ministries in 1993 and as general overseer have been leading their expansion since then. To what extent the presence of these powerful female leaders implies that Pentecostal-Charismatic Christianity challenges and transforms African gender ideologies is subject to debate (Soothill 2015).

The emergence and explosive growth of NPCs in the 1980s took place in a decade in which many African countries faced severe economic crises. The optimism of the 1960s that the new independent post-colonial African states would be able to provide social and political stability and economic development for their growing populations was seriously challenged. Against this background, the rise and success of the NPCs in a period of economic and other hardship has often been explained in instrumentalist ways. In these interpretations, NPCs attract a large following because they "enable people to cope with limited conditions and to take some measure of control over their own lives in a situation where other, official, institutions fail", and because they engender "hope, a renewed self-esteem, and a sense of empowerment, all of which enables converts to stand up to difficult circumstances" (Lindhardt 2015, 7). More generally, the popularity of NPCs is explained in relation to socio-economic processes such as urbanization and neoliberal capitalist economic reform. For example, the "break with the past" advocated by Pentecostalism is not just about breaking with a previous sinful lifestyle but also enables people to renegotiate traditional moral commitments to, and financial demands from relatives in the extended family and wider community. This corresponds with the process of individualization and the increasing shift towards the nuclear family in modern African urban life. In countries where the economic situation has gradually improved in recent decades, the continued popularity of NPCs has been explained by referring to the ways in which contemporary Pentecostalism legitimizes the quest for consumption and wealth among the growing urban middle classes. The links between Pentecostalism and the changing socio-economic circumstances in which it finds itself appear to be multiple, complex, and dynamic. This is captured in Dena Freeman's (2012, 28) observation that "Pentecostalism is able to cater for the spiritual needs of both the rich and the poor, the winners and the losers in the neoliberal turn".

As much as instrumentalist interpretations in terms of modernity and neoliberal capitalism provide important insight into the appeal of NPCs among many Africans, few adherents will explain their attraction to Pentecostalism in such terms. Hence, Lindhardt (2015, 7) emphasizes that it is equally important to "give careful consideration of the religious factors that give NPCs a competitive advantage over other churches and secular institutions". Indeed, converts are likely to refer to the inspiration and empowerment they receive through worship and preaching at a particular church, or to the power of God they witness in the healing and deliverance performed by a particular prophet. Thus the subsequent sections discuss two important features of contemporary Pentecostalism: their teaching of the prosperity gospel, and their emphasis on healing, deliverance and spiritual warfare.

The prosperity gospel

One key characteristic of NPCs relates to a theological development in African Pentecostalism in recent decades, with an increasing prominence of what is variably called the faith gospel, the prosperity gospel, or the gospel of health and wealth. These terms can have slightly different yet overlapping meanings, but in general they refer to new religious understandings that centre on the belief that material, physical, professional and relational well-being are an integral part of salvation and are a sign of true faith and of God's favourability towards the true believer. Thus, in contrast to the classical Pentecostal emphasis on personal salvation and on holiness, understood as a sober lifestyle and a withdrawal from "the world", the NPCs tend to preach that salvation is not only about the hereafter, but also (and in some cases, especially) about the here-and-now. This is often framed in a language of divine blessings – in terms of physical health, material abundance, success in one's career, business and other areas of life – as a right to be claimed by the born-again Christian. As Paul Gifford summarizes this idea:

> Every Christian should now share in Christ's victory over sin, sickness and poverty. A believer has a right to the blessings of health and wealth won by Christ, and he or she can obtain these blessings merely by a positive confession of faith.
>
> (Gifford 2004, 48)

On the one hand, material blessings may be claimed as a right, while on the other hand they are seen as the reward for fulfilling one's Christian duties, especially the duty of paying tithes (that is, donating 10 per cent of one's income to the church). When the promise of prosperity is not fulfilled, this is usually explained with reference to witchcraft, demonic curses, or otherwise spiritual causes from which one needs to be delivered.

Critics argue that the prosperity gospel is a contemporary illustration of the Marxist argument that religion is the opiate of the people, and that the emphasis on tithing enables successful Pentecostal pastors to shamelessly enrich themselves at the expense of their often poor followers. However, in the eyes of these followers, the well-off preachers to which they pay their tithes may in fact embody the middle class aspirations they have themselves. In that case, the prosperity gospel can be seen as legitimizing "the quest for materialism, power, and prestige" sought by many Africans in the post-colonial era and in a consumerist capitalist context (Ojo 2012, 307).

Another criticism is that the prosperity gospel has been imported from America and is "a foreign element to African Christianity" (Gifford 1990). Although an American influence cannot be denied, one could argue that the prosperity gospel has become so popular precisely because it resonates with local African worldviews, in which religion is holistic and in which spiritual power is linked to material and physical wellbeing. Like indigenous religions, the prosperity gospel presents the principle that spiritual blessing always takes material form (wealth, healing and fertility). Against this background, the spread of the prosperity gospel can be seen as another example of the "creative processes of appropriation and contextualization" through which Christianity is "rendered meaningful and relevant to Africans" (Lindhardt 2015, 9). Its spiritual explanation of the lack of success helps people to make sense, in a modern idiom, of their ongoing struggle with poverty and their difficulty to make progress. In addition to spiritual solutions such as deliverance, many NPCs also provide more practical assistance – such as small loans to set up businesses, and workshops to develop entrepreneurial skills – for people to actually make progress in life.

Healing, deliverance and spiritual warfare

Another aspect typical of many contemporary NPCs is the centrality of healing and deliverance practices as well as of spiritual warfare. The three main categories used here – healing, deliverance and spiritual warfare – cannot be clearly distinguished as the boundaries are rather fluid. For instance, Matthew Ojo identifies four "spheres of healing" that, in varying degrees, can be found among African Pentecostal-Charismatic organizations: (1) physical healing; (2) relief from evil, witchcraft and the worlds of spirits; (3) healing over the socio-economic difficulties of the individual; (4) healing of the political and socio-economic conditions of the nation (Ojo 2012, 306). These spheres at least partly overlap with the four "areas of deliverance" that, according to Birgit Meyer, can be found in NPCs, again in varying degrees: (1) deliverance from the immediate past, that is, from sinful attitudes defining one's life before becoming born-again; (2) deliverance from the ancestral past, that is, from ancestral curses running through one's lineage; (3) deliverance from occult bondages, which are the result of one's involvement in indigenous religions and in religious or spiritual "sects" (e.g. Jehovah Witnesses, Mormons, Freemasonry, but also Hinduism, Buddhism and Islam); (4) deliverance from demonic control and influence, as a result of one's exposure to demons (Meyer 1998, 323–5). It appears that healing and deliverance are related and partly overlapping practices, because they both presume a cosmology in which evil spirits and demons exercise real power over people, which can only be combatted by evoking the power of God.

This enchanted cosmology, which is often seen as a key factor in the appeal of NPCs to many Africans, is characterized by what scholars have called the paradox of dis/continuity. Aptly capturing this paradox, Joel Robbins states that "Pentecostalism preserves traditional spiritual ontologies at the same time that it demonizes them" (Robbins 2010, 160). In other words, as much as Pentecostalism opposes indigenous religions, it does not deny the real powers that witches, ancestors and other spirits can have over people within African indigenous religious worldviews. Instead of denying, Pentecostalism reframes these beliefs in a Christian discourse about the Devil, thus assigning demonic agency to the spiritual forces of indigenous religions. At the same time it provides people with spiritual means of protection against evil spirits, because the power of God is believed to be stronger than the power of the Devil. This combination of acknowledging the realities of evil forces and providing people with means of spiritual empowerment and protection may explain the appeal of NPCs to many Africans.

As much as evil or demonic power operates at the level of individuals who are then subjected to rituals of healing and deliverance, it also operates at a larger scale – holding grip over communities, neighbourhoods, cities, societies, nations and even international bodies. This is where spiritual warfare comes in, as a Pentecostal-Charismatic methodology for "purification, neutralization and sanctification" of physical, public, social and political space (Lindhardt 2015, 21). Spiritual warfare refers to a wide range of material and symbolic practices through which Pentecostals discern evil spirits in particular areas, spaces and institutions, and defeat these through God's power. Examples range from playing gospel music in minibuses as a way of endowing them with divine protection, to prayer walks through a neighbourhood known to harbour prostitution in order to cleanse the streets of immorality; from overnight prayers and intense fasting in the run up to elections in order for the God-chosen candidate to win, to prophesying against the United Nations because they would be promoting gay rights in Africa.

What distinguishes neo-Pentecostalism is not the belief in the realities of evil spirits and in the power of spiritual counter-practices as such (as this can be found in the AICs, too), but the particular forms in which these beliefs are expressed. NPCs tend to centre on specific charismatic figures – men, and occasionally women, of God who are believed to have received a special "anointing" with extraordinary spiritual powers. The language, imagery and sound used by these figures to demonstrate and exercise this anointing are styled in particular ways, in order to create impressions of spectacular performances of divine power. As much as this style preserves African indigenous worldviews as noted above, it is also highly contemporary and global as it makes use of a range of modern media techniques, light and sound effects, and of performances and rhetoric inspired by American, Brazilian or Korean charismatic pastors (see Chapter 15).

Feature: Mountain of Fire and Miracles Ministries

A well-known example of a PCC specialized in deliverance is the Mountain of Fire and Miracles Ministries (MFM). The founder and general overseer, Daniel K. Olukoya, was trained as a microbiologist and received his PhD from a UK university, before he discovered the power of God working through him. Started in 1989 as a prayer group in Lagos, Nigeria, MFM had its first church service in 1994 and since then has implemented a strategy of establishing "a network of branches in every state capital, local government headquarters, senatorial district and locality" within the country (MFM n.d.). It has now grown into a global Pentecostal organization that claims to be present on every continent, in a total of 66 countries. Its Lagos inner-city headquarters is a transformed slum area where the Sunday morning service is attended by about 100,000 people. At the outskirts of Lagos, the church has established a Prayer City, where hundreds of thousands of people gather for non-stop prayer and deliverance. Rosalind Hackett explains the enormous appeal of MFM by referring to the constant battle of survival – against crime, corruption, pollution, poverty, traffic and violence – that defines life in mega-cities such as Lagos and that leaves people feeling highly vulnerable and insecure. "In light of this, Olukoya's narratives and depictions of nefarious spiritual powers, causing suffering and preventing self-realization in this modernizing world, appear as powerful metaphorical representations of living conditions for the majority of Lagosians" (Hackett 2011, 121). In a similar way, his narratives apparently also speak to the social and spiritual insecurities – for instance, in relation to migration, visa problems, illegal residence status – faced by people attracted to MFM in other parts of the world.

The MFM website, the circulation of many publications and sermons by Olukoya as well as videos of his performances, give a good insight into the discourse of deliverance and spiritual warfare used in the church. MFM's mission statement talks about the church's commitment to training believers "in the art and science of spiritual warfare, thus making them an aggressive and victorious army for the Lord", and to turning "the joy of our enemies to sorrow, which is why we would always have a Deliverance ministry wherever we are" (MFM n.d.).

Analysing Olukoya's teachings, Hackett (2011, 120) writes that he "provides a *local* theory of supernatural agency which can plausibly account for deviance and misfortune in the lives of individuals, families, communities, nations, nay even the global community". Where Hackett seeks to understand and to render intelligible the reasons why a deliverance ministry such as MFM is so appealing to many Africans, Paul Gifford is more explicit in his critique of MFM. He argues that Olukoya's theology is anti-modern as it reflects a "totally primal Christianity" in which the primary cause of anything is a spiritual force; such a form of Christianity, in his opinion, "does little to empower church members individually" and "does even less to challenge Nigeria's totally dysfunctional socio-political structures" (Gifford 2014, 117, 130–1). These divergent interpretations not only reveal different approaches to the study of religion in Africa, but also different notions of modernity, the question being whether modernity is necessarily disenchanted or whether primal (or enchanted) worldviews can simultaneously be modern.

Pentecostalism, politics and public culture

One of the interesting things about contemporary Pentecostal-Charismatic Christianity is that its impact and influence reaches far beyond the confines of churches and the religious domain as it is traditionally conceived. Traditional boundaries such as those between church and state, religion and politics, religious and secular culture have become increasingly blurred and, in fact, inadequate in the face of what has been called the "Pentecostalization of the public sphere in Africa" (Lindhardt 2015, 20). This process of Pentecostalization refers to the incorporation of Pentecostal ideas, forms, discourses and practices into other spheres of cultural, social, public and political life. Earlier in this chapter we already referred to the Pentecostalization of the mainline churches, but also non-Christian religious organizations in Africa have been influenced by Pentecostal styles, especially revivalist Islamic movements. A fascinating example of this can be observed in a photography project by Akintunde Akinleye and Marloes Janson, which reveals the very similar charismatic and embodied styles of worship in the above-discussed Mountain of Fire and Miracle Ministries and the Muslim Nasrul-Lahi-Fatih Society of Nigeria (NASFAT), also in Lagos (Akinleye and Janson 2014). This example calls into question a strict distinction between Christianity and Islam by foregrounding the emerging convergences in aesthetic styles between both traditions.

Other studies of Pentecostalization call into question the idea of the public sphere as a rational and neutral or secular space by demonstrating how Pentecostal worldviews shape public and political debates. Similarly, public spaces in African cities, such as parks and stadiums, are frequently taken over by massive prayer rallies and revival meetings; vehicles for public transport are decorated with bumper stickers stating that "this bus is protected by the blood of Jesus"; shops and restaurants are labelled with names such as "Full of Blessings Enterprises" (Figure 5.1). Moreover, Pentecostal styles influence popular culture and the entertainment industry (see Chapter 15). On the one hand, the liberalization of the media sector was an opportunity for many NPCs to launch their own radio and TV programmes as well as publishing houses. Yet film production companies, even if not run by Pentecostals, also started producing films touching on Pentecostal themes and representing Pentecostal worldviews, while in the meantime gospel has come to dominate the popular music scene.

At a more explicitly political level, early Pentecostalism tended to emphasize the biblical command to submit to governmental authorities, as these are instituted by God (Romans 13). As such, Pentecostal churches were often a-political, in a context where the established churches, such as the Catholic Church,

Figure 5.1 Internet cafe with a Pentecostalite name in Lusaka, Zambia (Adriaan van Klinken, 2011)

often took a stance against authoritarian regimes and promoted democracy. More recently, however, neo-Pentecostal churches appear to have abandoned the idea that the church should not be involved in "worldly affairs" such as politics, and they have developed new forms of political engagement and political language, often in an explicitly religious guise. Thus, contemporary Pentecostal rhetoric is very much concerned, not just with winning individual souls, but with "claiming the land for Christ" and "dedicating the nation to God". According to Ruth Marshall's (2009) in-depth study in Nigeria, Pentecostalism embarks on a large-scale programme of born-again conversion which aims to target and transform people and model them into ideal Christian citizens which can then change the character of the nation at large. Of course, this raises critical questions about the ways in which Pentecostals perceive democracy and religious freedom (see Chapter 8).

The earlier discussed belief in spiritual warfare also has profound political ramifications. From a Pentecostal perspective, politics is a primary field where the cosmological battle between God and the Devil takes place, and techniques of spiritual warfare are deployed to combat the influence of Satan in the life of the nation. Concrete examples of this can be seen, for instance, in the way Pentecostals relate to Islam, or engage in debates about homosexuality. As a result of Pentecostal political influence, one country in Africa has officially been declared a "Christian nation": Zambia. In many other countries a similar Pentecostalization of political culture and of nationalist ideologies can be observed (see Chapter 8).

Feature: Prophet David Owuor

Prophet David Owuor has become a highly prominent figure in Kenya's religious landscape since he established the Ministry of Repentance and Holiness in 2004. Being academically trained and having worked as a scientist in Israel and the United States, he claims to have been called by God to return to his native country. God wanted him to save the Kenyan nation, as well as the Kenyan church, from moral and spiritual decay. Addressing this decay, he not only points at "sins" such as abortion, homosexuality, adultery and witchcraft. He also explicitly targets fellow Pentecostal pastors and their prosperity gospel, which he sees as deceptive. He himself relentlessly preaches a message of repentance from sin, calling upon people to (re)dedicate themselves to God and lead a holy lifestyle. His preaching is combined with prophetic warnings of divine wrath coming over Kenya if the country does not repent. Owuor became particularly popular after the post-election violence erupting in Kenya after the disputed December 2007 presidential elections. Claiming to have predicted these violent clashes, and emphasizing that the violence would not have happened if only people had listened to his message, Owuor introduced himself on the national stage as a man of God who could bring healing, reconciliation and peace to a divided and wounded nation. In the run up to the next general election, in 2013, he held a National Prayer and Repentance event in Nairobi, which was attended by nearly all the presidential candidates and thousands of Kenyans. At this event, Owuor not only prayed over the candidates, but also made them publicly swear to respect the outcome of the election and to uphold peace.

A salient feature of Owuor's ministry is that it does not seek to establish churches but instead creates "national altars". Usually in the open air such as in parks and stadiums, according to Damaris Parsitau "these are not churches but any space that is claimed, cleansed and used for worship, fasting, repentance and prayer meetings" (Parsitau 2015, 193–4). Hundreds of such altars can now be found all over the country. This is where the followers of the prophet meet, not seldom dressed in sackcloth or other sober dresses as an expression of repentance and of their readiness for the second coming of Christ. Especially when Owuor himself visits one of these altars, large numbers of people gather with high expectations of the powerful prophesies and miracles that he will deliver. Other Kenyans, however, are suspicious of Owuor, as they call into question his spiritual authenticity as well as the origins of his wealth.

With his strong criticism of prosperity preachers and his emphasis on repentance and holiness, Owuor distinguishes himself from contemporary Pentecostalism and carves out a unique space. At the same time the personality cult around him corresponds with the neo-Pentecostal emphasis on the pastor or prophet as a uniquely anointed and divinely gifted figure. He further has greatly contributed to the invention of a neo-Pentecostal political narrative of Kenya as a nation born-again, in which "repentance, forgiveness, and peace lead to God's favour and prosperity – both national and personal" (Deacon 2015, 207).

Conclusion

This chapter has provided an account of the religious orientation of contemporary Christianity in Africa, especially its Pentecostal-Charismatic character. It should be emphasized that NPCs come in many different varieties: they may preach different shades of the prosperity gospel, and they may understand and practise healing, deliverance and spiritual warfare in different ways. In all their variety, they have however pushed African Christianity in new directions, navigating new ways of expressing and experiencing the Christian faith both in relation to African indigenous religious worldviews and to the challenges and opportunities represented by modern processes of social, cultural and economic change.

One development that cannot remain unnoticed is the globalization of African Pentecostalism, with many churches having become transnational denominations that are active, not only in a range of African countries but also in other continents. Thus, branches of originally African NPCs nowadays can be found all over Europe and North America, as well as in other parts of the world, where they contribute a unique flavour to established forms of Christianity. The leaders of these churches are part of, and contribute to, a global circuit in which Pentecostal ideas and practices circulate and develop. Within Africa, there are no signs yet of a diminishing popularity of Pentecostal-Charismatic Christianity. Part of the success of this movement is that it is highly creative, dynamic and innovative. It constantly gives space to the birth of new initiatives and the emergence of new charismatic figures that appeal to people in the ever-changing cultural, economic, social and political circumstances of African societies.

Questions for discussion

- Do you agree with Gifford that the enormous concern of many contemporary NPCs with evil spirits and demons makes these churches "primal" and "anti-modern", or do you think that this religious worldview is compatible with, and shapes modernity in Africa? What are your considerations?
- What are the consequences and implications of the Pentecostalization of the public sphere in African societies, both for the way the public sphere operates, and how it is usually understood? How do you evaluate this process in relation to democratic principles such as freedom of expression and religion?
- What are the chances, and what are the risks, for NPCs in Africa to remain a relevant religious factor that continues to appeal to new generations?

References (*indicates recommended reading)

Akinleye, Akintunde, and Marloes Janson. 2014. "The Spiritual Highway: Religious World Making in Megacity Lagos", SOAS University of London. https://www.soas.ac.uk/gallery/spiritual-highway/ (accessed 30 September 2017).

*Anderson, Allan. 2015. "'Stretching Out Hands to God': Origins and Development of Pentecostalism in Africa". In *Pentecostalism in Africa: Presence and Impact of Pneumatic Christianity in Postcolonial Societies*, edited by Martin Lindhardt, 54–74. Leiden: Brill.

Asamoah-Gyadu, Kwabena. 2005. *African Charismatics: Current Developments within Independent Indigenous Pentecostalism in Ghana.* Leiden: Brill.

Deacon, Gregory. 2015. "Driving the Devil Out: Kenya's Born-Again Election", *Journal of Religion in Africa* 45/2, 200–220.

Freeman, Dena. 2012. "The Pentecostal Ethic and the Spirit of Development." In *Pentecostalism and Development: Churches, NGOs and Social Change in Africa*, edited by Dena Freeman, 1–40. New York: Palgrave MacMillan.

Gifford, Paul. 1990. "Prosperity: A New and Foreign Element in African Christianity", *Religion* 20/4, 373–388.

*Gifford, Paul. 2004. *Ghana's New Christianity: Pentecostalism in a Globalizing African Economy.* London: Hurst & Co.

Gifford, Paul. 2014. "Evil, Witchcraft, and Deliverance in the African Pentecostal Worldview." In *Pentecostal Theology in Africa*, edited by Clifton Clarke, 112–131. Egune: Wipf and Stock.

Hackett, Rosalind. 2011. "Is Satan Local or Global? Reflections on a Nigerian Deliverance Movement". In *Who Is Afraid of the Holy Ghost? Pentecostalism and Globalization in Africa and Beyond*, edited by Afe Adogame, 111–132. Trenton: Africa World Press.

Kalu, Ogbu. 2008. *African Pentecostalism: An Introduction*. Oxford: Oxford University Press.

*Lindhardt, Martin. 2015. "Introduction: Presence and Impact of Pentecostal/Charismatic Christianity in Africa". In *Pentecostalism in Africa: Presence and Impact of Pneumatic Christianity in Postcolonial Societies*, 1–53. Leiden: Brill.

Marshall, Ruth. 2009. *Political Spiritualities: The Pentecostal Revolution in Nigeria*. Chicago: University of Chicago Press.

Meyer, Birgit. 1998. "'Make a Complete Break with the Past': Memory and Post-Colonial Modernity in Ghanaian Pentecostalist Discourse", *Journal of Religion in Africa* 28/3, 316–349.

Meyer, Birgit. 2004. "Christianity in Africa: From African Independent to Pentecostal-Charismatic Churches", *Annual Review of Anthropology* 33, 447–474.

Mountain of Fire and Miracles Ministries (MFM). N.d. "About MFM", http://www.mountainoffire.org/about# (accessed 29 September 2017).

Ojo, Matthews. 2012. "Pentecostal and Charismatic Movements in Modern Africa." In *The Wiley-Blackwell Companion to African Religions*, edited by Elias Bongmba, 295–309. Malden: Wiley-Blackwell.

Omenyo, Cephas. 2005. "From the Fringes to the Centre: Pentecostalization of the Mainline Churches in Ghana", *Exchange* 34/1, 39–60.

Parsitau, Damaris. 2015. "Embodying Holiness: Gender, Sex and Bodies in a Neo-Pentecostal Church in Kenya – Body Talk and Cultural Identity in the African World." In *Body Talk and Cultural Identity in the African World*, edited by Augustine Agwuele, 181–201. London: Equinox.

Robbins, Joel. 2010. "Anthropology of Religion." In *Studying Global Pentecostalism: Theories and Methods*, edited by Allan Anderson, Michael Bergunder, Andre Droogers and Cornelis van der Laan, 156–178. Berkeley: University of California Press.

Soothill, Jane. 2015. "Gender and Pentecostalism in Africa". In *Pentecostalism in Africa: Presence and Impact of Pneumatic Christianity in Postcolonial Societies*, edited by Martin Lindhardt, 191–219. Leiden: Brill.

6   Islamic Reform Movements in Africa

Introduction

As elsewhere in the Muslim world, Islamic reform movements are not a new phenomenon in Africa. Islamic reform movements have emerged in numerous sub-Saharan African countries as a result of the crisis of modernity and globalization of the 20th century. Their goal is to reform the various Muslim communities and societies in the region. However, Islamic reform movements in Africa have not presented a consistent model of reformism as evident from the heterogeneous approach of the various movements. In this complexity it is possible to find "modern" reform movements amongst the Sufi brotherhoods as demonstrated "with the movement of Ibrahim Niass in West Africa since the 1930s, the movement of Alawi scholars in East Africa since the 1890s or the Qadiriyya-Nasiriyya of Northern Nigeria since the 1950s" (Loimeier 2006). Further, there are countries in sub-Saharan Africa with a long tradition of Islamic reform movements, "such as Senegal, Northern Nigeria or Zanzibar", and others where reform movements have had a minimal function, "such as in Ivory Coast or Ethiopia" (ibid.).

The major desire of these movements is to live up to the ideal-type of Islam founded on the Qur'an and *sunna* (the authoritative practice of Prophet Muhammad). Hence in different changing circumstances, renewal (*tajdid*) and reform (*islah*) have involved a call for the return to what is perceived as the fundamentals of Islam. In their advocacy, they were opposed to the prevailing practices in their respective societies that they interpreted to be against the ideal Islamic teachings and principles. Therefore, in this chapter the phrase "reform movements" would be used in reference to both the renewal and reform groups that appeared within the African sub-continent.

Background of Islamic reforming ideology in Africa

To understand the nature of Islamic reforming movements, it is vital to take into consideration the message–human relationship model (see Voll 1982). The Qur'an provides Muslims with the foundation of the message–human relationship that identifies two important elements: first, the existence of the message and nature of that message; second, the role of the human being in implementing that message. The first element accentuates the existence of a consistent message from the divine source, which takes its ultimate and complete form in the Qur'an itself. The second element is the function of the human in relationship to the unchangeable message. Islam holds that specific human beings identified as prophets and messengers conveyed the permanent message to humanity, and Muhammad was the seal in the chain of the prophets. Despite the end of the period of the prophets, the basic framework of the two elements of an unchanging message and a human agency continued. Therefore, according to Islamic reforms, the post-prophetic human agent appeared to call upon Muslims to realize an already existing message of the Qur'an (see Voll 1982). Thus, Islamic reformers in various parts of the Muslim world emerged to perform the human agent role in relation to the permanent message that was earlier performed by prophets. In different historical experience of the Muslim community, Islamic reform movements took various forms that included either being more message-oriented or more human-oriented. Sub-Saharan Africa, for instance, has witnessed both the message-oriented and the human-oriented styles of reform movements as evident in the jihad of Usman dan Fodio of Nigeria and the Mahdi movement of Muhammad Ahmad of Sudan respectively.

In Africa too, Islam has been reinterpreted and re-appropriated by the different Muslim communities. As discussed in Chapter 3, Islam has experienced considerable growth in the second half of the 20th century and into the 21st century due to numerous conversions. The resultant "African Islam", which is grounded in local social practices, is a way of life for most Muslims in Africa. It is inseparable from divination and "magic", and embraces Qur'anic talismans of the locally trained Islamic scholars for protection and healing purposes. Alongside this "popular" Islam, are the numerous "Sufi orders largely oriented toward mystical quest" (Bregand 2007, 122). All over sub-Saharan Africa, "this understanding of Islam has been contested since the 1970s by graduates of Arab Islamic universities who, deriving authority exclusively from both the Qur'an and the sunna … want to eradicate everything which does not stem from these texts" (Bregand 2007, 122). The reform movements' condemnation of Sufi spirituality has a certain secularizing tendency by encouraging a "rationalization of religion and society, with the rejection of all kinds of magic as superstition" (Loimeier 2006). However, this dismissal should not be interpreted to imply that the reform movements completely ceased to address Africans' concerns and anxiety with witchcraft. Rather the Qur'an acknowledges the reality of witchcraft and provides remedy through Qur'anic recitation of certain texts, an approach emphasized by the reformists.

The determination to reform Islam in Africa has some of its roots in Saudi Arabia with Muhammad Abd al-Wahhab (1703–1792), himself inspired by Ibn Taymiyya (1263–1328) and an advocate of a literal form of Islam. More precisely, Islamic reformism refers to the movement which, from the middle of the 19th century up to the years 1935–1940, addressed the issue of modernity, and whose best known leaders were Jamal al-Din al-Afghani (d. 1897), Muhammad Abduh (d. 1905) and Rashid Rida (d. 1935). "By modernity they meant the mastery of science and of technological progress, which they deemed necessary without reservation", but "accompanied by a return to the religion of the pious ancestors (*al-Salaf*)", Denise Bregand (2007, 123) observed. Thereafter, other Muslim thinkers have influenced the evolution of Islamic thinking in a more political direction, among them Abul a'la Maududi (1903–1979), who founded the Jamat-i-Islami in the Indian sub-continent in 1941, and Hasan al-Banna (1906–1949), who founded the Muslim Brotherhood in Egypt in 1929, as well as Sayyid Qutb (1906–1966). All these Muslim personalities have continued to influence contemporary African Muslims in the continent.

Despite the complexity of the situation, which makes it difficult to demarcate the extremes within this expansive "reform" movement in Africa, Islamic reform within the continent encompasses a spectrum ranging from a liberal reformism, which is open to the present social order, to the militaristic and normative fundamentalism with a Wahhabi tendency – the perceived purest form of Islamic ideal. The appeals to these reform movements are varied and they include, generational tension between newly trained Muslim youth and traditional conservative *ulama*; local Muslims' search for empowerment by embracing global Islam; dynamics presented by the emergence of the Pentecostal movement leading to Muslims' unified response; and opposition to Western modernity by adopting a global Islamic identity, which is distinct from Christianity.

Militaristic and normative fundamentalism with a Wahhabi tendency

Sub-Saharan Africa has witnessed both the message-oriented and the human-oriented styles of reforming movements as evident in the jihad of Usman dan Fodio (1754–1817) of Nigeria and the Mahdi movement of Muhammad Ahmad (1844–1885) of Sudan respectively, both of which were influenced by the works of al-Wahhab. Both these movements appeared during the pre-colonial era. While dan Fodio's jihad placed minimal emphasis on the character of the leadership, the Mahdi movement, in contrast, gave greater prominence to the charismatic nature of the leadership and the special role of the leaders in the process of religious revitalization. The founders of both movements began as religious scholars concerned by the perceived corrupt state of Islamic life in their societies (Voll 1982).

After receiving his Islamic education from various teachers, dan Fodio began teaching and preaching in 1774, covering his home state Gobir and also the neighbouring states of Kebbi and Zamfara in the present day northern Nigeria. With the failure of the political leadership in Gobir to apply Islam in all spheres of life within the state, dan Fodio broke ranks with the royal court and returned to Degel to preach to his followers. Expressing his frustration, dan Fodio criticized the local (Hausa) rulers for condoning polytheism, worshiping fetishes and believing in the powers of talismans and divination. He also denounced "traditional" customs, the free socializing of men and women, dancing at burial feasts and inheritance practices that he believed were contrary to Islamic law (Maishanu 1999).

In early 1804, he declared jihad, and in the wars that followed, he was able to defeat the rulers of Gobir, Kano, Katsina and other Hausa states by 1830. His appeal for justice and morality succeeded in rallying both the Fulani and the downtrodden in Hausa society against the local leadership. As a consequence of the jihad warfare the entire Hausaland was subdued and the resultant regime that was founded came to be known as the Caliphate of Sokoto. The jihad movement succeeded in fortifying the practice of Islamic law (sharia) within the dominion established by dan Fodio and became the source of law before European colonization (Maishanu 1999).

Today, there exist in Africa a heterogeneous Islamic reforming group with a Wahhabist tendency. They include a major group like Yan Izala, and other smaller ones such as Ahlal-Sunna (people of the Sunna), Ansar Sunna (helpers of sunna) amongst others. Other Muslims may refer to this heterogeneous group as "Wahhabis", however "they do not define themselves in terms of the founders of that ideology, Ibn Taymiyya or al-Wahhabi; rather they strictly observe rules which they have brought back from universities in Medina or Kuwait and insist on holding as closely as possible to the texts" (Bregand 2007, 125–6). Their major ambition is to promote the "awakening" of correct practice of the faith amongst the local Muslims. Yan Izala movement is the most influential group with a Wahhabist tendency in sub-Saharan Africa, whose ideology and activities contributed to the application of sharia criminal law in the states of northern Nigeria in the 1990s. In its desire to be a pan-Islamic movement in Africa, Yan Izala has spread as far as Benin.

Members of the Wahhabism tendency groups in Africa are highly visible in public where they are recognized by women's wearing of *jilbab* (outer garment completely covering a woman from head to feet), and over calf-length pants for men; some of the men wear turbans, and also keep beards trimmed to a "regulation length" (Bregand 2007, 126). Although one need not be a Wahhabist to criticize the contemporary global order, their discourse is clearly anti-Western in tone. Their criticism is also placed on inappropriate usage of scientific progress, decline of family values and moral depravity. In their assessment "the moralization or regeneration of society will lead to the regeneration of public life" thereby advocating for "a flawless social morality" (Bregand 2007, 128).

Feature: Yan Izala movement in Nigeria

According to Roman Loimeier's (1997) extensive study on the Yan Izala movement, the Muslim organization in Nigeria was launched in 1978, but because it was rejected by many Nigerians it was not officially recognized until 1985. Since the focus of the organization was to fight *bid⊠a* (religious innovation) in the society, Sheikh AbuBakr Gumi (1922–1992) believed that the ideal name for the organization would be *Jamā⊠at Izālat al-Bid⊠a wa-Iqāmat al-Sunna* (Society for Removal of Un-Islamic Innovation and Re-establishment of the Sunna of the Prophet). There is no doubt about the crucial role that Sheikh Gumi played in the establishment of the Izala organization, due to his religious and political influence on Nigerian Muslims since the 1960s. Due to Sheikh Gumi's stiff opposition to the Sufi brotherhoods, the establishment of an organization that was critical of the Sufi traditions was necessary, thereby providing him with a base to undertake his activities. Thus, the persistent rivalry between Sheikh Gumi and the Sufi leaders in Kaduna encouraged the establishment of the organization, which served as an effective way to the opposition of the Sufi brotherhoods.

The appearance of Yan Izala is related to the social, religious and political complexities of the late 1970s. Specifically, the Izala protest was against three major Muslim groups in the society: "the ulama who abandoned Islam and followed mystification and innovations, the majority of the Muslims who followed their sheikhs blindly (Arabic: *taqlid*), and finally the group of traditional rulers (like emirs) who kept practices that were non-Islamic" (Amara 2011, 161). Since Islam in Nigeria, historically speaking, spread due to the efforts of the Sufi tradition, particularly the Qadiriyya and the Tijaniyya, it was essential for the Yan Izala to develop a strategy of arresting the Sufi dominance, which came in the form of taking control of the local mosques. During its initial years the movement focused on recruiting followers and preachers amongst the Muslim population who denounced Sufi brotherhoods' affiliation and practices regarded as *shirk* (associating the divinity of God with other beings). In its programme, the organization put emphasis on the Qur'an and sunna as the basic reference of the faith.

According to the organization's constitution, its activities are summed up in these ten objectives (quoted from Amara 2011, 168–9):

1   Returning to the Quran and the sunna following al-Salaf al-Ṣāliḥ in faith, worshipping, human transactions, and in all fields of life;
2   Showing Muslims their religion and inviting them to follow its rules;
3   Warning Muslims against polytheism, innovation, new ideas of atheists and communists;
4   Unify Muslims under the same faith and same path in order to establish an *umma* organized under one flag and one Imam;
5   Purify the Islamic Society from polytheism, innovations, myths, ... etc. in order to create a comfortable atmosphere in which to educate generations of Muslims;
6   Establish "the good Muslim" who is far from polytheism, fundamentalism and belief in myths;
7   Free the Muslim world from its enemies who destroyed the unity of Muslims;
8   Warn Muslims against sectarianism;
9   Al-Taṣfiya wa'l-Tarbiya [clearance and education];
10 Attempt to set up an Islamic society and practice the rule of God on earth. This is the path of Izala in Nigeria. The organization invites people in- and outside the country to assist in propagating the message of Islam.

Salafiyya: modern Islamic reform movements

Salafiyya is perceived as a progressive reform movement aiming at the revitalization of Islam and Muslim societies in the modern era. Accordingly, the term conveyed a flexible religious approach that was associated with Islamic modernism
ideas of major reformist personalities who are mentioned earlier: al-Afghani,
Abduh, and Rida. Within the frame of Islamic modernism, according to Rida,
salafiyya was associated with distinguished personalities dedicated to modern
reform and their sense of moderation, which encouraged them to advance con-
ciliation between Islam and the various attainments of Western civilization. In
other words, Islamic modernism was a flexible approach to Islam that allowed a
balance between rationality and revelation, arriving at an intermediate position
between blind imitation of the West and Islamic conservatism (Lauziere 2010).

In sub-Saharan Africa, "it is difficult to speak of one organized group or
movement called Salafiyya" because "it is a 'trend', or an Islamic orientation
within the Muslim community" (Amara 2011, 149). In numerous Muslim societies in Africa, many proponents of salafiyya ideas operated individually since
salafiyya as an organized group does not exist in the continent. In Nigeria, the
emergence of salafiyya ideas is attributed to the struggle against colonization, the
response to Sufism and in the context of global struggle linked to the Iranian
Islamic revolution of 1978 (ibid., 148). Through their mosque sermons, promotion of education (including women's education) and appropriation of media
tools such as cassettes/VHS-cassettes to disseminate their views, their ideas were
embraced by both the educated and non-educated Muslims in society.

In Kenya, the diffusion of Islamic reformist ideas modelled on Salafiyya
modernism is strongly associated with Sheikh al-Amin b. Ali Mazrui (1891–
1947). Confronted by numerous challenges experienced by Muslims in
coastal Kenya in the late 19th century, and coupled with their low social
status in society attributed to the community's reluctance to embrace
modern education, Sheikh al-Amin appeared on the local scene to champion
reforms. Influenced by the ideas of modern Islamic reformers, which
emerged in Egypt at the end of the 19th century, al-Amin sought ways of
reinterpreting their thoughts on the modernization of Islam within the local
context to address the predicaments of the Kenyan Muslims during the early
decades of the colonial period. In the generation after Sheikh al-Amin, the
Zanzibari sheikh Abdallah Salih al-Farsi (1912–1982) emerged as the agent
of Muslim reformist thought in East Africa. Like Sheikh al-Amin, al-Farsi
also condemned through his writings and mosque sermons certain practices
considered as *bid'a*. He encouraged Kenyan Muslims to advance their religious knowledge in prestigious educational institutions in the Islamic world.
Upon completion of their studies, "in the 1980s they returned to Kenya as
graduates of the Islamic University of Medina (Saudi Arabia), al-Azhar
University in Cairo, and the Islamic University of Omdurman (Sudan), to
continue the work of Islamic reform" (Seesemann 2006, 235). Some of the
practices regarded as "innovation" and strongly criticized by the proponents

of Salafiyya ideology in Kenya included: religious beliefs and practices involving magic, belief in spirits and possession cults; extravagant funeral ceremonies or visiting the tombs of persons regarded as saints; and "the celebration of Prophet Muhammad's birthday (*mawlid*)" (Seesemann 2006, 235–6).

Feature: Modern reforming ideas of Sheikh Al-Amin Mazrui in Kenya

Al-Amin bin Ali Mazrui represents a category of Muslim intellectuals in East Africa who were not just mere importers of ideas unfolding in other parts of the Islamic world, but who were "innovator[s] who selectively chose and adapted certain useful modernist themes" relevant to society (Pouwels 1981, 330). Unlike in West Africa, there were no violent confrontations that accompanied the reforming ideas in the East African region. There were no jihads like those evident in West Africa in the 18th and 19th centuries. East African Islamic modern reformers started as a minority "movement" of Arab elites who were familiar with the 19th century developments. Al-Amin was the first East African Muslim to "fully embrace modernist Islam, to write about it, and to promote it publicly" (Pouwels 1981, 331). It was probably during his academic sojourn in Zanzibar, an island on the East African coast and centre of Swahili culture, that he was initially exposed to some of the Egyptian reform papers popular with some of the earlier Zanzibari *ulama* (Islamic scholars).

He established himself as a modern Islamic scholar through his activities as an author and educator as demonstrated in his two publications in Kiswahili language, *Sahifa* and *al-Islah*. Both publications included regular editorials intended to make Muslims embrace new, "progressive" ideas in education without antagonizing the core Islamic values. One way in which he was interested in preserving Islam against cultural erosion was by promoting the study of Arabic. To this end, he introduced new methods in instruction that emphasized language comprehension rather than simple memorization of religious texts. Many Muslims of Arab descent who were well versed in the Islamic primary sources publicly renounced various aspects of local indigenous Muslims as un-Islamic. And, along with a rejection of certain African indigenous beliefs and practices they denounced local religious leadership (Mraja 2011; Pouwels 1981).

Similarly, al-Amin was concerned that the local Swahili Muslims were not living in accordance with the principles of Islam, and thereby, there was need for them to return to the correct path by studying and understanding the Islamic sources, which would guarantee authentic comprehension of the revelation, personal health, and worldly success. Consequently, he censured local customs and *walimu* (local religious teachers) whenever they contravened the Orthodox view. Swahili indigenous medicine and its practitioners (*waganga*) were condemned on the allegation that they turned the local

Muslim away from the right path. As indigenous religious values and the charisma (*baraka*) of the *shurafa* (sing. *Sharif*; honorific title for descendants of Prophet Muhammad or his family) came under attack, new doubts about the relevance and efficacy of the traditional religious education arose. In Mombasa, Kenya, a growing number of Muslims found Islamic religious training to be backward and an obstacle to progress (Mraja 2011; Pouwels 1981).

Fearing for the future, al-Amin realized that Kenyan Muslims had to be convinced of the relevance of Islam to what he perceived as an increasingly secularized society. He argued that Islam did not enjoin a renunciation of worldly affairs, but rather allowed Muslims to concern themselves with both the earthly life and the hereafter. Borrowing cues from Abduh and Rida, al-Amin felt that it was crucial for Muslims to become skilled in Western science and technology in order to progress. He urged the local Muslims to acquire knowledge in these sciences by advocating for the establishment of Muslim academies where modern subjects would be taught alongside the traditional religious sciences (Figure 6.1). To him such an endeavour was akin to engaging in a "holy" war (Mraja 2011; Pouwels 1981).

Figure 6.1 Muslim Academy, Riyadha Mosque, Lamu, Kenya (Hassan Ndzovu, 2017)

However, this modernist understanding of *salafiyya* as used in this section, differs from the popular descriptions of contemporary "salafism", which is a label used in referring to Muslim purists who embrace a rigid religious approach similar to "Wahhabism". "Due to their will to fight (even against other Muslims, including Salafi-oriented scholars)" (Loimeier 2018, 294), and their emphasis on violent jihad, we have described such movements as Salafi-Jihadi-minded reform groups. This category has come to present the most public and controversial face of Islam in contemporary sub-Saharan Africa, and includes movements like Boko Haram (in northern Nigeria), al-Shabaab (in Somalia) and other religio-political groups operating in northern Mali (see Chapter 9). Within sub-Saharan Africa, the Salafi-Jihadi-minded movements of reform gained prominence around the 2000s, when they began to challenge the political legitimacy of the leaders of their respective countries by demanding for the establishment of Islamic caliphates. In his description of these groups, Loimeier (2018, 295) posits:

> All of these jihad-minded movements of reform were led by religious scholars (ulama) who were linked with a Sufi order. They thus represent a tradition of militant Sufism that has been largely neglected in Western academic analyses, although these movements of reform continue to inform Muslim politics in sub-Saharan Africa to this day. In contrast to their historical predecessors, contemporary jihad-minded groups have adopted anti-esoteric positions and have developed a record of destroying the tombs of Muslim saints, and even mosques, in northern Mali, in north-eastern Nigeria and in Somalia.

Neo-reformist movements

The neo-reformist movements of Hassan al-Bana (1906–1949), an Egyptian imam and founder of the Muslim Brotherhood, and Abul a'la Maududi (1903–1979), an Indian philosopher and imam and founder of the religious political movement, Jamaat-i-Islami, saw the Islamic community of the 20th century confronted with numerous challenges. They recognized the internal flaw of the community, the external threat posed by Western political power and the value of science and technology. The neo-reformists completely denounced everything associated with the West and instead declared the absolute self-reliance of Islam. For their part, modern Islamic reformers strived to provide an Islamic justification for selective borrowing from the West. However, neo-reformist movements like the Muslim Brotherhood of Egypt (est. 1929) and Jamaat-i-Islami (est. 1941) sought their answers only within the Islamic faith. It was their conviction that if Muslims were true to their religion by shunning Western secularism and materialism then they were assured of a perfect guidance and success in all aspects of life (Esposito 2005).

In Africa, the most recent generation of Islamic reform (or neo-reformist) movements, such as the Jamaat 'Ibad ar-Rahman (the society of the servant of the Merciful) in Senegal, the Islamic Movement in Northern Nigeria or the various groups of the Ansar as-Sunna in East Africa, "are more critical of the secular, laicist state and have in some cases made it the main object of their criticism" (Loimeier 2006), while others like the Tabligh Jamaat in The Gambia and the Intellectualist reform movement in Ethiopia are less vocal against the state. Due to the failure of the post-colonial states in initiating tangible development strategies and providing social services, certain neo-reformist movements have in some case turned into political organizations. In contrast to the leading representatives of earlier generations of Muslim reformers like Sheikh dan Fodio, Sheikh Gumi or Sheikh al-Amin, the majority of the recent generation of reformers has no training as religious scholars, but instead they were the product of the state education systems. Consequently, "many of the leading representatives of the new movements are teachers, bureaucrats, engineers, technicians, scientists or doctors, and they no longer define themselves as *ulama* or scholars of Islamic law, but as Muslim intellectuals, 'professors' or teachers" (Loimeier 2006).

Jamaat Ibad-ar-Rahman (JIR), the neo-reformist movement, was established in 1978 by Alioune Diouf and was officially recognized in March 1979 by the Senegalese state. The organization has gained considerable public attention and attained social influence, particularly in the field of education and social welfare. In the area of Islamic education, the JIR strived "to establish schools that taught Arabic and Islamic sciences as well as the subjects taught at state schools" (Loimeier 2000, 180). During the fifth JIR national congress in 1991, Sidi Khali Lo lamented that "the only way out of the country's crisis was to be found in the Muslim's reorientation towards the prescriptions of the Quran and the Sunna" (Loimeier 2000, 181). In that congress, the movement criticized the "secular orientation of the state, the policy of family planning, gambling and the habits of conspicuous consumption prevalent at family festivities, as well as high taxation and deficient religious education in schools", adding that "the deterioration of the general living conditions" was "deplorable" (Loimeier 2000, 181).

The history of Jamaat Tabligh in The Gambia is associated with the efforts of Imam Dukureh (d. 2000), who studied in Saudi Arabia. After completing his studies, the imam embarked on a *da'wa* initiative in his native village, making the people more aware of their religion by disparaging the local ways of practising Islam. The majority of the villagers did not embrace his reformist ideas except for a few individuals. Strikingly, Tabligh Jamaat in The Gambia is popular with the local population, especially the youth. Despite the *da'wa* efforts of the group embraced by the local Mandinka group, "these local Muslims are often considered 'outsiders' on account of their ideas, practices and dress code" (Janson 2005, 455). The movement has significant attraction for the Gambian youths who have been exposed to Western-secular education. "The attraction of the movement for the young people may be explained partly by the serious economic depression in The Gambia and its drastic social effects that influence the ways the youths perceive their lives", Marloes Janson (2005, 455) observes. Conspicuous to this movement is its appeal to the youth and insistence "that women undertake missionary tours and deliver public speeches" (ibid., 452), which is a contradiction of the public role of women as held by the traditional conservative *ulama*.

What made the neo-reformist movement appealing to the Muslim masses was that it mixed the worldview that informed the activism of the Wahhabism reformist groups, with the holistic vision of Islam articulated in theory by modernists like al-Afghani, Abduh and Rida. The result was an ideology grounded exclusively on Islam, one that presented Islam as a timeless, rational, comprehensive faith whose transcendent message was relevant to Muslims in both their earthly life and hereafter.

Feature: The Intellectualist Islamic reform movement in Ethiopia

Terje Østebø's (2008) study on the Intellectualist reform movement in Ethiopia states that this movement does not possess any organizational structure in the strict sense because it developed around certain personalities who were advancing certain ideas rather than initiating a specific movement. Initially, it began in the early 1990s among Muslim students in Ethiopia's institutions of higher learning around the city of Addis Ababa. Informally, the movement acted as the Muslim student movement in the country, agitating for their welfare in addition to organizing lectures and study circles. Gradually, the movement was able to exert influence outside the learning institutions through public lectures and regular contributions to various publications. Despite the movement losing significant foothold in the university's campuses, it has remained a kind of elitist organization, with its leaders and supporters comprising mostly of university graduates, youth and urban intellectuals. Arguably, the Intellectualist reform movement is mostly an urban occurrence whose base, the urban youth, have had the opportunity to obtain formal secular education before joining universities in Addis Ababa. Apart from religious education, these Muslim youth are more exposed to urban life and secular education than their counterparts in the rural areas. After joining universities and receiving lectures on religion as well as exposure to diverse trends in Islam, the Muslim youth soon found themselves participating in discussions on Islamic virtues in relation to divergent facets of modern life (Østebø 2008).

Gradually the Intellectualist reform movement developed an ideological attachment to the Muslim Brotherhood, where the views of al-Banna were disseminated among its members. Though the Muslim Brotherhood was not officially launched in Ethiopia, its ideas were selectively chosen and interpreted to fit the Ethiopian context. This was reflected through the spread of Muslim Brotherhood literature, public lectures and articles in the magazine *Bilal*. Despite this affection for the Muslim Brotherhood, the Intellectualists were careful not to exhibit any direct association with the movement for fear of victimization by the state. In their advocacy, the Intellectualists have constantly insisted that Islam is a comprehensive religion, relevant for all aspects of life and Muslims are expected to be active in all sectors of societal and political life. Therefore Muslims should actively participate in their capacity as members of society, and their religiously inspired conduct would lead to a society influenced by Islamic virtues. Referring to past discrimination, the Intellectualists have campaigned for equal representation of Muslims in public life and for the creation of a political environment facilitating mutual respect and coexistence between Muslims and Christians in the country (Østebø 2008).

Within the Ethiopian context, the Intellectualist reform movement is the most elaborate and articulate on political views bedevilling the country. Significant is the Intellectualists' view on the nature of the political environment appropriate to address the interests of the Muslims in Ethiopia. This can be understood against the background of the long history of Ethiopia being seen as a Christian nation. Instead of expressing the classical views of the Muslim Brotherhood, advocating for the fusion of Islam and politics, they support the establishment of a secular government that in their view guaranteed the rights of the country's different religious communities. At the same time, to foster Muslim unity they were against the existing federal structure's recognition of Ethiopia's ethnic plurality, which in their view is an obstacle to national unity. These views fit in with their political agenda. To overcome the ethnic barrier, the Intellectualist reform movement began to openly advocate Muslim unity regardless of their ethnic affiliation, arguing that Islam surpasses the boundaries of ethnicity. Ostensibly, the Intellectualist reform movement is not confined to any particular ethnic group since it is seemingly attracting followers from a variety of ethnic groups. However, the majority of its leaders and supporters derive from Amharic-speaking areas, such as Wollo, Gondar and other parts of northern Ethiopia. Over time, the movement has sought affinity with indigenous Sufi traditions where ideas of indigenous Sufi scholars and reformers are interpreted as representations of an Ethiopian Islam. While Sufism has been condemned by various reform movements in Islamic history, the Intellectual movement considers the country's Sufi's tradition as a common Muslim heritage, significant in the construction of an Ethiopian Islamic identity (Østebø 2008).

Conclusion

The chapter has demonstrated that reforming movements have been a dominant theme for Muslims in Africa as they responded to both internal and external forces that challenged their faith and social order. Despite the divergent Islamic reform movements in Africa, what unites all of them is the endeavour to create a just and appropriate society for Muslims, that is, a society that would enable Muslims to live in accordance to the dictates of their faith, in a world that is characterized with growing modernization viewed by many Muslims to be "Westernization". Islam was used effectively in the formation of Islamic socio-political reform organizations and movements. The various reform movements attributed the perceived marginalization of the Muslim community to the abandonment of the dictates of the faith, and therefore advocated Islamic reform to bring about social and moral reform.

Questions for discussion

- What are the similarities and differences between Pentecostal Christian and Islamic reform movements, and what explains their direct appeal among the youth?
- Whether one understands Islamic reform movements as essentially religious, social or political depends on the particular context. Look into one case in Africa and examine it accordingly.

References (*indicates recommended reading)

Amara, Ramzi Ben. 2011. The Izala Movement in Nigeria: Its Split, Relationship to Sufis and Perception of Sharia Re-Implementation. PhD Dissertation, Bayreuth University.

Bregand, Denise. 2007. "Muslim Reformists and the State in Benin." In *Islam and Muslim Politics in Africa*, edited by Benjamin Soares and Rene Otayek, 122–136. New York: Macmillan.

Esposito, John. 2005. *Islam: The Straight Path*. Oxford: Oxford University Press.

Janson, Marloes. 2005. "Roaming about for God's Sake: The Upsurge of the Tablīgh Jama'at in the Gambia", *Journal of Religion in Africa* 35/4, 450–481.

Lauziere, Henri. 2010. "The Construction of Salafiyya: Reconsidering Salafism from the Perspective of Conceptual History", *International Journal of Middle East Studies* 42/3, 369–389.

*Loimeier, Roman. 1997. *Islamic Reform and Political Change in Northern Nigeria*. Evanston: Northwestern University Press

Loimeier, Roman. 2000. "The Islamic Reform Movement and the State in Senegal", *Journal of Religion in Africa* 30/2, 168–190.

*Loimeier, Roman. 2006. "Islamic Reform Movements in Sub-Saharan Africa: Religious Renewal and Social Change", Quantara.de. https://en.qantara.de/content/islamic-re form-movements-in-sub-saharan-africa-religious-renewal-and-social-change (accessed on 5 June 2018).

*Loimeier, Roman. 2018. *Islamic Reform in Twentieth-Century Africa*. Edinburgh: Edinburgh University Press..

Maishanu, Hamza Muhammad. 1999. "The Jihad and the Formation of the Sokoto Caliphate", *Islamic Studies* 38/1, 119–131.

Mraja, Mohamed Suleiman. 2011. "Sheikh al-Amin Mazrui (1891–1947) and the Dilemma of Islamic Law in the Kenyan Legal System in the 21st Century", *Journal for Islamic Studies* 31/1, 60–74.

Østebø, Terje. 2008. "The Question of Becoming: Islamic Reform Movements in Contemporary Ethiopia", *Journal of Religion in Africa* 38/4, 416–446.

Pouwels, Randall. 1981. "Sh. Al-Amin B. Ali Mazrui and Islamic Modernism, 1875–1947", *International Journal of Middle East Studies* 13/3, 329–345.

Seesemann, Ruediger. 2006. "African Islam or Islam in Africa? Evidence from Kenya." In *The Global Worlds of the Swahili: Interfaces of Islam, Identity and Space in 19th and 20th Century East Africa*, edited by Roman Loimeier and Ruediger Seesemann, 229–250. Berlin: LIT Verlag.

Voll, John. 1982. "Wahhabism and Mahdism: Alternatives Styles of Renewals", *Arab Studies Quarterly* 4/1–2, 110–126.

Part II

Topical Issues of Religions in Africa

7 Religion, witchcraft and modernity in Africa

Ambivalent forces and moral values

What is the nature of witchcraft in Africa? What is its place in "religion"? How can ideas about the reality and danger of witches be sustained in today's world? The answers to these questions are critical and complex. They go to the heart of African ideas about personhood and morality that shape everyday life.

In indigenous African worldviews, it is essentially the human being, not God or the devil, that is responsible for evil. Projects that fail despite all efforts, undiagnosed pains or incurable illness, and especially untimely death are all thought to be caused by the occult manipulations of spiritual forces by witches. While witchcraft believers can accept *how* a misfortune or affliction occurred (as the result of an overt cause such as accident or disease, for example), this does not explain *why* undeserved suffering happens. The deeper reason is that it was provoked by the jealousies and perverted desires of witches to see human good thwarted. Their interventions on the spiritual plane have effect in the material world, and they work those powers towards evil ends. This understanding of "the problem of evil" sets the subject of African witchcraft squarely in the sphere of ethics, a central concern of religious reason and practice. The very understanding of witchcraft as the will and behaviour of beings that seek to undermine the good of the human community constitutes a baseline for moral reasoning

For this very reason, however, African indigenous religions have often been mistakenly *reduced* to witchcraft beliefs. Until relatively recently,

> any religious activity by Africans that did not have some clear equivalent in the practice of contemporary European Christians risked being vaguely consigned to the category of "witchcraft" ... indigenous healers and specialists were described as "witch-doctors" ... without any deep consideration of the *moral value* attached to such practices.
>
> (Ellis 2007, 35; emphasis added)

This chapter shows that the concept of witchcraft is central to African moral systems of thought and illuminates deeply held values. It also demonstrates that witchcraft is not a static and timeless phenomenon; rather, current manifestations of witchcraft belief are deeply linked to modernity and reflect very contemporary evils.

Who or what is a witch?

Witchcraft beliefs vary among the countless indigenous cultures across the sub-continent, but consistent similarities exist nevertheless. Simply put, in African traditions witches are people purported to have the capacity to manipulate spiritual power towards their desired ends, and who may choose to do so for evil. In the vast anthropological literature on the subject, some distinguish between sorcery and witchcraft, with the former being defined as a learned technique applied with evil intention, and the latter being an innate power that is sometimes launched by unconscious forces, and fuelled by antisocial feelings. Others state more simply that sorcery is an observable practice while witchcraft is invisible and therefore necessarily remains a theory or conjecture. In both cases, it is the threat of their presence and potential that is most pertinent to the human community.

According to popular folklore, witches are ambiguous, liminal beings, inhabiting a human body but able to transmute themselves into birds or other animals. They live in human society by day but operate at night on an invisible plane. Usually the term "witch" is applied to those considered to be entirely evil and destructive. But for those who understand witchcraft as an innate quality of spiritual power (and sometimes even as organic substance that resides in an individual's vital organs and activates those innate powers from within), the term "witch" may also apply to any person with supernatural capacities with potential for good or evil. Ultimately, both the mysterious powers of witchcraft and the persons who draw on them are viewed with ambivalence. First we will deal with the purely negative conceptions of witchcraft, and then with the broader views and their contexts.

Most African folklore represents the witch as the embodiment of evil predators. They are "soul eaters" who attack their human victims in the spiritual realm, causing them to suffer on the material plane. It is said that when they feed on the soul of a victim the body wastes away and dies. A typical description of the witch can be found in the following explanation of the vernacular term *mfiti* used by the Chewa of Malawi:

> The mfiti witch is addicted to evil and abominable practices. To be an mfiti is to be a particular kind of man or woman. The mfiti kills for the love of killing, or to sate a lust for feasting on human flesh. He or she kills to repay commensal gifts of the flesh of other witches' kin. These witches want to bring misery and death to others simply because they can. The mfiti has extraordinary powers, capable of amazing feats like flying through the night on a witchcraft airplane while leaving a physical body asleep in bed at home. These witches enjoy the company of fellow witches and seek to convert others to their vile practices, including their abominable sexual predilections, picking on children since they are least able to resist. The

mfiti, in this way, occupies a distinct status and represents a particular mode of being: at once human and not human, both superhuman and sub-human.

(Ashforth 2015, 24–5)

The witch is *superhuman* insofar as he or she is empowered with mystical capacities, but *sub-human* as the antithesis of all that characterizes society. The witch and witches' doings are abominable, monstrous, an anathema to the propagation of humanity and the flourishing of community. Witches cause women's infertility, crop failure, even natural disaster that destroys property and takes human life.

In every detail, witches betray and invert the norms of human society and its fundamental values. Witches belong to associations and initiation into the coven requires the sacrifice of a member of an initiate's maternal family whose soul is shared in a feast. The idea of "cannibalism" is in itself a shocking violation. The choice of the victim among maternal kin is a particularly depraved transgression of ethics because, especially in societies that are matrilineal (in which descent is traced through the mother's line), the bond between a mother and her children is so sacred that one's primary duty is not to one's spouse or children but to one's maternal siblings. When witches feast together they are said to turn their backs to one another, inverting the most natural form of human communion.

People accused of being witches are often those who display anti-social sentiments such as anger or jealousy, or whose behaviour conveys that they are too self-sufficient: they are reclusive, arrogant, or ungenerous. From a socio-political perspective, the threat of accusation is a means of keeping people in line, making sure they behave according to society's moral mandates.

Making sense of witchcraft

In the late 19th and early 20th centuries Western scholars deemed almost all ideas and activities that were foreign to them to be "rooted in ignorance and irrationality" (Geschiere 2013, xv). Witchcraft beliefs and practices in Africa seemed an especially riveting example. Focus on the ghastly folklore imagery and questionable anti-witchcraft remedies like talisman and "juju" only reinforced the artificial distinction between "the primitive" and the supposedly more sophisticated philosophies that constituted "religion". Even to this day "the very notion of witchcraft … has exoticizing implications" (ibid.), that is, it serves to represent Africa as "Other" of the assumedly enlightened West. Currently, news media feature stories of shocking abuses of women and children accused of witchcraft in Africa, or deadly efforts to exorcise them. Interest in tantalizing details of the frightening and bizarre can overshadow the attempt to understand what witchcraft means in Africa and eclipse the possibility of seeing the phenomenon as a kind of moral response to acute suffering in the contemporary world.

By the same token, the central place of witchcraft in African thought gave it pride of place in modern anthropology as one of its most prominent subjects. Scholarship on witchcraft in Africa has a long pedigree, beginning with a now classic study by British anthropologist E.E. Evans-Pritchard (1937), *Witchcraft, Oracles and Magic among the Azande*. It sought to appreciate how witchcraft worked rationally in African systems of thought, fitting logically into a given cultural world of meaning. Evans-Pritchard also drew a distinction between ideas about witchcraft and magic. The former is an innate capacity to have supernatural power over natural forces while the latter is a learned practice in which physical elements are manipulated to affect the spiritual realm. Sorcery is magic applied towards evil ends. In the 1950s and 1960s scholars tried to make sense of African witchcraft in terms of its social function. They focused on the dynamics of witchcraft accusations, or the threat of being accused, as a means of suppressing jealousy and other anti-social affect. Especially in small-scale societies that rely on harmonious relations, witchcraft thereby reinforced social order (Middleton and Winter 1963).

While it was long presumed that the "superstitions" of witchcraft belief would wither under modernity, it has become apparent in the 60 years since the independence of former African colonies that beliefs about witchcraft endure. In fact, witchcraft rumours, accusations and practices for protecting against witchcraft attacks ("anti-witchcraft") all seem to be very much *on the rise* in the decades since the end of colonialism, even and perhaps especially in urban contexts.

Since the 1980s, scholars featured this notable escalation in fear about witchcraft and the sense that its evil had broadened in scope as the prime example of the unanticipated direction that modernity has assumed. The object was not to imply that African traditions are "backward", resisting rationality, empirical science or technological know-how. Rather they demonstrated how witchcraft beliefs were "creatively refashioned to suit new situations" in response to social change (Moore and Sanders 2001, 11).

For those living outside a context in which it is taken seriously as a reality, witchcraft may be considered "a matter of 'belief,' an issue pertaining to the domain of the cognitive" (Ashforth 2015, 10). However for insiders to a culture that views witchcraft as the source of evil, the invisible threat is real. Fears are well-founded in face of inexplicable fiascos introduced with modernity: increasing poverty, new deadly epidemics like HIV/AIDS, the ravages of civil war, and the acute suffering of refugees. Reference to witchcraft is a regular, daily occurrence throughout sub-Saharan Africa. Disquieting reference to witches' secret and sinister practices is everywhere, a backdrop of everyday life. It is the subject of gossip and rumour within families as well as on the political scene.

Anti-witchcraft: ambiguous powers and persons

In the face of the threat that witches pose, Africans turn to special practitioners to counter their force. Diviners investigate the deeper causes of affliction and expose witchcraft that may be its source. They offer remedies in the form of "medicines", substances like protective amulets and charms that supposedly protect their users from witches' attacks or free them from their snares. Since physical illness has a spiritual component, in practice the functions of diviners and traditional healers overlap (see Chapter 12).

Scholars have tended to make a radical distinction between diviner-healers, who use their powers for good, and witches, who act only for evil. But the opposition is simplistic and misleading. Diviners and witches draw on the same preternatural powers (that is, forms of power outside or beyond the norms of nature) and invisible forces. Diviners may also inherit their craft or be indoctrinated into their practice in the world of dreams, where witches are also said to recruit their numbers. Therefore their power may be just as innate and unconsciously derived.

Not only do diviner-healers operate using the same spiritual means as witches, some acknowledge that they also can use them to attack and kill a spiritual enemy, justifying it as a defensive and protective act. "To the Maka [of Cameroon] it is self-evident that the *nganga* [diviner-healers] themselves must be deeply involved in the very *djembe* [witchcraft] they are supposed to combat ... one has to kill in order to be able to heal" (Geschiere 2013, 73). Many Africans consider that the diviner-healer is necessarily a witch of a superior order. According to the Maka, "It is owing to their extremely developed *djembe* that [diviners] can 'see' what the witches are plotting, that they can overcome them and force them to lift their spell" (Geschiere and Fisiy 1994, 329). This implies that a diviner may become a witch *at will*, using power for the advancement of a client, but potentially at the expense of another. However, others maintain that diviners belong to guilds and take oaths that preclude them from using their powers for evil. For these reasons, most apply the term "witchcraft" exclusively to the evil exercise of occult spiritual power.

The place of witchcraft in African religions: a moral concern

The paradoxical conception of witchcraft as a simultaneously negative and positive force is prevalent in the popular social imaginary. While witchcraft is mostly spoken of in a negative way, in common parlance the term "witch" may refer to any person perceived to have uncanny abilities, suggesting that their extraordinary powers are derived from occult sources. In joking banter or gossip, a person with inordinate success, exceptional intelligence or creativity, or uncanny luck is said to be a witch. Such ambiguity makes the nature of witchcraft more inscrutable.

The problem is exacerbated by the fact that indigenous terms that supposedly distinguish among powers are actually just as opaque. An example is the occult power *sékè*, celebrated among a number of peoples in the lagoon region of southern Côte d'Ivoire:

> The power [of witchcraft called *awa*] is the very same as that of anti-witchcraft. Characteristics of the latter (*sékè* in Alladian and Ebrié) are just

as applicable to the power of aggression; *sèkè* is sometimes stronger than *awa*, but *it is of the same nature*. At this point the theory becomes ambiguous and sometimes confusing: *sèkè* is a power of legitimate defense, but it is of the same nature as *awa; it can at any time change purely and simply into awa*; in the extreme the anti-witch can very well be suspected of witchcraft.

(Augé 1976, 130, emphasis added)

Africans constantly struggle to contend with the ambiguity of witchcraft. It goes to the heart of African understandings of personhood and the exercise of free will. While a person is a cultivated human being who contributes constructively to society for the collective good, a witch who uses power to undermine the social fabric is categorized as a *non-person*. Thus, witchcraft is more than a "belief", a naïve and misguided conviction about the existence of persons with the ability to exercise power. It is a worldview that holds that the source of evil in the world is not God or the devil, but the wicked agency of a certain category of human being with power in the spiritual realm.

Women's innate power as guardians of the moral order

Witchcraft is sometimes conceptualized as an organic substance that resides in the individual. The AbaGusii of Kenya, for example, maintain that it resides in the liver, while for the Akan of Ghana it is considered to be a white worm-like substance that resides in the stomach. In other words, it is as much a bodily as a spiritual phenomenon.

In West African traditions women are commonly considered to be inherently endowed with an uncanny force, ambiguous in nature. Among the Yoruba of Nigeria, for example, it is thought that, "if it is *according to their 'secret'* that women give birth, it is also with their 'secret' that they take life, by consuming the life essence of their kinsfolk. ... witchcraft, like fertility, is endemic to Yoruba womanhood, *all women are potential witches* ..." (Apter 2007, 94, emphasis added). The "secret", however, is not women's procreative capacity. Their innate power *manifests* in maternity, but is even greater on the invisible plane. It is a moral force that only a female elder who is beyond childbearing can fully assume. Therefore, "women are thought to become even more powerful after menopause, when menstrual blood ceases to flow" (Drewal 1992, 179). At this stage they fully embody their spiritual power and become guardians of the moral order.

Although Yoruba understand that certain female elders are witches (*aje*), one refrains from referring to them with that term in order to avoid offending them. Instead they are called "the Mothers". This epithet does not refer to any actual maternity, nor is it a sentimental term of endearment. It is a respectful title honouring their power that is both revered and feared.

Feature: Yoruba Gelede, the celebration of witches in Nigeria

The Yoruba masking festival *Gelede* is the means by which society honours the Mothers. Celebrated in playful pantomime, the Mothers are "seduced" so that they will channel their extraordinary power (*ase*) for the good of the community (Drewal 1992, 179).

Considered to possess as commanding a force as the ancestors or even the gods, the Mothers' power surpasses the capacity of one sex to contain it. After menopause women commonly sprout chin hairs, a sign of divine dual-sexed nature. Gelede masks represent the Mother as a bearded woman. The beard indicates the status, knowledge and wisdom of an elder but more over "a bearded woman [is considered to] possess extraordinary spiritual power" (Drewal and Drewal 1983, 71). This image of ambiguous gender represents the double world – natural and occult – in which they operate.

The other Gelede mask represents the Mother as a bird with a great, bloodied beak grasping a snake. It alludes to the folklore that witches transform themselves at night into birds to hunt and kill their prey. One Yoruba praise name for the Mothers refers simultaneously to their double gender and their transformative powers: "the 'owners of two bodies' (*abâra méjì*)" (Drewal and Drewal 1983, 11). The two masks together show the Mothers' double moral capacity. They have the potential to be ruthless but they are also like the ancestors, "freed of the human weaknesses and conditions of pettiness" and therefore "have special responsibilities for establishing the moral order of society" (Olupona 2001, 57). For this reason they are called the "'owners of the world' (*oní l'oní aiyé*)" (Drewal and Drewal 1983, 11). Some Gelede masks depict the head of the Mother sustaining the social order: the market, the family, and food production (see Figure 7.1).

The Yoruba also say that, "the power of the mothers is equal or superior to that of the gods ... the mothers own and control the gods" (Drewal and Drewal 1983, 8). When the Gelede mask of the great Mothers appears it is accompanied by the masquerades of two of the most important of the divinities: *Ogun*, the God of iron, a smith who shapes the world, and *Eshu*, the trickster known to wreak havoc on it. They show constructive and destructive powers working simultaneously.

Among the Abidji of Côte d'Ivoire, elderly women are also presumed to have innate powers ascribed to all witches, and the capacity to channel them for the good. Considered the living embodiment of the ancestors, they enforce the moral order and drive out evil. In times of war, epidemic or other moments of social distress, women elders protect society by performing a rite of anti-witchcraft called Egbiki. It is performed at night, under the cover of darkness, for it is both forbidden and dangerous, especially for men, to view it. Women strip naked, pound the ground with old pestles, and curse witches who send evil

Figure 7.1 A Gelede mask of the Mother with its superstructure showing her sustaining the dynamics of the world: the market, the family and food production (© The British Museum)

to the village. They wash their genitals and sprinkle the bathwater on the ground as a "trap" to snare the witches (see Chapter 13). It exposes the evil-doer by causing witchcraft to turn against its sender. The innate power of the witch is said to be an actual substance lodged in the belly, so if a witch were to persist with an attack despite the women's warning and curse, the substance would turn against the evil-doer and the witch's abdomen would visibly swell.

Egbiki can be simultaneously construed as an intensely moral condemnation of evil and also as an act of "anti-witchcraft" that draws on the same ambiguous occult forces.

Witchcraft accusations and justice in a world of witches

Despite the prevalent belief that women possess potentially beneficial powers, they are increasingly the targets of anti-witchcraft violence. "Because [academic witchcraft studies] often devote insufficient attention to the *moral* aspects of witchcraft [they] may risk contributing to the stigmatization of people who are accused of being witches, with at times fatal consequences" (Ter Haar 2007, 15 emphasis added). All over Africa women, especially elderly women, have been disproportionately accused of witchcraft, leading to cruel punishment ranging from banishment to torture and death. The frequency with which women are targeted has led some to see witchcraft accusations as a special category of violence against women.

An incident in northern Ghana exemplifies a case in which elderly women, who might once have been deployed to protect the community from evil, were victimized. When an epidemic of meningitis in 1997 led to almost 600 deaths, a campaign to root out the witches responsible ensued. The violence against the women accused of causing the illness was so widespread that it attracted international media attention. An official inquiry revealed that aggression against female witchcraft suspects was commonplace in the area and often resulted in murder. By 2001 up to 8,000 people, mostly elderly women, had been stigmatized, banished, or had taken refuge from their persecutors in "witch sanctuaries" (Adinkrah 2004, 328; see Figure 7.2).

One reason for the new wave of accusations is that legal reforms abolished the procedures once used by local chiefs and diviners to adjudicate cases of witchery, as well as systems for counterchecking complaints that formerly guarded against false accusations. Legal measures such as the Witchcraft Suppression Act of 1957 in South Africa forbade accusation, leaving people to take matters into their own hands. "People became more vulnerable to witchcraft accusations and accused witches lost any chance they had for a fair trial under customary law" (Ludsin 2003, 88). Vigilante justice is swift and violent.

However, the use of criminal courts to adjudicate witchcraft accusations proved no more effective in producing peace and justice. In Cameroon in the 1980s state courts accepted "the declarations of nganga [diviners] and other healers as proof" of the validity of an accusation, and those convicted received heavy prison sentences and fines solely on the basis of such testimony (Geschiere and Nyamnjoh 1998, 84). This failed to uproot belief in witchcraft or reassure the populace that the danger was contained, since witches' powers are presumably just as effective behind bars. Moreover, the courts changed the role of the diviner from healer and mediator to social menace: "the nganga, the expert of old on the subject of containing witchcraft, becomes a disciplinary figure who drags his 'suspects' before the gendarmes" (ibid., 88).

Figure 7.2 Some of the accused who found refuge in a "witch camp" in Ghana (© Nyani
Quarmyne/Panos)

Currently, "lurid tales of grotesque violence serve as a rallying cry for the
well-intentioned in their efforts to curb what they call 'witchcraft violence' or
'witchcraft abuse'" (Ashforth 2015, 6). Human rights organizations have pres-
sured states to combat witchcraft accusations and their violent consequences.
"Committees' recommendations range from calling upon states to 'challenge
traditional views' ... to requiring that states investigate the torture and killing
of suspected witches and prosecute the perpetrators" (Mgbako and Glenn 2011,
394). But asking the state to dispel deeply embedded cultural beliefs or to
punish those who believe they are acting for the common good has proved both
futile and dangerous. Moreover, the state itself has been accused of complicity
in witchcraft.

Witchcraft and the African state

In the years immediately following independence, African states wishing to
adopt a positive African identity tended to bracket the belief in witchcraft,
denigrate it as "backward", and treat it as an obstacle to their primary business,
fostering "development" in the model of the west. Some considered witchcraft
"as a very dangerous form of 'subversion' of those aims" (Geschiere and Fisiy
1994, 325). During Africa's economic boom years however (from the 1970s to
the late 1980s), the appearance of inexplicable new wealth among the elite led
to a general feeling that witchcraft was gaining ground. Witchcraft became the
prime idiom through which many Africans made sense of the invisible forces of

globalization. Rich businessmen and corrupt civil servants were understood to be witches who gorged themselves on the lifeblood of labourers.

> The image of the greedy, pitiless witch feeding on the populace came to refer to the devouring world of consumption and corruption. These idioms of ingestion and incorporation involve deep transmutations of blood, flesh, and bodily organs into accumulated wealth, whether in bundles of cash or truckloads of commodities.
>
> (Apter 2012, 25)

Popular ideas about witchcraft also inform perceptions of political power and the identification of African statecraft with witchcraft is ubiquitous. It is generally believed that political leaders make human sacrifice to secure their positions, and African leaders build fearful reputations on these rumours. Therefore, Geschiere and Fisiy (1994, 323) warn that "witchcraft in modern politics is certainly no joke".

State figures have also used witchcraft belief as an effective tool for political repression. For example, in Togo in 1991 empirical evidence and public first-hand testimonies revealed that President Eyadéma and his entourage "killed, tortured or [illegally] detained [many people] for the alleged practice of witchcraft, including considerable numbers of people from the President's native village" (Ellis 1993, 471). But their cruel persecution also signalled the President's own firm belief in the power of witchcraft to threaten his regime. Some politicians in Eyadéma's administration resorted to sorcery and the witchcraft of specialists who purportedly preserved or increased their power by spiritual means. When a mob ransacked the home of one feared Togolese government minister, they "discovered under his bed a human foetus preserved in a jar", a sign of engagement in witchcraft practice (Ellis 1993, 472). Popular fear of the state as witch is therefore well-founded.

Since the 1990s, as the promise of development turned to despair and revolt, civil war disrupted a number of African countries. The state itself took on the characteristics of a witch, seeming to thrive on pitiless destruction while horrific violence and bloody slaughter fed its cruel appetite for power. During Côte d'Ivoire's civil war in 2011 satirical images featured political rivals with blood dripping from their mouths. Witchcraft continues to operate in Africa both as an indispensable instrument of political control and as an image of unscrupulous greed for personal power. It is such a persistent theme that Wyatt MacGaffey (2000, 63) proposes that we "begin to think of it as a theory of power, a political theory".

Christian approaches to witchcraft beliefs

Catholic and mainline church missionaries tended to deny the reality of witchcraft and the efficacy of magic. By contrast, Protestant Pentecostalism flourished in Africa in part because it promoted the view of an ongoing spiritual battle between good and evil. Instead of dismissing the fear of witchcraft, Pentecostal-

Charismatic Christianity in Africa reinforced it. Many of these churches claim to combat witchcraft through the power of the Holy Spirit and make spiritual healing and exorcism their focus. In seeming accord with indigenous African worldviews, church leaders trace disease to demonic affliction and spiritual oppression (Adinkrah 2004, 330). All-night prayer vigils for protection against witches, and exorcism of those who confess are regular features of worship in Pentecostal churches or those influenced by the charismatic movement (see Chapter 5).

Neo-traditional prophetic movements also castigate witches as utterly evil but seek to combat witchcraft using the same powers and spiritual means:

> In November 1998, ... two elderly women, both 85 years old, were pro-nounced witches by a "prophet" of a "healing church." According to the report, the two women were subsequently forced to drink concoctions prepared by the prophet "in a bid to exorcise them of the witchcraft." The two women died shortly after consuming the potion.
>
> (Adinkrah 2004, 342)

The Catholic Church is not immune from involvement in witchcraft accusation and exorcisms of demons. In the capital city of the Democratic Republic of the Congo, Kinshasa, priests perform painful and dangerous practices intended to exorcize the forces of witchcraft that supposedly lurk in unsuspecting con-gregants, especially children. But if the purging is not deemed successful, those stigmatized – even infants – are exiled and abandoned to their own devices on the streets. The abuse and abandonment of accused children in Malawi and Angola also seem driven by the strain of urban capitalism on families who cannot support them, and the violence of armed conflict that destroyed com-munities. In an interview Filip de Boeck, an anthropologist who has written about "child witches" in the Congo, called this is "a thoroughly modern phe-nomenon that is shaped by global capitalism. Contrary to older forms, the witchcraft 'new style' is experienced as being wild, random and unpredictable" (De Boeck in Fagge 2015).

It should come as no surprise that the Churches are sometimes accused of being a haven for witches. And by logical extension the Church "has become in itself a form of witchcraft" (Newell 2007, 464). If Churches are not actively practising anti-witchcraft and Christians are admonished to abandon the tradi-tional practices believed to protect them, congregants fear that they are laying themselves open to easy assault.

Conclusion

As we can see, witchcraft did not disappear with "modernity". Not only do witchcraft rumours and recourse to anti-witchcraft techniques persist in bus-tling cities, but witchcraft has also become a means to account for the crushing, invisible forces of modernity itself.

Today completely novel forms of witchcraft circulate in the popular imagination. An example is *famla* or *ekong* that arose in Cameroon in the 1990s. Its perpetrators, the nouveaux riches, do not feed on their victims' souls, as in older conceptions of witchcraft attacks. Instead they supposedly <u>transform them into zombies to work on invisible plantations,</u> the source of their otherwise inexplicable newfound wealth (Geschiere and Nyamnjoh 1998, 74). Zombie rumours suddenly appeared in Lusaka, the capital of Zambia as well (Mildnerová 2016). Scholars interpret such new images of witchcraft as <u>reflections of the capitalist exploitation of labour and its devastating ramifications</u> (Moore and Sanders 2001).

Since the 1990s anthropology has treated the renewed and reinvigorated expressions of the occult as a signal of "the indigenization of modernity" (Geschiere 1997). The appearance of new forms of witchcraft in the cities, and the rise of accusations in the context of Pentecostal movements that have swept the continent demonstrates that "modernity" is not one homogeneous experience but takes on multiple faces as it is shaped by local cultural realities. Witchcraft is part and parcel of African <u>modernity</u>, not separate from it.

Questions for discussion

- Recognizing that witchcraft belief is often used by Westerners to argue that African societies are "backward", make the case that it is an integral part of modernity instead.
- How might changes in the economy account for increasing witchcraft accusations against elderly women?
- Do parallels between African and European folklore about witchcraft make it easier or harder to understand its place in modernity?

References (*indicates recommended reading)

Adinkrah, Mensah. 2004. "Witchcraft Accusations and Female Homicide Victimization in Contemporary Ghana", *Violence against Women* 10/4, 325–356.

Apter, Andrew. 2007. *Beyond Words: Discourse and Critical Agency in Africa*. Chicago: University of Chicago Press.

Apter, Andrew. 2012. "Matrilineal Motives: Kinship, Witchcraft, and Repatriation among Congolese Refugees", *Journal of the Royal Anthropological Institute* 18/1, 22–44.

Ashforth, Adam. 2015. "Witchcraft, Justice, and Human Rights in Africa: Cases from Malawi", *African Studies Review* 58/1, 5–38.

Augé, Marc. 1976. "Savoir Voir et Savoir Vivre: Les Croyances à la Sorcellerie en Côte d'Ivoire", *Africa: Journal of the International African Institute* 46/2, 128–136.

Drewal, Henry John, and Margaret Thompson Drewal. 1983. *Gẹlẹdẹ: Art and Female Power among the Yoruba*. Bloomington: Indiana University Press.

Drewal, Margaret Thompson. 1992. *Yoruba Ritual: Performers, Play, Agency*. Bloomington: Indiana University Press.

Ellis, Stephen. 1993. "Rumour and Power in Togo", *Africa: Journal of the International African Institute* 63/4, 462–476.

Ellis, Stephen. 2007. "Witching-Times: A Theme in the Histories of Africa and Europe." In *Imagining Evil: Witchcraft Beliefs and Accusations in Contemporary Africa*, edited by William Olsen and Walter Van Beek, 31–53. Trenton: Africa World Press.

Evans-Pritchard, E.E. 1937. *Witchcraft, Oracles and Magic among the Azande*. Oxford: Clarendon Press.

Fagge, Nick. 2015. "'They Accused Me of Killing and Eating My Grandmother': Agony of Congo's 50,000 'Child Witches' Who Are Brutally Exorcised to 'Beat the Devil out of Them'", *Daily Mail Online*, 19 October 2015. http://www.dailymail.co.uk/news/a rticle-3276057/My-grandmother-died-said-witch-drink-salt-water-stuck-fingers-throat-p ieces-saidF-d-eaten-Congo-s-child-witches-exorcised-devil-beaten-them.html (accessed 10 July 2018).

*Geschiere, Peter. 1997. *The Modernity of Witchcraft: Politics and the Occult in Post-colonial Africa*. Translated by Peter Geschiere and Janet L. Roitman. Charlottesville: University Press of Virginia.

Geschiere, Peter. 2013. *Witchcraft, Intimacy, and Trust: Africa in Comparison*. Chicago: The University of Chicago Press.

Geschiere, Peter, and Cyprian Fisiy. 1994. "Domesticating Personal Violence: Witchcraft, Courts and Confessions in Cameroon", *Africa: Journal of the International African Institute* 64/3, 323–341.

Geschiere, Peter, and Francis Nyamnjoh. 1998. "Witchcraft as an Issue in the 'Politics of Belonging': Democratization and Urban Migrants", *African Studies Review* 41/3, 69–91.

Ludsin, Hallie. 2003. "Cultural Denial: What South Africa's Treatment of Witchcraft Says for the Future of Its Customary Law", *Berkeley Journal of International Law* 21/1, 62–111.

MacGaffey, Wyatt. 2000. "Aesthetics and Politics of Violence in Central Africa", *Journal of African Cultural Studies* 13/1, 63–75.

Mgbako, Chi Adanna, and Katherine Glenn. 2011. "Witchcraft Accusations and Human Rights: Case Studies from Malawi", *George Washington International Law Review* 43, 389–418.

Middleton, John Beattie, and Edward Henry Winter. 1963. *Witchcraft and Sorcery in East Africa*. London: Routledge.

Mildnerová, Kateřina. 2016. "The Modern Forms of Witchcraft in Zambia: An Analysis of Local Witchcraft Narratives in Urban Settings of Lusaka", *Religio* 24/1, 19–51.

*Moore, Henrietta, and Todd Sanders, editors. 2001. *Magical Interpretations, Material Realities: Modernity, Witchcraft and the Occult in Postcolonial Africa*. London: Routledge.

Newell, Sasha. 2007. "Pentecostal Witchcraft: Neoliberal Possession and Demonic Dis-course in Ivoirian Pentecostal Churches", *Journal of Religion in Africa* 37/4, 461–490.

Olupona, Jacob. 2001. "To Praise and to Reprimand: Ancestors and Spirituality in African Society and Culture." In *Ancestors in Post-Contact Religion*, edited by Steven Friesen, 49–71. Cambridge: Harvard University Press.

*Ter Haar, Gerrie. 2007. *Imagining Evil: Witchcraft Beliefs and Accusations in Con-temporary Africa*. Trenton NJ: Africa World Press.

8   Religion, power and politics in Africa

The relation between "religion" and "politics"

Where in Western contexts religion and politics are often seen as distinct categories, in African societies they are deeply intertwined and refer to interconnected and overlapping spheres. Indeed, any neat distinction between religion and politics reflects a secular framework in which religious belief and practice is perceived to be a private affair, marginalized in (if not excluded from) the public sphere and not supposed to play a political role. However, even in European and North American societies that have gone through processes of secularization, religion and politics are not always as neatly separated as is sometimes suggested. Obviously this is even more the case in Africa, where religion historically and today has great political significance. Hence it is surprising that much of the academic literature on African politics pays very little attention to religious belief and practice, reflecting a blind spot for (if not a secular bias against) religion in much of the social sciences.

Stephen Ellis and Gerrie ter Haar, in their book *Worlds of Power: Religious Thought and Political Practice in Africa*, present a definition of religion as "a belief in the existence of an invisible world, often thought to be inhabited by spirits that are believed to affect people's lives in the material world" (Ellis and ter Haar 2004, 3). This definition allows understanding the close relation between religion and politics in Africa, as it draws attention to the widespread belief that "all power has its *ultimate* origin in the spirit world" (ibid., 4). Because power, fundamentally, is of a spiritual nature, religion and politics are interconnected realms. Admittedly, political institutions and structures in most contemporary African countries are shaped on the basis of a formal distinction between religion and politics, which is a legacy of colonial governance. Yet the ways in which these institutions and structures are inhabited, engaged and operationalized are often informed by various forms of religious thought and practice. If that is the case for formal political processes, it is even more the case for informal political activities, or "politics from below" (Bayart, Mbembe and Toulabor 1992). As Ellis and ter Haar (2004, 2) put it, "it is largely through religious ideas that Africans think about the world today, and religious ideas provide them with a means of becoming social and political actors". In other words, religion is a source of social and political agency in the broadest sense of the word, which has implications for the understanding of social movements, political organizing and systems of governance at all levels in society. This chapter explores the complex intersections between religious thought and practice, on the one hand, and formal politics as well as politics from below, on the other. It focuses on contemporary contexts but begins by providing a brief historical perspective.

A historical perspective

Historically speaking, pre-colonial African societies had various political systems and structures, some more egalitarian and others more hierarchical. However, the general pattern was that "institutions of governance became more complex and structured over time", and "by 1500CE there were large and thriving chiefdoms and kingdoms across the continent" (Eldredge 2018, 137). The chief or king often performed both political and religious roles, and their power was believed to originate from ancestors, spirits and deities. A well-known example is the Asantehene, the ruler of the Kingdom of Asante (in present-day Ghana), who is symbolically seated on the Golden Stool, a royal and divine throne that according to Asante mythology descended from the sky. Interestingly, the Asante monarchy has survived colonialism and exists up to date, with the king continuing to perform certain political and religious roles particularly concerning mediation and peacekeeping (Müller 2013) (see Figure 8.1).

Other parts of West Africa have a pre-colonial history of Islamic states known as caliphates or emirates, where the rulers performed both political and religious leadership roles. An example is the Sokoto caliphate in Hausaland (present-day northern Nigeria). Although in the colonial period the sultan of Sokoto was subjugated to colonial rule, his office was not completely abolished and he was given a relative freedom to exercise his power. To date, the sultan remains an important spiritual leader for Muslims in Nigeria, and as such also continues to hold significant social and political influence. On the other side of the continent, the royal families that through the centuries governed the Christian kingdom of Ethiopia legitimized their rule by claiming descent from the Solomonic dynasty that begun with the first Ethiopian emperor, Melenik I (believed to be born out of the encounter between the queen of Sheba and the biblical king Solomon). Although the Imperial monarchy came to an end in 1974 and Ethiopia is now a republic, the legend of the Solomonic dynasty is still popular and continues to shape a narrative of Ethiopia as a Christian nation. These examples of pre-colonial African political institutions are very different, but what they have in common is that political leadership was religiously legitimized, and that there was no clear distinction between political and religious leadership roles. They also illustrate that in many cases, pre-colonial institutions continue to have contemporary political relevance and significance (Eldredge 2018).

Figure 8.1 The Asante king, known as Asantehene (© Jake KY Anderson / Alamy Stock Photo)

In the colonial period, European colonizers introduced modern state forms, government structures, and political institutions in most parts of Africa. Although colonial administrations made use of Christian missions for the project of "civilizing the natives", the formal political structures were, for lack of a better word, "secular". This was reflected in a formal separation between church and state, and in the installation of a legal-rational, bureaucratic state system. Yet political resistance movements against colonial rule frequently made use of religious language and symbols. For example, in the British colony of Kenya the secret anti-colonial movement Mau Mau (1952–64) made use of oath rituals, hymns and even a creed derived from both Kikuyu indigenous religion and Christianity (Lonsdale 1998).

After independence, post-colonial states inherited and largely adopted the colonial structures. Although in the following decades political systems in many countries did change – for instance from multi- to single-party democracy in the 1970s–1980s, and then back to multi-party democracy again in the 1990s in countries such as Kenya, Tanzania and Zambia – they generally continued to adhere to the basic principles of the modern (secular) state. However, the ways in which post-colonial African statesmen and politicians operate within these structures often constitute a creative negotiation of these principles. Ellis and ter Haar (2004, 86) discuss a whole range of examples of African heads of states who "believe in the power of the invisible world just as their subjects do, seeking forms of power commensurate with the importance of the positions they seek to defend and of the burdens they have to discharge". Among these examples is Mathieu Kérékou, President of Benin (from 1972 to 1991 and again from 1996 to 2006), who not only flirted with Marxism and promoted a socialist philosophy, but also made use of ritual practices from Vodun, the indigenous religion of Benin, while at a later stage he came under the influence of a *marabout* (spiritual expert) from Mali who claimed to have received esoteric knowledge from the devil. The same marabout, Mohamed Amado Cissé, also provided ritual services to President Mobutu of Zaire (now known as the Democratic Republic of the Congo) and President Bongo of Gabon. By the time Kérékou became president again in 1996, he had reinvented himself as a born-again Christian, possibly because that would appeal more to voters. Another example is Kenneth Kaunda, President of Zambia (1964–1991) who developed a socialist ideology that he branded "Zambian humanism". As the son of a Presbyterian evangelist, Kaunda publicly profiled himself as a devout Christian yet also developed a close relationship with two Indian gurus who, as his spiritual advisors, were secretly on the payroll of the government and had significant influence in political affairs.

The identification of African statecraft with witchcraft is also ubiquitous. For instance, the late President Félix Houphouët-Boigny of Côte d'Ivoire, who was "widely considered one of the most successful and enlightened African heads of state and known as a staunch Catholic, was nevertheless privately devoted to secretive traditional religious practices throughout his career", with reports suggesting that "he may have carried out ritual killings, and that his death in

1993 was followed by mortuary slayings designed to send servants with him to the next world" (Ellis and ter Haar 2004, 80). Several other prominent African politicians are rumoured to be involved in secret societies such as the Freemasons or the Rosicrucians, which is often seen as the source of their political power as well as economic wealth. Discussing many examples, Ellis and ter Haar argue that all over Africa, heads of state and prominent political figures may build a progressive and modern public image, but in the meantime resort to various spiritual and religious means of maintaining and protecting their political power.

Feature: President Zuma calls upon the ancestors

A more recent illustration of how perceptions of spiritual power play a role in politics is Jacob Zuma, President of South Africa (2009–2018). Zuma had cultivated a profile in which he skilfully combined an evangelical Christian and a Zulu traditionalist identity (the Zulu people are the largest ethnic group in South Africa). In 2012, Zuma was under threat of losing the support from his political party, the African National Congress (ANC), among others because he was associated with corruption. If Zuma had lost his position as ANC President, he would have very likely subsequently also lost his chances for re-election as South African president. (In South Africa, the ANC is the largest political party, so its leader is almost automatically also elected as head of state.)

Interestingly, during this period of political turmoil against him, Zuma, according to media reports, participated in a ceremony that the elders of his clan, deep in rural Zulu land (in the province of KwaZulu-Natal), had organized for him. The ceremony exemplifies the argument of Ellis and ter Haar quoted above, about religion and politics being interconnected because of their shared concern with spiritual power. During the ritual, 12 cows were slaughtered and incense was burnt, while Zulu warriors in traditional dress danced and sang, and many bystanders joined in prayer for Zuma to win a second term as president. The elders of the clan led the prayers, directing them to the ancestors:

> We are appealing to you, our great grandfathers and grandmothers, to protect your son, Gedleyihlekisa [Zuma's traditional Zulu name]. We appeal to you all, Nxamalala [name of Zuma's home town] ancestors, to be with him, to guide and protect him against those ganging up against him. ... We know that you will not forsake him. His enemies will not win. ... His journey ahead is bumpy but we appeal to you, our forefathers, to be with him. Protect your son against those who want to see his demise. You are the ones who chose him among us to lead the country and you cannot forsake him.
>
> (Joy Magazine 2012)

The sacrifice of cows and the offering of incense are important rituals in Zulu indigenous religion to propitiate the ancestors. Interestingly, the same rituals were performed on the eve of the 2010 FIFA world cup in the Soccer City stadium in Johannesburg, by traditional diviners and healers, reportedly with the threefold intention of "unifying people, welcoming visitors, and appeasing ancestors" (Chidester 2012, 180). Both occasions demonstrate that, even in a country often considered to be the most modern on the continent, religious ritual is performed for public and political purposes, in order to mobilize spiritual power and seek the blessing of the ancestors. In the words of David Chidester (2012), cases like these illustrate how in post-apartheid South Africa with its internationally acclaimed progressive constitution, religion has gone "wild", with indigenous religious practices re-emerging in the public sphere in new forms, often mixed with Christian and other religious beliefs and symbols.

Zuma, for those readers curious to know, in 2012 managed to maintain his position as ANC President and in 2014 was re-elected as President of South Africa. One might think that the ancestors had been favourable towards him and that their powers had protected his political career. However, in 2018 his career came to an end, as Zuma was forced to resign from his office.

Christianity, democratization and political engagement

After independence, the relationship between political and religious institutions needed to be renegotiated. Under colonialism, Christian churches held a privileged position as providers of education, health care and other crucial social and public services. After independence, in many countries the post-colonial state tried to take over these responsibilities, especially when their economies were initially flourishing. For instance, in Zambia many of the mission schools were nationalized, with churches and other religious institutions being somewhat relegated to the religious sphere (strictly defined). Thus, effort was made to formally separate "religion" from "politics", although religious leaders would typically be invited to attend and perform certain roles in official state ceremonies.

Shortly after independence, in the late 1960s and throughout the 1970s, political leaders and heads of state in a range of African countries gradually developed authoritarian tendencies and entrenched personal dictatorships by strengthening single party regimes. Initially, Christian and Muslim religious leaders kept a low public profile while the political elites who assumed power through competitive elections at independence sought to end such elections and further restricted the freedom to disparage their unpopular policies. To a certain extent, religious leaders were convinced by politicians that unchecked freedoms and competitive political processes would lead to ethnic conflict, thereby hampering economic development in their respective states. Other leaders remained largely silent not because they favoured those unpopular policies, but because they wanted to maintain a cordial working relationship with African governments. They also lobbied to regain their original role in the provision of education and healthcare, which was helped by the situation of economic decline in the 1970s as a result of which many governments struggled to provide basic social services and were happy to relegate these to the church.

Only when political repression intensified and the economic crisis became more severe, in the 1980s, did religious leaders take on a more explicitly political role, publicly critiquing their governments and heads of state. Especially Catholic and mainline Protestant church leaders were at the forefront of what has been called "a second liberation, as the peoples of Africa tried to throw off the political systems that had increasingly oppressed and beggared them" (Gifford 1995, 1). In Francophone countries such as Benin, Congo, Gabon, Togo and Zaire, Catholic bishops in the late 1980s presided over national conferences that were supposed to transition dictatorships into democracies. Meanwhile, in Kenya, Madagascar and Zambia, the Council of Churches (mostly representing mainline Protestant churches) in each of these countries played a key role in critiquing dictatorial regimes and in democratic transitioning processes. Although it is difficult to generalize, Pentecostal Christian leaders often played a more ambivalent, if not reactionary role in these dynamics of democratic change (Ranger 2008). Typically claiming that they did not want to engage in politics, they often ended up de facto condoning the regimes in power and resisting democratic change. For instance, during the clamour for multiparty democracy, these church leaders actively supported the repressive leadership of Jerry Rawlings in Ghana (1979–2000) and Daniel arap Moi in Kenya (1978–2002). Both presidents took advantage of the divisions evident in the religious sector for their own political gains, and they increased these divisions by offering financial support and other privileges to the Pentecostal leaders supporting them. The conflicting stances taken by Christian leaders in the process of democratic change had partly to do with historical divisions and pragmatic considerations, yet fundamentally it reveals the different political-theological orientations that exist within Christianity in Africa: a form of Christianity committed to democracy and concerned with social justice, versus a form of Christianity claiming to be a-political and to prioritize "saving souls". In more recent decades, Pentecostal churches have largely moved beyond their traditional a-political stance and have engaged democratic structures in order to pursue their political ambitions. However, these ambitions at their core sometimes seem more concerned with theocracy (rule of God) than with democracy (rule of the people), as demonstrated in the example of Zambia below.

Feature: Zambia as a Christian nation

As mentioned earlier, the first president of Zambia, Kenneth Kaunda, came under the influence of two Indian gurus – a secret that increasingly became public knowledge. It was a key reason why Kaunda in the 1980s began to lose the support of a growing constituency of voters: the members of Pentecostal churches. In fact, Kaunda lost political support much more widely, including from the highly influential Catholic Church and from the mainline

Protestant churches, for two other reasons: his government failed to respond adequately to the severe economic crisis that had hit the country from the late 1970s, and because the system of single-party democracy (introduced in 1972) developed into an increasingly repressive regime. Almost all Christian denominations and their representative bodies (the Zambian Episcopal Conference, the Council of Churches in Zambia, and the Evangelical Fellowship in Zambia) joined hands with other civil society organizations, forcing Kaunda to move to multi-party democracy and to hold free elections, which took place in November 1991. In these elections, Kaunda was overwhelmingly defeated by trade union and opposition leader Frederick Chiluba.

Chiluba, who identified as a born-again Christian, was most enthusiastically supported by Pentecostal churches in the country. Once voted into office, the first thing he did was organize a cleansing ceremony, with pastors praying in each room of State House in order to chase out the evil spirits associated with Kaunda and his gurus. The ritual was motivated by "the belief that we inhabit a spiritual world in which opponents can use spiritual power to cause harm" (Phiri 2008, 101). Having moved into his presidential residency, Chiluba soon held another ceremony in State House during which he declared Zambia to be a Christian nation:

> On behalf of the people of Zambia, I repent of our wicked ways of idolatry, witchcraft, immorality, injustice and corruption. I pray for the healing, restoration, revival, blessing and prosperity of Zambia. On behalf of the nation, I have now entered a covenant with the living God ... I submit the Government and the entire nation of Zambia to the Lordship of Jesus Christ. I further declare that Zambia is a Christian nation that will seek to be governed by the righteous principles of the Word of God.
>
> (Phiri 2008, 103)

The declaration can be seen as reflecting a typical Pentecostal political theology: the idea of born-again conversion is applied to the nation as a whole and becomes a political project that is believed to bring about national redemption in the form of healing, blessing and prosperity for the country. The idea that the Zambian nation and its government are subjected to Jesus Christ suggests that, principally, Zambia is no longer a democracy but a theocracy, indeed governed on the basis of "the Word of God".

Chiluba's declaration was enthusiastically welcomed by the Evangelical Fellowship of Zambia, yet the Catholic Church and most of the mainline Protestant churches were sceptical if not negative, and have remained so until today (Hinfelaar 2011). This may have been partly because of their concern about the growing political influence of Pentecostal churches in the country, which threatened their established position. Yet their response also indicated an adherence to the formal principle of the separation of church and state, and a concern about the implications of the declaration for religious freedom in the country. Despite their opposition, four years later (in 1996) the declaration was enshrined in a preamble to the Zambian Constitution, with a text that acknowledges Zambia's status as a Christian nation as well as the commitment to upholding freedom of religion. Since then, there have been ongoing debates about the legal and political meaning of the declaration, but also in the latest amendment of the constitution (2016) the status of Zambia as a Christian nation was maintained. The social and political consequences of Chiluba's declaration included foreign policy decisions that encouraged ties with Israel while cutting relations with Iran and Iraq; creating increased tension between the Muslim minority and the Christian majority, as Muslims felt increasingly threatened in the new state context; encouraging an influx of missionaries into Zambia and holding evangelistic crusades at government expense; creating a government department of religious affairs; and providing discretionary funding to churches and other social organizations that support the president. More recently, it also has had serious implications for the question of human rights in relation to sexual minorities, with the prevailing public and political argument being that gay rights can never be accepted in a Christian nation (van Klinken 2014). In the meantime, Chiluba has long been ousted out of office, his self-declared Christian administration being associated with a legacy of severe corruption.

Zambia is a relatively early example of a trend that has manifested itself throughout the continent: Pentecostal political engagement inspired by an ideology of Christian nationalism. The same trend was apparent in Kenya where Pentecostal churches, in the process of drafting a new constitution, lobbied (unsuccessfully) for the acknowledgment of Kenya as a Christian nation, and then (again unsuccessfully) campaigned against the draft constitution in the 2010 referendum, warning that it would allow for Islamic kadhi courts, abortion and homosexuality (Deacon 2015). In Nigeria, which has led the Pentecostal revolution on the continent, Pentecostal leaders have engaged with Muslim leaders in a battle for the soul of the nation, using born-again conversion as a programme to bring about social and political redemption (Marshall 2009).

Islam, democratization and political engagement

As mentioned earlier in this chapter, in certain parts of Africa Islam has been long present and there exists a pre-colonial history of Islamic states. However, only in the 20th century, Islam spread to new areas and was more widely adopted on the continent (cf. Chapter 3). In the colonial period, conversion to Islam for some people was politically motivated: it was an act of resistance against Western imperialism in the forms of colonialism and missionary Christianity (Wright 2013). In the same way, certain Islamic reform movements in contemporary Africa emphasize Muslim identity in order to distinguish themselves from the originally Christian but secularized West, which tends to be seen as morally degraded.

When looking at the relation between Islam and politics in the contemporary period, which is our focus in this chapter, it is important to acknowledge the relatively recent spread of Islam in much of Africa, which took place more or less simultaneously with the spread of Christianity. Indeed, in many countries there is a clear competition between these two religions (and to some extent also indigenous and neo-traditional religions) for public visibility and political influence. This competition was stimulated by the processes of political liberalization, an expanding public sphere, and greater freedom of expression and association occurring in many African countries from the early 1990s. As René Otayek and Benjamin Soares point out, these dynamics facilitated a renewed political engagement in Muslim communities:

> In the 1990s, Muslim religious leaders in sub-Saharan Africa were largely absent from the initial debates about such issues as human rights, multiparty rule, and the rule of law in many countries. That would, however, soon change. With greater spaces for political expression, many African Muslims eagerly and actively engaged in political debate, often as concerned citizens who happened to be Muslim and sometimes as Muslim activists, even as Islamists. But only a minority of Africans seem to advocate political Islam or Islamism as an agenda.
>
> (Otayek and Soares 2007, 13)

Muslim political engagement has taken different forms. In some countries, such as Kenya, Muslim religious leaders during the 1990s teamed up with mainline Christian religious leaders to call for greater respect for civil liberties and for multiparty democracy. Also in other countries with majority, or significant minority Muslim populations, such as Mali, Nigeria, Senegal and Tanzania, there is evidence of Islamic leaders supporting pro-democracy movements (Dowd 2015). However, in the same countries there is also evidence of more radicalized forms of political Islam, or Islamist movements, which tend to pursue a political project at odds with democracy. Especially in Nigeria, Sudan and Somalia, these movements have gained considerable ground. Under their influence, various Muslim-majority states in the northern part of Nigeria around the year 2000 decided to implement *sharia* (Islamic penal laws) in their official legal system, in a context where Islam historically played an important role in the construction of identity and in political organization (Sanusi 2007). In Sudan, since the early 1980s, the government had actively pursued the Islamization of the country, introducing an Islamic constitution that recognized sharia law – a move that gave rise to intense and long-lasting interreligious conflict, and finally led to the secession of the Christian-dominated southern part of the country in 2011 (Ahmed 2007). Most other countries in sub-Saharan Africa have been able to curtail the influence of Islamist movements, not least because of the "ability of the secular state – even when relatively weak – to coerce, repress, and exclude its critics, Islamist or otherwise" (Otayek and Soares 2007, 14). Frequently, this coercion and repression of Islamism by African states happens with the support of post-9/11 "war on terror" funding and strategies from the US.

Feature: Politicization of Islam in Kenya

Muslims in Kenya are a minority of about 10–12% of the population. Yet they have actively participated in the country's political processes. Since the ushering in of multiparty politics in the 1990s, Kenyan Muslims' political engagement experienced significant transformation. With the transition to democratic politics, the role of politicized Islam has become more visible. The most serious attempt to mobilize Kenyan Muslims politically was with the formation of the Islamic Party of Kenya (IPK) in the early 1990s. According to Hassan Ndzovu (2014, 87),

> The party had declared that its aim was to bring about a just constitutional government that upholds the ideals of democracy, human rights, and removal of all forms of discrimination at all levels. It wanted to be recognized like any other political party in Kenya so that it could participate in elections, to make the system more open and honest rather than demolishing the existing system.

The IPK emerged "as a political lobby for the interests of Muslims, rather than as a means for Islamist political objectives" (Ndzovu 2014, 87). The criticism of President Moi's leadership formed a common ground between IPK and other opposition parties. Together, they wanted to remove Moi from power due to his poor track record, which was associated with bad governance, corruption and abuse of power. Fearing that the party would influence Muslims' political direction in the country, the government refused to recognize IPK as a political party. More so, ethnic and racial differences between Muslims were manipulated by state machineries to severely weaken their efforts to present a united political voice. Through alleged state support, an alternative Muslims' political party appeared, the United Muslims of Africa (UMA), to diffuse the popularity of IPK. The UMA presented itself as the authentic voice of the "African" Muslims, as opposed to the "Arab" element purportedly dominating the IPK. This distinction served to reinforce the idea of Muslims on Kenya's east coast being "Arab" and not truly "African" due to the long history of Arab influence and settlement in that region.

Nevertheless, there are occasions when Kenyan Muslims are united, especially when they feel that their right to observe their religion is threatened. For instance, during the Kadhi court debate (2004–2010), Muslims displayed a high degree of unity. Kadhi courts are based on Islamic law and concerned with issues of marriage, family, inheritance and succession for

Muslims in Kenya, dating back to the pre-colonial period. In the process of drafting a new constitution, a group of Pentecostal Christian clergy campaigned for the Kadhi courts not to be recognized. Muslim leaders resisted the campaign and demanded constitutional recognition of the courts, arguing that these play an important role in the preservation of their identity. Many Muslims perceived opposition to the Kadhi courts as externally inspired. "They suspect that it forms part of the Western agenda to fight proxy wars with Muslims all over the world since 9/11" (Ndzovu 2014, 133).

Though the contours of Muslims' engagement in Kenyan politics are complex, they seem to encourage a politicization of Islam as a way of making sense of their historic marginalization, which shapes their understanding of the country's politics and state policies. In recent years, the activities of militant Islamist movements such as al-Shabaab (from neighbouring Somalia) in Kenya have fuelled a public backlash against Muslims in the country, as well as anti-terrorist campaigns from the government of which Muslims have become targets.

Conclusion

This chapter has demonstrated that in African contexts, religion and politics cannot be considered distinct categories and separate spheres, as they are closely interconnected. The key reason for this is that both religion and politics are concerned with power, and that from an indigenous religious perspective, power is inherently spiritual. This deeply rooted belief continues to shape the ways in which many people in Africa today, including those who identify as Christian or Muslim, understand and engage with "the political". Another key factor is the way in which religious identity has been politicized in many African societies, during colonialism and since independence, as a result of local processes of social and political change as well as global religious dynamics such as the emergence of neo-traditional religious movements, revivalist forms of Christianity and reformist forms of Islam. This chapter has only made a beginning to explore these complex intersections, making it clear that one cannot seriously understand religion in Africa without taking politics into account, and vice versa.

Questions for discussion

- This chapter quoted Ellis and ter Haar (2004, 2) stating that "it is largely through religious ideas that Africans think about the world today, and religious ideas provide them with a means of becoming social and political actors". How would you support, or oppose, this claim, with reference to indigenous religions, Christianity and Islam?
- Many observers argue that religion is an obstacle to democracy in Africa. How would you assess such a claim?

- Why do you think that much of the academic literature on African politics pays very little attention to religion, and what conceptual rethinking is required to change this?

References (*indicates recommended reading)

Ahmed, Einas. 2007. "Political Islam in Sudan." In *Islam and Muslim Politics in Africa*, edited by Benjamin Soares and René Otayek, 189–208. New York: Palgrave Macmillan.

Bayart, Jean-François, Achille Mbembe and Comi Toulabor. 1992. *Le Politique par le bas en Afrique noire. Contributions à une problématique de la démocratie*. Paris: Karthala.

Chidester, David. 2012. *Wild Religion: Tracking the Sacred in South Africa*. Berkeley: University of California Press.

Deacon, Gregory. 2015. "Kenya: A Nation Born Again", *PentecoStudies* 14/2, 219–240.

*Dowd, Robert. 2015. *Christianity, Islam, and Liberal Democracy: Lessons from Sub-Saharan Africa*. Oxford: Oxford University Press.

Eldredge, Elizabeth. 2018. "Pre-Colonial Political Institutions: Relevance for Contemporary Africa." In *The Palgrave Handbook of African Politics, Governance and Development*, edited by Samuel Ojo Oloruntoba, Toyin Falola, 137–158. New York: Palgrave Macmillan.

*Ellis, Stephen, and Gerrie ter Haar. 2004. *Worlds of Power: Religious Thought and Political Practice in Africa*. Oxford: Oxford University Press.

Gifford, Paul, editor. 1995. *The Christian Churches and the Democratisation of Africa*. Leiden: Brill.

Hinfelaar, Marja. 2011. "Debating the Secular in Zambia: The Response of the Catholic Church to Scientific Socialism and Christian Nation, 1976–2006." In *Christianity and Public Culture in Africa*, edited by Harri Englund, 50–66. Athens: Ohio University Press.

Joy Magazine. 2012. "Zuma Calls on the Spirits". *Joy! Magazine Online*. http://www.joymag.co.za/newsitem.php?newsID=272 (accessed 28 April 2018).

Lonsdale, John. 1998. "Kenya." In *The Encyclopedia of Politics and Religion* (vol. 2), edited by Robert Wuthnow, 441–444. London: Routledge.

Marshall, Ruth. 2009. *Political Spiritualities: The Pentecostal Revolution in Nigeria*. Chicago: University of Chicago Press.

Müller, Louise. 2013. *Religion and Chieftaincy in Ghana: An Explanation of the Persistence of a Traditional Political Institution in West Africa*. Münster: LIT Verlag.

Ndzovu, Hassan. 2014. *Muslims in Kenyan Politics: Political Involvement, Marginalization and Minority Status*. Evanston: Northwestern University Press

Otayek, René, and Benjamin Soares. 2007. "Introduction." In *Islam and Muslim Politics in Africa*, edited by Benjamin Soares and René Otayek, 1–24. New York: Palgrave Macmillan.

Phiri, Isabel. 2008. "President Frederick Chiluba and Zambia: Evangelicals and Democracy in a Christian Nation." In *Evangelical Christianity and Democracy in Africa*, edited by Terence Ranger, 95–130. Oxford: Oxford University Press.

Ranger, Terence, ed. 2008. *Evangelical Christianity and Democracy in Africa*. Oxford: Oxford University Press.

Sanusi, Lamido Sanusi. 2007. "Politics and Sharia in Northern Nigeria." In *Islam and Muslim Politics in Africa*, edited by Benjamin Soares and René Otayek, 177–188. New York: Palgrave Macmillan.

van Klinken, Adriaan. 2014. "Homosexuality, Politics and Pentecostal Nationalism in Zambia", *Studies in World Christianity* 20/3, 259–281.

Wright, Zachary Valentine. 2013. "Islam and Decolonization in Africa: The Political Engagement of a West African Muslim Community", *The International Journal of African Historical Studies* 46/2, 205–227.

9 Religion, conflict and peace-building in Africa

Introduction

Previously, conflicts in African societies tended to be explained primarily in terms of ethnic tensions. But recently, religion is emerging as a major driver of conflict. This is largely because ethnic identity is increasingly subsumed under religious identity. This does not insinuate that ethnicity lost its critical power in national politics of a state, only that religion is now emerging as a serious divide increasingly threatening the unity of some of the post-colonial states. Sub-Saharan Africa is particularly vulnerable to religious clashes since politicians tend to exploit religious language in order to gain political credibility. This has precipitated large-scale religious conflicts in certain states. The unity of the post-colonial state, of course, has always been contested, as the modern African state is a colonial invention, with boundaries of most countries being randomly assigned.

This chapter, therefore, examines the multifaceted connections between religion and conflict, as well as peace dynamics. It examines the role of the religious sector in strengthening social divisions that lead to instability. But, also aware that in various ways religion can also be a unifying force, the chapter analyses the bridges built by religious actors in Africa to increase social cohesion, without neglecting the divisive power of religious discourse. The link between religion and conflict is, accordingly, explored by viewing religion as a cause of structural violence through discrimination and exclusions. Undoubtedly, religious identities can establish serious barriers, aggravating violent conflict within a state where some sections of the population claim to be adhering to the absolute true religion.

The three religious traditions studied in this book have variously contributed to the numerous conflicts witnessed on the continent. In the post-colonial era, for instance, the long Sudanese civil conflict was interpreted as a war that involved the Muslim North and the African indigenous religionists and Christians residing in the South (Ahmed 2007); during the Rwandan genocide of 1994, most Christians were killed within the compounds of the church buildings (Longman 2001); the present war in Somalia spearheaded by the Salafi-jihadi-minded group, al-Shabaab has been framed as a struggle for liberating the "occupied" Muslim land (Ndzovu 2017). One of the prominent jihadi organizations in sub-Saharan Africa is Boko Haram (meaning "Western education is forbidden"), which was responsible for the much publicized kidnapping of school girls in northern Nigeria. While the sporadic violence between Christians and Muslims in Nigeria continues (Dowd 2015), in Cote d'Ivoire the two civil wars that erupted in 2002 and after the 2011 election were driven by conflict between the predominantly Muslim North and largely Christian South (Conteh 2011). Exploring these complex histories and dynamics, the following sections survey the role of African indigenous religions, Christianity and Islam in situations of conflict as well as peace-building.

African indigenous religions

Indigenous religions are not institutionalized in the way Islam and Christianity are, and therefore do not usually play a role in situations of conflict as institutional bodies. However, that is not to say that they are not relevant to the question of religion, conflict and peace. As Ezra Chitando and Joram Tarusarira (2017, 5) argue,

> The dominant narrative in the study of religion in Africa is that African indigenous religions are non-violent, peaceful and seek to promote healing and integration. In this paradigm, it is militant missionary religions such as Islam and Christianity that promote violence. Such an approach misses the key learning that no religion is violent in and of itself: only the determination of individuals and groups acting in the name of a particular religion is relevant as to whether/the extent to which a religion can be appropriated and deployed to perpetrate violence.

Chitando and Tarusarira challenge the romanticization of African indigenous religions by discussing the conflict-ridden context of Zimbabwe. They specifically examine how a popular Zimbabwean song that draws on indigenous religious imagery, has been performed to justify "sacred violence" and to "evoke feelings of hostility against imagined or actual political enemies" (ibid., 6). Indeed, a review of literature on both historical and contemporary African contexts does provide further evidence that indigenous religious beliefs, symbols and practices have been used for political purposes and as tools in cases of conflict.

In different countries, Africans mobilized to oppose colonial discrimination by appealing to African nationalism, often inspired by indigenous religious language and symbol. While some Africans took spiritual refuge from the attack by colonial administrators and missionaries in their indigenous religions, others embarked on an armed struggle against the oppressors through instrumentalizing indigenous religions as ideological weapons. The resistance was mostly organized by traditional rulers, whose right to rule was based on indigenous traditions, as illustrated by the case of the Ashante Wars (1873–1884) in present day Ghana; the Anglo-Zulu War of 1879 where the Zulus under King Cetschwayo defeated the British forces in contemporary South Africa; and the

Matabele War of 1893 in which the Ndebele under King Lobengula fought against the British settlers in contemporary Zimbabwe. In other cases, indigenous beliefs in magic, spirit possession and witchcraft were critical for motivating and offering protection to the combatants involved in the struggle (Møller 2006). During the colonial period in the Democratic Republic of the Congo (DRC), nationalist movements emerged that combined religion, politics and the revitalization of indigenous culture as a strategy to defeat colonial rule and recapture political power. For instance, the Kingunza (prophetic) movement used songs to bring down the ancestral spirits that would offer assistance in the struggle, which according to them was fought not by guns "but with music, prayers and bodies" (Covington-Ward 2016, 72). Yolanda Covington-Ward (2016, 73) argues that, "Through performative encounters, the Kingunza movement used a type of spiritual legitimacy gained from the spiritual realm to subvert Belgian colonial authority".

The reliance on indigenous religious beliefs, institutions and practices in the context of conflict was again manifest in the post-colonial era. Driven by the desire to be "authentic", Mobutu Sese Seko, who from 1965 to 1997 was President of Zaire (present day DRC) declared, "We are embarking on our cultural liberation … the reconquest of our African, Zairian soul. We men of black skin have had imposed on us the mentality of quite a different race. We must become authentic Africans, authentic blacks, authentic Zairian" (Rayapen 1989, 55). Mobutu capitalized on Africans' respect for ancestral customs to attack the symbolism of the Christian church in the country. Consequently, he dropped his Christian name and asked the people to go back to their local African culture, grounded in indigenous religions.

The appeal to African indigenous religions was also evident during the civil wars that ravaged the continent in the post-colonial era. Though most of these wars with religious elements have generally been associated with Islam and Christianity, African indigenous religions have also contributed to conflicts among citizens. During the Biafra civil war (1967–1970), some of the proponents of secession from the Nigerian state (mostly the Igbo people) resorted to seeking the assistance of indigenous experts in magical powers who could "influence the course and outcome of the war in their favour" (Conteh 2011, 54). Nonetheless, they were eventually defeated by government forces. In the Liberian civil war (1989–1997; 1999–2003) most of the leaders of warring groups were purportedly endowed with supernatural powers due to their ability to communicate with supernatural forces. In fact,

> some Liberians held the belief that the late Liberian head of state, Samuel K. Doe (1980–1990), during the early stages of the Liberian civil war, was impervious to bullets, and had the power to disappear in the face of danger through the help of some West African sacred specialists.
>
> (Conteh 2011, 56–7)

This raises the question as to what happened to his supernatural power, as the war culminating in his assassination. The two rebel movements active in Uganda in the 1980s – the Holy Spirit Mobile Forces of Alice Lakewena (1956–2007) and the Lord's Resistance Army inspired by Joseph Kony (b. 1961) – were together regarded as "prophetic movements" and "armies of God" fighting to eradicate the evils of world. The two movements were entrenched in African indigenous religions that "were renewed in the face of war and upheaval" (Kastfelt 2005, 12–13).

In Sierra Leone, the Revolutionary United Front's (RUF) insurrection, led by Foday Sankoh (1937–2003), embarked on a civil war in 1991 against the government. Though many RUF rebel fighters wore Christian crosses and rosaries or Islamic Qur'anic talismans on the battlefield, a majority of them believed that the traditional charms prepared by indigenous specialists were effective in making them resistant to the enemy's bullets. Due to lack of proper coordination by the state to subdue the RUF rebel forces, the government called upon "all citizens, especially those in the hinterland, to use whatever traditional means or power they had to combat the rebels" (Conteh 2011, 62). The emergent "traditional warriors" formed by various ethnic groups "used not only conventional arms and witch guns but through spiritual means used killer bees to attack and destabilize the rebels" (ibid.). Due to the indigenous charms provided to them, the "traditional warriors" allegedly "possessed the supernatural ability to turn daylight into darkness to prevent the rebels from seeing" them, giving the former "the upper hand in the war" (ibid.). Similarly, the RUF rebel forces consulted the services of African indigenous specialists to counter the defence strategies of the "traditional warriors". Thus, both the warring factions solicited the protective traditional-magical charm, the *huronko/ronko*, believed to be efficacious in the battlefield. Clearly, declarations about possessing supernatural ability by opposite camps in Africa seem to be a common way to instil fear and weaken the fighting spirit of the opposing forces.

Christianity

Like African indigenous religions, Christianity has also been observed to exercise power and exacerbate conflicts within the continent. It is critical to keep in mind that historically speaking, in most of sub-Saharan Africa, Christianity was introduced during the colonial period. Although conversion to Christianity was generally not enforced through the use of physical violence, missionary Christians and their converts benefited from the power inequalities that were inherent to the colonial political context. European missionaries "increasingly took top positions and placed a ceiling on those available to Africans" (Rayapen 1989, 54). Moreover, both colonial governments and Christian missions exercised more subtle forms of violence, including epistemological violence towards local cultures and indigenous religions by deeming these to be inferior to Western traditions. At the same time, during the colonial period Christianity also emerged as a context for practices of resistance by colonial subjects. For instance, Christian converts that broke away from the European dominated mission churches established independent churches (see the example of the Lumpa Church, Chapter 2). Others joined colonial resistance movements such as the Mau Mau in Kenya (Lonsdale 2002).

Given the prevalence of racism, even those Africans who converted to Christianity were considered inferior to Europeans by missionaries. The racial violence that was more or less explicit in colonial governance and missionary Christianity in Africa generally, became particularly visible in Southern Africa, with the various forms of racial politics and systems of Apartheid (racial segregation) in Namibia, Zimbabwe and most famously, South Africa. In 20th century South Africa, the Afrikaners imposed their white supremacy over black Africans by using the Old Testament to justify the doctrine of Apartheid in the country. The term "Afrikaners" refers to that part of the white population in South Africa that has its roots in the history of continental Europeans (mostly Dutch, German and French) that arrived in the 17th century and settled in the region. Gradually they developed their own language, culture and identity strongly based in their Protestant (to be precise, Calvinist) religious tradition. According to the Afrikaners, "they were a chosen people, set apart by their migration and their suffering, just like the ancient people of Israel", and therefore, "the idea of equality with black Africans because of commonality of faith" was interpreted as blasphemous (Rayapen 1989, 55).

Apart from the historical contexts of colonialism and apartheid, Christian beliefs and practices have frequently played a critical role in situations of conflict and violence in post-colonial African societies. Even in a country where more than 90 per cent of the population is Christian, such as Rwanda, the country's various churches have been criticized for their involvement in the 1994 genocide (Møller 2006). The genocide involved the Hutu majority against the Tutsi minority, both of which generally practise Christianity. Historically, during the colonial rule, the Belgians exacerbated the divisions between the two ethnic groups by favouring the Tutsis in terms of accessing higher education and holding positions of power. Following independence in 1962, the Hutu began a process of discriminating and eliminating Tutsi – killing thousands and forcing hundreds of thousands to flee the country. While in exile the Rwandan Tutsis formed the Rwandan Patriotic Front and initiated onslaught against the Hutu-led government. After years of fighting, the government retaliated by embarking on a genocidal campaign against Tutsi living in the country. One of the ideas of the Christian Church, the Hamitic myth (the notion of the "lost tribe of Israel", derived from the Old Testament) was used by the Hutu to portray the Tutsi as alien conquerors from Ethiopia, to which country they should return. This call was demonstrated by dumping their dead bodies into the river Nyabarongo that leads to Ethiopia (ibid., 34). Ironically, the missionaries and the colonialists used this same myth to put members of the Tutsi community in positions of leadership in the years before independence.

Feature: The churches' sanction of genocide in Rwanda

A study by Timothy Longman (2001; 2010) reveals how to a certain extent the Christian churches in Rwanda were complacent in the 1994 genocide witnessed in the country. It is estimated that the majority of the Rwandese were killed on the "sacred grounds" of the country's churches, which served as killing fields. When ethno-political violence exploded in the country after the assassination of President Juvenal Habyarimana in 1994, most of the minority Tutsi ethnic group rushed into the Catholic and Protestant churches for refuge. This did not stop the Hutu extremists through their wide network of youth militia, the Interahamwe, to pursue the Tutsi even into the churches and engaged in the process of eliminating them.

If both the Hutu and Tutsi are Christians, how could this violence happen? Obviously, the division on the basis of ethnicity was stronger than the sense of unity on the basis of a shared Christian faith. While the churches were not the principal architects of the Rwandan genocide, their entanglement in ethnic politics prepared the Rwandese to overlook the sanctity of church premises and participate in the murders of Tutsi without feeling that their actions were against the principles of their faith (Longman 2010). Without doubt the organizers of the Interahamwe death squads in various localities involved prominent church leaders together with other church employees. Narratives about the militias attending mass prior to embarking on their killing missions, and about some of the killers pausing during the massacres to pray at the altar, indicate that murderers considered their actions to be sanctioned by the church teachings. Rather than being mere "neutral" player, the Christian churches in Rwanda provided crucial support for the genocide (Longman 2001).

While President Habyarimana found his hold on power challenged by opposition activists who exposed his corruption and questioned his legitimacy, church leaders in the country also found their own authority undermined. The churches' support for the genocide, therefore, can be comprehended within this context of church authority being eroded. The challenge to their authority made church leaders sympathetic to the notion of a "Tutsi menace" that extremist Hutus promoted following Habyarimana's assassination. In supporting the genocide, church personnel considered the assault on Tutsis and their associates as a struggle to protect church authority and subsequent power (Longman, 2001; 2010).

Since the church leaders did not condemn the rising Tutsi pogrom in the country, but instead exhibited their own anti-Tutsi bigotry, their persistent support for the Hutu-led regime was interpreted as approval of the anti-Tutsi message. Church officials provided credibility to those organizing the genocide by calling on their members to support the new government. As a result they did not officially censure the tarnishing of churches' sacred grounds, creating the impression that they supported the massacres. In different parts of the country, several clergies lured Tutsi into churches knowing that they would be attacked and killed by the Interahamwe militias. In this unfolding scenario, the church personnel engaged in the violence and justified the killing as a defensive action necessitated by the invasion of Tutsi-dominated rebel forces (Longman 2001). (See Figure 9.1.)

Islam

Some of the reform movements that appeared among African Muslim communities (see Chapter 6) have developed into Salafi-jihadi groups that employ violence in attaining their political objectives. One of the main reasons for the recent decline in peace in some parts of Africa is the increased jihad activity, driven by certain Salafi-jihadi groups such as Boko Haram in Nigeria, al-Shabaab in Somalia and Kenya, the Movement for Monotheism and Jihad (MUJAO), and al-Qaeda in the Islamic Maghreb (AQMI) in Mali and parts of West Africa among others. These and similar Islamic groups in Africa have insisted on the "jihad of the sword" as a means for the establishment of an Islamic state in their respective countries. They have relied on interpretation of selective texts of the Qur'an to support their agenda. The complexity of the links between Islam and violence in sub-Saharan Africa is clearly highlighted by the experience of al-Shabaab in Somalia, which since its formation has

Figure 9.1 Ntrama church altar. 5,000 people seeking refuge in this church were killed during the Rwandan genocide (courtesy of Scott Chacon, 2006)

advocated for the creation of a State governed by Islamic law (Love 2006, 628). During the Sudanese civil war, Islamic concepts and symbolism were also applied by the Islamist government to justify the application of violence in their effort to eradicate the *dhimmis* (second class citizens, such as African indigenous religionists and Christians) through jihad warfare (Kastfelt 2005). This determination was religiously sanctioned in 1992, when prominent Islamic clerics issued a religious decree (*fatwa*) that legalized jihad in Southern Sudan. As a consequence of this declaration, the Islamist government of Sudan launched a military onslaught against the southern Sudanese, which was strongly resisted by the latter (Conteh 2011).

In Nigeria, tension between Muslim and Christian communities has deepened social animosities and continues to ignite periodic fatal attacks. Islam was introduced in the present northern Nigeria by the 10th century, while Christianity arrived in the southern regions in the mid-19th century. Throughout the colonial period, the two regions were separately governed and the remnants of this British policy are evident in the contemporary tension between Muslims and Christians in the country (Vaughan 2016). In the first two decades of the 21st century, conflicts between Christians and Muslims have seemingly intensified in the country, accelerating in 1986 when the Nigerian government announced that it had joined the Organization of Islamic Cooperation (OIC) membership. This decision was interpreted by Christian leaders as a strategy to give Islam prominence in the country. Muslim leaders, on the other hand, have been concerned about what they perceive as attempts by Christians, especially Pentecostals, to claim Nigeria as a Christian nation. Thus, the tensions and conflicts between Christian and Muslim communities in Nigeria are, on the one hand, deeply rooted in (pre-)colonial histories and policies, and on the other hand, in the post-colonial emergence of religious revivalist and reformist movements which are both concerned with the "contest for public space" and with exercising political influence in a context of economic, social and political instability (Ojo 2007).

The introduction of Islamic law (sharia) in the predominantly Muslim states of northern Nigeria in the late 1990s further increased tension between Muslims and Christians in the country. By the year 2003, sharia law had been entrenched in the constitutions of twelve states in the northern region. Christians living in these states felt they were being rendered second class citizens. Consequently, Christians, especially Pentecostals, began to mobilize "to fight attempts to Islamize Nigeria" and instead strengthened "their efforts to make Nigeria a Christian territory" (Dowd 2015, 100). In addition, since the 1980s Salafi-jihadi groups, in particular Boko Haram, with their rallying calls for the establishment of an Islamic state and the rule of God, have appeared in the country inflicting wide scale destruction in northern and central Nigeria (Voll 2015). Among the various groups that have been involved in the 2012 Malian conflict are the Salafi-jihadi movements of AQMI and MUJAO whose desire was to ensure the creation of an Islamic caliphate in the country. Comparatively, Boko Haram, al-Shabaab and the different religio-political Malian groups have all "managed to gain territorial control over parts of their respective countries, a fact that reflects their quest for spatial segregation" (Loimeier 2018, 294). Although these movements are associated with violence, Roman Loimeier (2018, 297) has observed:

> A central question regarding the development of *jihad*-minded groups is the question of why such groups have found support in local populations despite the fact that they represent extremely narrow doctrinal positions that are rejected by a majority of Muslims due to their literalist limitations and despite the fact that such groups often establish a regime of terror and extreme justice.

As elsewhere in Africa, the Salafi-jihadi leaders resort to Islamic texts to rationalize their brutal actions, which demonstrate their calculated ability to frame violence in Islamic terms. This scenario has compelled moderate Muslims to come forward and pre-empt this manipulation of Islamic knowledge. For instance in Kenya, Muslim leaders, through organizations like the Supreme Council of Kenya Muslims, the Center for Ihsan and Educational Development, and Building Resilience against Violent Extremism (BRAVE) have come up with programmes to counter the jihadi ideology. BRAVE has particularly been instrumental in running anti-jihadi campaigns on media and social media platforms with anti-extremism messages.

Feature: Al-Shabaab as a jihadi organization

Since the collapse of SiadBare's (1919–1995) government in 1991, Somalia has distinguished itself as an incubator for violent Salafi-jihadi groups and an exporter of jihadi ideology in the East African region. One of the prominent movements that appeared to fill the leadership vacuum is al-Shabaab. As a wing of the Islamic Courts Union (ICU), al-Shabaab seceded from the parent group and embarked in spearheading jihadi against the "enemies" of Islam that would culminate with the establishment of the Islamic caliphate. The movement has increasingly aligned its approach to attain this broader cause, aiming at exporting its interpretation of Islam in the region (Gatsiounis 2012).

The group continues to operate across much of southern Somalia, undertaking a number of assassinations and attacks against Somalia authorities. The group portrays itself as the "defender" of the Islamic faith and a resistor of "infidel forces" who under the African Union mission are mandated to restore peace in the country. Al-Shabaab's harsh leadership inspired by a literal interpretation of Qur'anic texts has outlawed what was formerly ordinary and normal, for instance, using gold and silver dental fillings, or women's wearing of bras. In some case, they have beheaded those it accused of embracing Western ideals (Gatsiounis 2012).

In the nearly ten years since it emerged from the shadows to announce itself as a potent new party to Somalia's complex civil conflict, al-Shabaab has developed into a strong organization, mentoring a new cohort of Salafi-jihadi leaders and fighters, grounded in al-Shabaab's ideological belief and military doctrine of violence. Gradually, the movement has succeeded in increasing its activities beyond Somalia's borders to the point that al-Shabaab metamorphosed into a transnational Salafi-jihadi organization. In 2010 the organization's first major attack outside Somalia was witnessed in Uganda, whose forces constituted the backbone of the African Union force in Somalia. Within Kenya, al-Shabaab's affiliated Salafi-jihadi groups like Jaysh Ayman, al-Hijra and al-Muhajiroun of East Africa have caused agony among citizens. Between 2013 and 2015 several attacks targeting non-Muslims in Nairobi as well as in the north-eastern and coastal regions were reported. Al-Shabaab claimed responsibility for all the attacks, justifying the killings as a reaction to Kenya's occupation of Muslim land (Somalia) and the discrimination against its Muslim citizens (Ndzovu 2017; Gatsiounis 2012).

In Ethiopia, the growing number of Ethiopians (mainly ethnic Somalis and Oromos) in al-Shabaab's ranks has allowed for the development of distinct units, willing to execute attacks against their country. However, the most fertile new ground for al-Shabaab's ideology may be Tanzania. The Salafi-jihadi group has largely used Tanzania as a place of refuge and recruitment, as well as coordinating attacks elsewhere in the region. Al-Shabaab's key associate in that country is the Ansar Muslim Youth Centre (AMYC). This is a loose network of extreme Salafi-jihadi preachers linked to certain mosques, Islamic social centres and schools, funded by certain like-minded businessmen and supported by numerous cells of armed youth scattered throughout the country. There is no doubt that al-Shabaab is transforming into a regional Salafi-jihadi group as demonstrated by the acceptance of non-Somali members. The movement is not any more a Somali jihadi-minded group, but it is on the verge of becoming an indisputably transnational organization with membership from across the region (Gatsiounis 2012).

Religious initiatives for conflict resolution and peace-building

Some of the events illustrated above stand in contrast to the positive role that religious organizations and religious leaders have played in initiating peace over the years. Some of the greatest peace makers of the 20th century in Africa include religious organizations such as the All Africa Conference of Churches, the Centre for Christian-Muslim Relations in Eastleigh (Kenya), the Acholi Religious Leaders Peace Initiative in Uganda and the Salam Sudan Foundation. Several initiatives for conflict resolution and peace-building in Africa, such as the Programme for Christian-Muslim Relations in Africa (PROCMURA) and the Truth and Reconciliation Commission of South Africa, have been founded on religious principles since non-violence and peace is part of all the religious traditions.

Although various religious groups in Africa have carried out violence in the name of their faiths, evidence also reveals that religion is a critical force in the mediation of peace. There are numerous illustrations of peace-making by religious leaders due to the respect accorded to them in Africa. Thus, "their elevated status allows them to effectively take on the role as mediators", particularly "during times of national crises" (Conteh 2011, 64). For instance, in the first Liberian civil war, Christian clergy under the umbrella of the Liberian Council of Churches intervened in early 1990 to seek resolution to the conflict. Later in June 1990, a move seen as "inclusive" brought the religious leaders of Christianity and Islam together, but to the exclusion of African religionists, to mediate peace agreement. Due to a hard line taken by the protagonists to the conflict, the two mediations collapsed (Conteh 2011).

Within the South African context, certain Christian churches were at the forefront of the struggle against Apartheid and the implementation of reconciliation and peace. After the end of Apartheid and the first democratic elections in 1994, the new South African government established a Truth and Reconciliation Commission (TRC) under the leadership of Anglican Archbishop Desmond Tutu, which became a model for peace-building on the continent and beyond. Based on the African principal expressed as "I am because you are", the TRC approached reconciliation from an indigenous African perspective based on the belief in the sanctity of human life, which is bestowed by God, and which also enables human beings to be responsible moral beings in community with others (see Chapter 11).

It appears that the religious traditions of sub-Saharan Africa – indigenous religions, Christianity, Islam – all have a strong potential to recognize fundamental human values. One exponent of religious efforts at reconciliation and peaceful coexistence is the case of PROCMURA.

Feature: The Programme for Christian-Muslim Relations in Africa

Previously identified as Islam in Africa Project (IAP), the Programme for Christian-Muslim Relations in Africa (PROCMURA) is one of the oldest interdenominational organizations in Africa. The organization's major objective is to create a genuine interfaith atmosphere among Muslims and Christians, and to encourage cordial neighbourliness, productive engagement and harmonious coexistence, which is not only a virtue in Christianity and Islam, but also of African indigenous religions. A group of Christian leaders came to the realization that the traditional concern of Christians with evangelizing and of Muslims with *da'wa* (propagation) activities hampered harmonious relations between adherents of the two faiths. Therefore, they formed the organization in 1956, which now works in eighteen countries across the continent (Ellingwood 2008).

PROCMURA has strived to attain its goals by organizing conferences, seminars and courses, publishing and sponsoring postgraduate studies.

These initiatives have made it possible for the organization to offer information to churches and theological institutions, to educate Christians about Islam and thereby promote the spirit of cooperation with Muslim neighbours. Due to the vast number of Christian denominations that exist in Africa, PROCMURA is both an interfaith and intra-faith organization. Since its initial years of formation, it has been run by a group of churches in Africa in consultation with a European liaison committee. Membership comprises the mainline Christian churches (Catholic, Orthodox and Protestant), as well as some Pentecostal and African independent churches (ibid.).

The organization's attitude towards Muslims was influenced by the developments taking place in post-colonial Africa, particularly the rapid expansion of both Christianity and Islam. Many sub-Saharan African countries have considerable populations of Muslims and Christians, representing both an opportunity and a challenge for Christian-Muslim relations. A report delivered by the General Adviser of PROCMURA in 1991 indicated that "Christian-Muslim relations [had] proved more complex and difficult than many had thought or hoped" in sub-Saharan Africa (quoted in Ellingwood 2008, 81). The collapse of the Sudan peace agreement in 1983 and the continuation of the civil war, and tensions caused by the debates over the introduction of sharia in Sudan and Nigeria, were cited as illustrations of hostilities that had proven difficult due to the increasing trend to view the conflicts within the religious dimension. There was fear that "the enviable model of religious tolerance" was "gradually eroding as the wind of intolerance blows across the African continent, threatening to turn the religiously tolerant societies into a volatile mix of religious aggression and bigotry" (ibid., 82).

In the process, PROCMURA has developed avenues for Christians and Muslims to talk about the local conflicts occurring due to hostilities in other parts of the world. These local conflicts were viewed as being linked not only to global hostilities between Muslims and Christians, but also to tribulations worsened by the rapid growth of both religions in the decades after the end of colonialism. While responding to the challenges facing Christians and Muslims in sub-Saharan Africa, PROCMURA formulated a number of approaches. One is that of undertaking scripturally-based study of issues, using the scriptures of both Christianity and Islam, addressing subjects ranging from personal and family interest, such as interfaith marriage, to political concerns (ibid.).

Conclusion

The chapter has shown that the beliefs, symbols and practices of African indigenous religions, Christianity and Islam have been part and parcel of situations of conflict in Africa. However, religions should not only be thought of as sources of violence. As demonstrated above, even within one faith tradition there exist different political ideologies and theologies, which can variably contribute to both violence and peace-building. Due to the demographic developments, in particular the growth of Christianity and Islam on the continent, efforts that seek to promote cordial relations between members of the two faiths should be welcomed. At the same time, the awareness of the deeply political nature of religions in Africa prevents us from naïve optimism and romanticization. Religious thought and practice will undoubtedly continue to be part of processes of conflict as well as peace-building on the continent.

Questions for discussion

- Search online for information about a current conflict in an African country and analyse the roles that religion (religious beliefs, institutions, leaders) plays in conflict and peace-building.
- Discuss the ways in which the changing role of religion in situations of conflict in Africa is shaped by global religious dynamics.

References (*indicates recommended reading)

Ahmed, Einas. 2007. "Political Islam in Sudan: Islamists and the Challenge of State Power (1989–2004)." In *Islam and Muslim Politics in Africa*, edited by Benjamin F. Soares and Rene Otayek, 177–186. New York: Palgrave Macmillan.

Chitando, Ezra, and Joram Tarusarira. 2017. "The Deployment of a 'Sacred Song' in Violence in Zimbabwe: The Case of the Song 'Zimbabwe Ndeye Ropa Ramadzibaba' (Zimbabwe Was/Is Born of the Blood of the Fathers/Ancestors) in Zimbabwean Politics", *Journal for the Study of Religion* 30/1, 5–25.

Conteh, Prince Sorie. 2011. "The Role of Religion during and after the Civil War in Sierra Leone", *Journal for the Study of Religion* 24/1, 55–76.

Covington-Ward, Yolanda. 2016. *Gesture and Power: Religion, Nationalism, and Everyday Performance in Congo*. Durham, NC: Duke University Press.

Dowd, Robert. 2015. *Christianity, Islam and Liberal Democracy: Lessons from Sub-Saharan Africa*. New York: Oxford University Press.

Ellingwood, Jane. 2008. "The Programme for Christian-Muslim Relations in Africa (PROCMURA): An Evolutionary Perspective", *The Muslim World* 98/1, 72–94.

Gatsiounis, Ioannis. 2012. "After Al-Shabaab", *Current Trends in Islamist Ideology* 14, 74–89.

*Kastfelt, Niels. 2005. "Religion and African Civil Wars: Themes and Interpretations." In *Religion and African Civil Wars*, edited by Niels Kastfelt, 1–27. New York: Palgrave Macmillan.

Loimeier, Roman. 2018. *Islamic Reform in Twentieth-Century Africa*. Edinburgh: Edinburgh University Press

Lonsdale, John. 2002. "Kikuyu Christianities: A History of Intimate Diversity." In *Christianity and the African Imagination: Essays in Honour of Adrian Hastings*, edited by David Maxwell and Ingrid Lawrie, 157–198. Leiden: Brill.

Longman, Timothy. 2001. "Church Politics and the Genocide in Rwanda", *Journal of Religion in Africa* 31/2, 163–186.

Longman, Timothy. 2010. *Christianity and Genocide in Rwanda*. Cambridge: Cambridge University Press

*Love, Roy. 2006. "Religion, Ideology & Conflict in Africa", *Review of African Political Economy* 33/110, 619–634.

Møller, Bjørn. 2006. "Religion and Conflict in Africa with a Special Focus on East Africa", *Danish Institute for International Studies Report* 6, 1–140

Ndzovu, Hassan. 2017. "The Rise of Jihad, Killing of 'Apostate Imams' and Non-Combatant Christian Civilians in Kenya: Al-Shabaab's Re-definition of the Enemy on Religious Lines", *Journal for the Study of Religions of Africa and Its Diaspora* 3/1, 4–20.

Ojo, Matthews. 2007. "Pentecostal Movements, Islam and the Contest for Public Space in Northern Nigeria", *Islam and Christian–Muslim Relations* 18/2, 175–188.

Rayapen, Lewis. 1989. "Religious Liberty in Africa", *International Journal on World Peace* 6/2, 49–60.

*Vaughan, Olufemi. 2016. *Religion and the Making of Nigeria*. Durham: Duke University Press.

Voll, John. 2015. "Boko Haram: Religion and Violence in the 21st Century", *Religions* 6, 1182–1202.

10 Religion and development in Africa

What is development, and what has religion got to do with it?

Africa is often considered an underdeveloped, or developing, continent, in contrast to other parts of the world, especially Europe and North America, which are considered to be developed. "Development", from this Western-centric perspective, is typically conceived of in largely socio-economic terms. It is part of a broader narrative of modernity according to which societies progress from a pre-modern to a modern stage, the latter being associated with high levels of (Western-style) education, technological advancement, scientifically informed healthcare systems and democratic nation-building. As Gerrie ter Haar (2009, 76) observes, "the modern idea of development has a genealogy in Western Christianity and can be seen as the secular translation of a millenarian belief whereby the kingdom of God is no longer projected in heaven but can be created on earth". Of course the idea of development has antecedents in the 18th and 19th centuries, when European missionaries and colonial governments started to "civilize" Africa – a continent they perceived as "primitive" (unsophisticated and rudimentary) – by introducing Western forms of education and health services. Yet only in the second part of the 20th century the development of Africa became a project, realized through programmes operating on the basis of scientific principles, with which both Western governmental and nongovernmental agents and the governments of newly independent African states were concerned. In spite of its Christian roots, this project of development was conceived of as secular, especially because the underlying narrative of modernity was shaped by the secularization thesis, the idea that with societies becoming modern, religion would be marginalized, privatized and perhaps even disappear completely. In the words of Barbara Bompani and Maria Frahm-Arp (2010, 5),

> Development in the twentieth century Western European model was seen as progress from a deeply religious, irrational and non-bureaucratic world, to a modern space in which material advancement was achieved through "sound" bureaucratic structures which led to secularization and the loss of the spiritual.

Religion, in other words, was generally considered to be a hindrance to development, and therefore tended to be overlooked as a relevant factor and force in the process of development. Only in recent years has this changed, with development agents increasingly acknowledging the significance of religious organizations, religious beliefs, and religious practices in the thinking about, and process of, development.

Taking religion into account in development has sometimes resulted in an instrumentalist approach, in which religious actors are included in development programmes that otherwise continue to operate on more or less secular principles. However, for development practice, and for development studies as an academic field, to truly make a religious turn, such an instrumentalization of religion falls short, as it seeks to *make use of* religion but fails to fully *understand* religion and its impact on development. Critical questions that need to be addressed are: "How do different religions define and critique development or understand development? Or, how is development shaped by religion, or religious movements/communities (re)shaped by development?" (Bompani and Frahm-Arp 2010, 5). Exploring these questions also implies acknowledging that African societies, in which religion plays such prominent roles, may develop in different ways than Western societies. In other words, there are alternative pathways of development that are not necessarily secular, and that are not narrowly concerned with socio-economic issues. Moreover, to understand the role of religion in development we should not only focus on religious organizations, but also on other vital categories: religious ideas, practices and experiences, as these – with all their complexities and ambiguities – are relevant to the possibilities as well as impossibilities of development in people's everyday lives.

Religious concepts of development

Contrasting secular and religious approaches to development, ter Haar identifies several key differences. These relate to an individual versus a more community-focused approach, a mechanistic versus an organic view of society, and a model based on competition versus one based on cooperation. Most importantly, she continues,

> for many religious people the spiritual dimension precedes the material one, in the sense that prosperity cannot be achieved without creating the spiritual conditions conducive to that goal. Hence, they consider inner transformation a necessary condition for social transformation, or even an actual source of it.
>
> (ter Haar 2009, 77)

A similar point is made by Stephen Ellis (2010, 25) when he states that "Africans have never ceased to regard material factors partly through the prism of religion, attempting to bring all the forces that shape their lives under human control". Further elaborating on this, he argues:

In societies where religion, politics and economics did not formerly exist as discrete categories, the forces of capital, the attachment of monetary value to objects, and the introduction of minted currencies were all experienced not merely as technical innovations, but in terms of a tectonic change affecting both the invisible world and the material one. Africa's entry into a capitalised world (or, conversely, the entry of capitalism into Africa) has therefore not in itself done anything to cause a separation between the perception of an invisible world that exists, distinct but not separate, con-joined with the visible world. It is by means of interacting with unseen entities, imagined in a variety of forms, that humans shape the world in which they live.

(Ellis 2010, 33–34)

Both Ellis and ter Haar point in the direction of an enchanted concept of development, in which human well-being is understood in a holistic sense and in relation to spiritual forces.

Such a conception of development can clearly be observed in indigenous religions. Here, ancestors, spirits, deities and God(s) are all considered as sources of spiritual power with a direct effect on the human realm; maintaining a harmonious relationship with these forces is therefore important in order to prosper in life (Alolo and Connell 2013). As Samuel Awuah-Nyamekye (2012, 80) writes with reference to the Akan people of Ghana:

[F]or the traditional Akan and, for that matter, African societies in general, development is related to the community's harmonious relationship with the Supreme Being, ancestors, the gods and the other spirit beings. … The Akan have a holistic attitude to life and thus they see development as any other human activity which aims at affirming life in a holistic way that will enable every generation to ensure its survival and be able to hand over the survival status to the future generation as directed by religion. Therefore, development in the view of the traditional Akan is the judicious utilization of resources (both natural and human) with the view to achieving growth and meaningful life for the present generation and the subsequent ones. In other words, development in the life and thought of the traditional Akan is a means of ensuring a holistic or all-inclusive well-being of human utilizing judiciously the total environment of the people from the religious or sacral point of view (human and economic development), but not a situation where there is economic growth at the cost of greater inequality, high unemployment, loss of cultural identity, consumption of foreign goods and depletion of resources needed by future generations.

This quotation illustrates several of the points made above, about religious forms of development being community-oriented, having an organic understanding of society, and having a holistic understanding of human well-being that comprises economic as well as social, cultural and religious dimensions. It is against this background that indigenous religions have recently been acknowledged as sources of beliefs, values and practices that are environment-friendly and that can be mobilized to promote ecologically sustainable forms of development (Mugambi 2017). Obviously this is crucial given the effects of climate change in Africa, and the related major developmental challenges such as food security, poverty and migration.

Integrated understandings of religion and development can also be found in Christian and Muslim communities in Africa. For instance, in traditional Muslim societies in the Sahara, Sufi orders historically played an important role, not only in providing spiritual leadership and promoting Islamic piety, but also in contributing to the social and economic welfare of the surrounding community. People would literally settle in the immediate neighbourhood of Sufi lodges in order to benefit from the spiritual, social and economic security they offered (Vikør 2002). Focusing specifically on contemporary Sudan, Rüdiger Seesemann (2002, 103–104) writes:

> [F]or the followers of the Sufi orders, worldly success depends on the blessings provided by the *shaykhs* – this can be taken as a further indication of the connection between the spiritual sphere and material matters. The believers visit a Sufi *shaykh* because of the latter's material and spiritual capacities. Neither the material nor the spiritual side of this relationship is necessarily formalised; the exact contents and the form of the interaction between the *shaykh* and his followers may indeed vary from case to case and over time.

The *shaykhs* (sheikhs) appear to perform a role somewhat similar to the chief in some of Africa's indigenous religious communities, such as the Akan. Here, the institution of chieftaincy is considered "as the earthly representative of the ancestors of the entire community" and therefore as holding sacred authority to provide spiritual, social, political and economic leadership (Awuah-Nyamekye 2012, 83). In a very different setting, contemporary neo-Pentecostal Christian pastors can also be seen as presenting a holistic view in which spiritual and material matters are connected, in the form of the prosperity gospel. In a highly modern guise, and perhaps on a more individualized basis, such pastors and their churches represent a "historical continuity ... [with] the traditional principle of investing in the invisible world, in the hope for future returns in the form of material prosperity" (ter Haar 2014, 17).

To conclude this section, there exists a strong tradition in African societies that conceives of development in terms of an enchanted worldview, in which the spiritual and material dimensions of life are closely connected, and in which prosperity and well-being are thought of holistically. This worldview also allows for misfortune, poverty and failure of development to be explained in spiritual terms, typically with reference to evil spirits, sorcery and, nowadays in particular witchcraft (Alolo and Connell 2013). In a fascinating study of communities in the Taita Hills of south-east Kenya, James Howard Smith (2008) has shown how the promise of a better world, presented by modern, neoliberal inspired development projects, gave rise to both hope and suspicion among the local people. As some people in the area gained in wealth while many others struggled to achieve development, the latter became disillusioned and explained the growing economic disparity in occult terms.

This led to a dramatic eruption of witchcraft accusations in families and communities, with witch-finders of all kind – from traditional diviners to Pentecostal preachers – doing good business. Ideas about witchcraft and development, Smith (2008, 5) argues, "operate in tandem", with the former being "the Other" of the latter. As discussed in Chapter 7, witchcraft is often seen as the source of otherwise inexplicable newfound wealth. One possible consequence of this culture of suspicion is that an individual might reject personal economic advancement, out of fear of being branded a witch.

Faith-based development organizations

The focus of this section shifts from religious-informed grassroots conceptions of development to more formal development work in Africa, and the role of faith-based organizations in this sector. Because indigenous religions are usually not institutionalized in the way that Christianity and Islam are, they are not typically engaged in formal development projects. However, sometimes NGOs (non-governmental organizations) do engage indigenous religious and community leaders (such as priests, diviners and chiefs) in development projects, for instance asking them to pour libation for the ancestors or to perform divination when a new project is launched. Indeed, some scholars have argued that acknowledging the significance of such indigenous religious rituals, as well as of indigenous knowledge more generally, is crucial to the success of development processes in Africa (Mawere 2014). However, the present section limits its scope to Islamic and Christian development activities.

With regard to Islam, there are a growing number of Islamic NGOs that are active in many parts of Africa. The activities of these organizations are said to represent an "entanglement of aid and *umma*" (Kaag 2007, 89). In other words, they combine traditional development and humanitarian aid work, such as medical assistance, food supply and education, with proselytizing activities through promoting particular forms of moral livelihood and instilling a sense of belonging to the *umma*, the notion of the global community of Islamic believers. As such, the work of these organizations can be seen as linked to broader processes of Islamization and Arabization of the region. In a 2004 review of Islamic NGOs in the central African country of Chad, Mayke Kaag counted eleven of them, six of them having Saudi origins, one Kuwaiti, one Libyan, and three Sudanese, with funding coming from these and other countries on the basis of the Islamic principles of solidarity and charity (*zakat* and *sadaqa*).

Interestingly, Kaag notes how these Islamic organizations consider the Christian NGOs as their competitors and vice versa, which illustrates the political and often geopolitical dimension of development activities. In fact, both

Islamic and (mostly evangelical) Christian organizations in Chad "suspect the other of having hidden political objectives or of being a political instrument in the hands of states or global power blocs" (Kaag 2007, 95). Rivalry, however, also exists among Islamic NGOs themselves. In his overview of Islamic organizations active in fields such as education, health, housing and agriculture in the West African countries of Ghana, Sierra Leone and The Gambia, David Skinner (2010, 103) observes "a pattern of competition for resources and political influence" and a "lack of Islamic unity" among the many organizations in these countries. This is due to divisions on the basis of ethnicity, country of origin, political affiliation, international links, different views of Islamic orthodoxy and tensions between traditional and modernizing forms of education. Similar divisions and tensions of course exist between Christian NGOs, often related to denominational differences. A noteworthy recent trend at the intersection of Islam and socio-economic development in Africa relates to the rise of Islamic finance on the continent. The principles on which Islamic finance is based are often argued to promote microfinance and encourage entrepreneurship among people who would otherwise not easily have access to financial capital (Muhammad Al Amine 2016).

Feature: Ghanaian Muslim women's empowerment

Many development programmes – both secular and religious – in Africa have specifically targeted women, out of a concern about gender inequality and the belief that women's empowerment is key to social and economic development. Many of these programmes are Christian-inspired, but there are also Islamic non-governmental organizations working in this area. One example is Annisaa Foundation in Ghana, the name being derived from an-Nisa, which is the fourth chapter of the Qur'an known for its numerous references to women. It was established in 2004 by a group of professional Muslim women in Ghana who wanted to contribute towards improving the status of the less privileged in society, particularly women and children. The organization's slogan is that "Service to mankind (sic) is service to Allah", which reflects a deeply religious motivation for the charity and development work they are doing.

A member of the Federation of Muslim Women's Associations of Ghana, Annisaa Foundation is specifically concerned with providing education to women and girls, and is involved in running several schools in the country. It also runs a mentoring and counselling scheme for young women seeking higher education. According to the organization:

> Education is key to liberating the under privileged and the vulnerable from poverty and social vices. Education would empower our youth to become responsible leaders, serve as role models and contribute towards national development. ... Although the number of educated Muslims especially women is rising steadily in Ghana, there is the need

to ensure that the trend continues and is sustained. Currently there are very few Muslims especially women occupying key positions. This trend is a result of low output in education of Muslims in the past decades. Annisaa Foundation helps bridge this gap by empowering and encouraging the youth especially young women to attain higher education.

(Annisaa Foundation nd)

Two things stand out in this quotation from Annisaa's website. First, a direct link is made between education as a key strategy to national development. This fits in with the above-mentioned more general concern in the development sector about women's relatively low levels of education hindering their full participation in society and limiting their socio-economic independence. The fact that it is an organization of professional women taking the initiative in empowering less-privileged women demonstrates a significant level of female agency and exemplifies Muslim women's role in community development in Ghana (Ammah 2015). Second, the quotation refers to the low level of education among Muslims in Ghana more generally. This has its origins in the colonial period, when education was dominated by Christian mission schools. Annisaa's objective of empowering Muslim women through education, therefore, is implicitly also an attempt to correct this relict from the colonial past and to increase the overall participation of Muslims in Ghanaian society, where they currently are a minority. In other words, promoting Muslim women's education appears to be a strategy in a religio-political project of strengthening the position of Islam in Ghana. (See Figure 10.1.)

With regard to Christianity, a major player in the sector of development is the Catholic Church. Historically speaking, the Catholic Church during and after the colonial period has established itself as a major player in education and healthcare in many African countries. According to Gifford (2015, 86, 90), in 2009, "there were claimed to be over 12,000 Catholic infant schools, 33,000 primary schools, and almost 10,000 secondary schools, plus about twenty universities", while the church also "operated 16,178 health centres, including 1,074 hospitals, 5,373 out-patient clinics" alongside orphanages, elderly homes, centres for mentally disabled people and rehabilitation centres. Where education and healthcare have always been core activities, in recent decades the Catholic Church has intensified its efforts and expanded its work terrain. As Nigerian theologian Stan Chu Ilo (2014, 189) explains,

[The role of the church in development] has become very prominent since the end of the Second Vatican Council in 1965. One of the reasons for this is the renewal of the self-understanding of the Church with regard to the social context in which the gospel is to be preached. Evangelization is

Figure 10.1 Young Somali woman at literacy class (© robertharding / Alamy Stock Photo)

integral and demands an immersion in the social conditions of the people who receive the good news.

The Second Vatican Council (1962–1965) was a series of meeting of all Catholic Bishops worldwide in Rome, where a new vision for the church and its mission in the world was developed. Discussions and decisions of the Council revitalized the tradition of Catholic Social Teaching, which is concerned with Catholic thinking about human dignity and the common good in society, addressing a whole range of socio-economic and political questions. This was reflected in one of the Council's official documents, *Gaudium et Spes*, the "Pastoral Constitution on the Church and the Modern World" (1965). In the aftermath of Vatican Council II, in Latin America and later to some extent also in Africa, liberation theology emerged. It is based on the notion that God is on the side of the poor, and that the mission of the church therefore is to work towards socio-economic justice. As a result of these developments, the Catholic Church in many African countries in recent decades has become more and more involved in activities that are broadly associated with development. Typically these activities are coordinated by Commissions for Justice and Peace and/or Commissions for Development which fall under the direct authority of the national conferences of Catholic bishops, while funding often comes from Western Catholic charities as well as secular development organizations.

Feature: Catholic Development Commission in Malawi

The Catholic Development Commission in Malawi (CADECOM) was established in 1984 as Caritas Malawi, and adopted its current name in 1999. The name change was to express the commission's commitment to not just being a relief organization but being involved in structural development work. CADECOM is one of the official commissions of the Episcopal Conference of Malawi, which is the body uniting the eight Catholic dioceses in the country. The organization works at three different levels: through a national office, regional commissions in each diocese, and local committees in each parish. Several of the programmes are funded by Catholic charities in Europe, Australia and the United States. CADECOM thus makes optimal use of the strengths of the Catholic Church: its strong presence in local communities across the country, its regional and national structures and political influence, and moreover its international connections and access to funding. CADECOM's mission statement is,

> To create awareness and empower disadvantaged men, women and the youth at all levels to undertake development which is integral, gender and environmentally sensitive, sustainable and which promotes justice, human dignity and self-reliance with the active participation of

the people themselves so that they take up the responsibility of their own destiny.

(ECMM nd)

In its 2008–2013 strategic plan, the organization lists a whole range of pro-grammes and activities, divided over five strategic areas: food security and nutrition; relief and rehabilitation; health and sanitation; environmental man-agement; HIV and AIDS and gender-based violence. Strikingly, the strategic plan reads like the plan of any other development organization, full of tech-nical development jargon. The only exceptions are the paragraphs about CADECOM's motivation, which refer to the creation of human beings in the image of God (Genesis 1: 27) and to Jesus' ministry aiming to bring good tidings to the poor, liberty to the captives, recovery of sight to the blind and freedom to the oppressed (Luke 4: 18–19). These biblical-theological notions serve to support the organization's notions of "integral development" and a "holistic approach to human life" (Catholic Development Commission in Malawi nd, 5, 19).

Overviewing activities such as those run by CADECOM and similar bodies in other countries, Paul Gifford observes a shifting balance in the work of the Catholic Church in Africa from evangelization to development. Acknowledging the way in which such development work is justified theologically, he is yet concerned that "Catholicism is becoming identified with those works rather than anything particularly religious" (Gifford 2015, 96). He concludes:

This [form of] Christianity brings not so much redemption as development. It is associated less with grace than with science and technology. It operates with a vocabulary not so much of atonement, sacraments, conversion, as one of micro-finance, capacity building, and women's empowerment. The virtues it promotes are accountability, transparency, and good governance, as much as faith, hope and charity. It operates as much from human rights reports and poverty-reduction strategies as from scriptures and creeds.

(Gifford 2015, 103)

Gifford suggests that a similar observation can be made of mainline Protestant churches (e.g. Anglican, Lutheran, Methodist and Presbyterian) in Africa, however with a crucial difference. Where the latter operate as national chur-ches, the Catholic Church is a global body with well-established international structures, which makes it easier to access development funding from the West. Another difference, specifically in the areas of HIV prevention and women's reproductive rights, is that the Catholic Church operates on the basis of ethical principles that are not necessarily shared by mainline Protestant development programmes, and certainly not by secular development bodies. With regard to the HIV epidemic in Africa, Ezra Chitando (2010) shows how the World

Council of Churches, as a global ecumenical body, has taken a very active role in working with mainline Protestant churches and organizations all over the continent, in order to make them "HIV competent". This included addressing delicate issues such as condom use and same-sex sexuality in a non-stigmatizing way. Thus at least in this area, the international networks within mainline Protestant Christianity encourage ethical standpoints different from the Catholic Church, which can have a direct effect on the respective intervention programmes.

Pentecostalism and spiritualized development

Pentecostal churches in Africa do not typically set up separate development bodies or faith-based organizations (although there are certainly exceptions). However, this does not mean that these churches are not involved in development in their own right. As Dena Freeman (2012a, 2) points out,

> African Pentecostals see development in terms of "What God wants for Africa", and most recently in terms of the gospel of prosperity. What God wants for Africa, they claim, is a continent blessed with health, wealth and abundance, where people work hard, pray hard and live upright moral lives. What the devil wants for Africa, however, is underdevelopment, poverty and suffering. And thus, along with hard work, development requires a "war against the demons", a notion that captures hearts and minds much more energetically than the NGO's rhetoric of the "war against poverty".

Pentecostalism, in other words, tends to conceive of development in an enchanted worldview, where social, economic and material well-being is affected by spiritual forces, in this case a dualism of God versus the Devil.

In the above quotation, Freeman refers to the Pentecostal emphasis on hard work and moral discipline. Indeed, the centrality of born-again conversion and the subsequent moral-spiritual programme of personal renewal is often considered as key to Pentecostalism's ability to affect change in individual people's lives, not just religiously but also socio-economically. This ability has further been associated with the charismatic and ecstatic nature of Pentecostal religiosity, which can empower and motivate people emotionally, spiritually and socially to make a break with their past and to transform their lives. It is in these ways that Pentecostalism is often seen to promote a particular ethic that supports the spirit of development in contemporary Africa, in a process that somewhat resembles the famous thesis of the sociologist Max Weber (2001) about the ethic of Protestantism supporting the spirit of capitalism in 16th and 17th century Europe.

As a case in point, Freeman discusses an example from the Gamo Highlands in Ethiopia, where a particular economic development project initiated by a secular NGO only became successful because of the conversion activities of

Pentecostal churches in the area through which people transformed their sense of self. The newly adopted Pentecostal values "fitted almost seamlessly with the capitalist values underlying the apple project, where hard work, self-discipline and independence would be crucial to succeeding as an apple entrepreneur" (Freeman 2012b, 173). The result of the project was, however, also that the degree of economic inequality in the area started to increase rapidly, with a class structure beginning to emerge in a society that used to be relatively egalitarian as it operated on the basis of an economy where wealth was redistributed in the community. This draws critical attention to the negative side-effects that development, in a neoliberal capitalist guise, can have.

Paul Gifford (2015) is much more sceptical, if not negative, about the contribution of Pentecostalism to African development. He distinguishes six "registers of victorious living" that can be found in Pentecostal circles: (1) a strong motivational message; (2) an encouragement of entrepreneurship; (3) the training of practical skills; (4) an emphasis on the prosperity gospel; (5) a focus on the "anointing" of the pastor; (6) a concern with defeating evil spirits. He acknowledges that the first three registers can, indeed, promote socio-economic development. However, he argues that in contemporary (neo-)Pentecostalism, the last three registers have gained much more prominence, giving rise to a deeply enchanted form of Christianity. Discussing the cases of Mountain of Fire and Miracle Ministries and of Winners Chapel International (both originally Nigerian), he argues that these churches undermine social capital, diminish personal agency, discount scientific rationality and therefore are obstacles to the advance of modernity and development in Africa – instead he finds them just "dysfunctional" (Gifford 2015, 67).

Gifford's account presents a sharp contrast between Catholicism (and mainline Christianity more generally) as being so deeply involved in development activities that it has become internally secularized and does not address people's spiritual needs, and Pentecostal Christianity as being so deeply involved in spiritual activities that it is too enchanted to contribute to development. In reality, the picture is far from black-and-white: after all, the Catholic and other mainline churches also provide religious services, and many of them have incorporated Pentecostal-charismatic elements in their church life, while many Pentecostal churches have recently become involved in more traditional development activities such as education and healthcare. For instance, Winners Chapel has set up two universities in Nigeria offering courses in subjects such as business, engineering, and social sciences, under the slogan: "Building new minds and creating a generation of world leaders who will feed nations and set standards" (Faith Tabernacle nd). A more fundamental problem is that Gifford appears to define development and modernity as being necessarily disenchanted, as if there is only one model for development: rational, secular Western modernity. This leads us back to the question we started with: what is development, and what has religion got to do with it? One could argue that contemporary Pentecostal churches, but also some recently emerging Islamic movements, such as the Muslim Nasrul-Lahi-Fatih Society of Nigeria (NASFAT), are in continuity with indigenous African worldviews in which the spiritual and material dimensions of life are closely interconnected. As such, they represent newly emerging African forms of modernity, with alternative (though not necessarily unproblematic) pathways of development.

Conclusion

This chapter has unravelled some of the complex intersections between development and religion in contemporary African societies. On the one hand, it has examined how different religious groups and faith-based organizations have been, and are today, involved in activities typically associated with socio-economic development. On the other hand, it has explored how both traditionally and in contemporary contexts, religious traditions and movements conceive of development in particular ways, integrating spiritual and material dimensions of life and therefore blurring the boundaries between "religion" and "development". The questions what, exactly, development is, how it occurs in African societies, and what religion has to do with this, will keep generating critical debate.

Questions for discussion

- In what ways is development in Africa "enchanted", and how does this relate to your own understanding of what development is and how it works?
- What advice would you give to an NGO planning a new development project somewhere in Africa, for which they want to engage with religious communities and leaders?
- Do you believe that religion, in the end, contributes to or hinders development in Africa? What are your considerations?

References (*indicates recommended reading)

Alolo, Namawu Alhassan, and James Astley Connell. 2013. "Indigenous Religions and Development: African Traditional Religion." In *Handbook of Research on Development and Religion*, edited by Matthew Clarke, 138–163. Cheltenham: Edward Elgar.

Ammah, Rabiatu. 2015. "Voices of Ghanaian Muslim Women in Dawah." In *Unraveling and Reweaving Sacred Canon in Africana Womanhood*, edited by Rosetta Ross and Rose Mary Amenga-Etego, 69–86. Lanham: Lexington.

Annisaa Foundation. nd. "What We Do." http://www.annisaafoundation.org/what-we-do/ (accessed 14 February 2018).

Awuah-Nyamekye, Samuel. 2012. "Religion and Development: African Traditional Religion's Perspective", *Religious Studies and Theology* 31/1, 75–90.

*Bompani, Barbara, and Maria Frahm-Arp. 2010. "Introduction." In *Development and Politics from Below: Exploring Religious Spaces in the African State*, edited by Barbara Bompani and Maria Frahm-Arp, 1–22. New York: Palgrave MacMillan.

Catholic Development Commission in Malawi, nd. *Strategic Plan 2008–2013: Empowering Communities.* https://episcopalconferencemalawi.files.wordpress.com/2009/03/cadecom-strategic-plan1.doc (accessed 10 February 2018).

Chitando, Ezra. 2010. "Sacred Struggles: The World Council of Churches and the HIV Epidemic in Africa." In *Development and Politics from Below: Exploring Religious Spaces in the African State,* edited by Barbara Bompani and Maria Frahm-Arp, 218–239. New York: Palgrave MacMillan.

Episcopal Conference of Malawi (ECCM). nd. "Catholic Development Commission in Malawi." http://www.ecmmw.org/new/commissions/cadecom/ (accessed 28 March 2018).

*Ellis, Stephen. 2010. "Development and Invisible Worlds." In *Development and Politics from Below: Exploring Religious Spaces in the African State,* edited by Barbara Bompani and Maria Frahm-Arp, 23–39. New York: Palgrave MacMillan.

Faith Tabernacle. nd. "Education: Universities." http://faithtabernacle.org.ng/education/universities/ (accessed 15 February 2018).

*Freeman, Dena. 2012a. "The Pentecostal Ethic and the Spirit of Development." In *Pentecostalism and Development: Churches, NGOs and Social Change in Africa,* edited by Dena Freeman, 1–38. New York: Palgrave Macmillan.

Freeman, Dena. 2012b. "Development and the Rural Entrepreneur: Pentecostals, NGOs and the Market in the Gamo Highlands, Ethiopia." In *Pentecostalism and Development: Churches, NGOs and Social Change in Africa,* edited by Dena Freeman, 159–180. New York: Palgrave Macmillan.

Gifford, Paul. 2015. *Christianity, Development and Modernity in Africa.* London: Hurst & Co.

Ilo, Stan Chu. 2014. *The Church and Development in Africa: Aid and Development from the Perspective of Catholic Social Ethics* (2nd edition). Eugene: Wipf and Stock.

*Kaag, Mayke. 2007. "Aid, Umma, and Politics: Transnational Islamic NGOs in Chad." In *Islam and Muslim Politics in Africa,* edited by Benjamin Soares and Rene Otayek, 85–102. New York: Palgrave Macmillan.

Mawere, Munyaradzi. 2014. *Divining the Future of Africa: Healing the Wounds, Restoring Dignity and Fostering Development.* Mankon: Langaa.

Mugambi, Jesse. 2017. "Africa: African Heritage and Ecological Stewardship." In *Routledge Handbook of Religion and Ecology,* edited by Willis Jenkins, Mary Evelyn Tucker and John Grim, 109–119. Abingdon: Routledge.

Muhammad Al Amine, Muhammad Al Bashir. 2016. *Islamic Finance and Africa's Economic Resurgence: Promoting Diverse and Localized Investment.* New York: Palgrave Macmillan.

Seesemann, Rüdiger. 2002. "Sufi Leaders and Social Welfare: Two Examples from Contemporary Sudan." In *Social Welfare in Muslim Societies in Africa,* edited by Holger Weiss, 97–115. Uppsala: Nordiska Afrikainstitutet.

Skinner, David. 2010. "Da'wa and Politics in West Africa: Muslim Jama'at and Non-Governmental Organizations in Ghana, Sierre Leone and The Gambia." In *Development and Politics from Below: Exploring Religious Spaces in the African State,* edited by Barbara Bompani and Maria Frahm-Arp, 99–130. New York: Palgrave MacMillan.

Smith, James Howard. 2008. *Bewitching Development: Witchcraft and the Reinvention of Development in Neoliberal Kenya.* Chicago: University of Chicago Press.

Ter Haar, Gerrie. 2009. *How God Became African: African Spirituality and Western Secular Thought.* Philadelphia: University of Pennsylvania Press.

Ter Haar, Gerrie. 2014. "Poverty and Prosperity in Africa." In *Religion and Development: Nordic Perspectives on Involvement in Africa,* edited by Tomas Sundnes Drønen, 11–26. New York: Peter Lang.

Vikør, Knut. 2002. "Sufism and Social Welfare in the Sahara." In *Social Welfare in Muslim Societies in Africa,* edited by Holger Weiss, 79–96. Uppsala: Nordiska Afrikainstitutet.

Weber, Max. 2001. *The Protestant Ethic and the Spirit of Capitalism.* London: Routledge.

11 Religion and human rights in Africa

The problem of human rights in Africa

Under this heading, one may expect to find a discussion of human right problems in Africa. Every year, Western human rights organizations and media publish reports about the status of human rights in African societies, and these reports are typically full of stories about the abuses of human rights on the continent. The rights of women, children, ethnic and religious minorities, people living with disabilities, people with albinism and of lesbian, gay, bisexual and transgender people, appear to be systematically violated, and Africa is often represented as a continent with a particularly poor record of protecting human rights. Often, this poor record is explained with reference to dominant cultural and religious traditions on the continent. Yet, although there certainly is reason for concern about issues relating to human rights in African societies, this chapter begins by discussing the problem of human rights in Africa from a different angle.

Human rights discourse itself – that is, the body of international documents of official human rights declarations, the traditions of thought underlying these documents, and the legal and political instruments implementing these declarations – in recent decades has become increasingly problematized from critical postcolonial perspectives. The postcolonial critique of the modern human rights discourse, especially of the Universal Declaration of Human Rights (adopted by the United Nations general assembly in 1948), is diverse, but centres around a number of key points: the idea of human rights is the product of a particular Western history; it is based on originally European, liberal and secular norms and values; declaring such human rights "universal" reflects Western centrism, if not Western superiority thinking; human rights instruments are often used as part of Western imperialist politics and serve to impose a neoliberal global modernity. It is beyond the scope of this chapter to discuss this critique in depth, yet we will discuss one exponent of it who specifically writes from an African postcolonial perspective: the Kenyan legal scholar, Makau Mutua.

In his book *Human Rights: A Political and Cultural Critique*, Mutua recalls how, when his parents converted to Christianity and he was baptized, he was required to choose a "Christian" name, that is, a European name because

African-sounding names did apparently not qualify. He uses this anecdote to draw a parallel between missionary Christianity and contemporary human rights politics:

> The same methods are at work and similar dispossessions are taking place, without dialogue or conversation. The official human rights corpus, which issues from European predicates, seeks to supplant all other traditions, while rejecting them. It claims to be the only genius of the good society.
> (Mutua 2002, xi)

Mutua goes on to argue how Western narratives about human rights in Africa tend to reinforce colonialist representations in which Africans are either savages (that is, brutal and barbaric offenders of human rights) or victims (that is, people whose rights are being violated by fellow Africans), with Western actors being represented as saviours (that is, rescuing the victims out of the hands of the savages). Mutua argues that much of the Western engagement in defending human rights in Africa serves "the redemption of the redeemers", by which he means that "whites who are privileged globally as a people – who have historically visited untold suffering and savage atrocities against non-whites – redeem themselves by 'defending' and 'civilizing' 'lower,' 'unfortunate,' and 'inferior' peoples" (Mutua 2002, 14). As an example of this dynamics at work, one may think of narratives about gay rights in contemporary Africa as presented in the BBC documentary *Uganda: The World's Worst Place to Be Gay?* (Mills 2011). Here, Ugandan gay people are represented as powerless victims persecuted by homophobic politicians, religious leaders and fellow citizens who do not recognize their human rights but instead criminalize them. This representation allows Western pro-gay rights audiences to denounce "African homophobia" without acknowledging its British colonial roots (in African countries that are former British colonies, anti-homosexuality laws were introduced during the colonial period), nor the role of American conservative Christians in fuelling anti-gay politics in Uganda and other African countries. It also reinforces the self-congratulatory idea that the West is perhaps the best place to be gay, ignoring that gay rights are a very recent phenomenon in Western societies and are far from fully achieved (as many African gay asylum seekers in Europe have painfully discovered).

Although Mutua develops a strong critique both of the Eurocentric traditions of thought underlying human rights discourse, and of the Western-imperialist ways in which human rights are being policed globally, he does not, in fact, reject the basic idea of universal human rights. Instead, he proposes to "re-open debate on the entire normative scheme of the human rights corpus and reconstruct it from the ground up" (Mutua 2002, xi). This global debate about, and reconstruction of, human rights should not be dominated by Western perspectives but instead take into account what diverse cultures can contribute to the understanding of human being in relation to society. Such an approach would reveal that Africa certainly has its own, distinct contribution to make, building on its "indigenous African rights traditions embodied in the wisdom of elders and sages" (Ibhawoh 2018, xii).

Inculturating human rights in Africa

Responding to the problem of human rights being perceived as Western outlined above, several scholars have engaged in rethinking human rights from African perspectives. Gerrie ter Haar refers to this as the quest for an "inculturation of human rights", which involves appreciating "the specific contribution of local cultures to the universal concept of human rights" and paying attention to the "role played by religion as an integral part of people's existence, inseparable from the social and moral order" (ter Haar 2009, 64). Other scholars describe a similar process with the term "vernacularizing human rights" (Ibhawoh 2018, 225). Ter Haar emphasizes that this is not just a theoretical exercise but is important because cultural and religious beliefs have the capacity to motivate people's behaviours. Further developing the idea of inculturating human rights, Abamfo Ofori Atiemo suggests that it is a creative process of negotiating the "global" – that is, the idea of universal human rights – and the "local" – that is, cultural, religious and social traditions that buttress and develop this idea in a contextually meaningful and effective way. In Atiemo's words:

> Inculturation of human rights does not mean the abolition of the local culture by the global one, or the assimilation of the local by the global, or the local culture seeking to preserve itself against the global. It is the two cultures – the global and the local – engaging each other in a creative encounter at the conceptual and the practical levels in order to discover, develop and use appropriate concepts, values and other aspects of the local culture for the enhancement of human rights in the local context and for the enrichment of the universal regime.
>
> (Atiemo 2013, 52)

Atiemo implements this approach in the context of the Akan and Ewe people in Ghana, exploring a whole range of traditional and contemporary Ghanaian cultural and religious beliefs, as well as social and political arrangements, which can be used to "translate" human rights in a locally meaningful idiom. He suggests that although human rights as a modern concept may be Western, in Ghana and in other African societies there are deeply rooted indigenous ideas about human dignity:

> Each person is thought to have been created by God with an independent soul that is said to carry something of God's essence. Each soul is viewed as unique in relation to other human beings and creatures and their unique destinies.
>
> (Atiemo 2013, 130)

The implication of this view is that "every human being is believed to be in a continuous, unbreakable relationship with the kinship group and to be a member of the wider community, which is said to include the gods and the ancestors" (Atiemo 2013, 131). This was reflected in the indigenous legal, social and political arrangements, which sought to ensure the protection of human dignity.

Similar indigenous conceptions of human dignity have been identified by other scholars, such as Francis Deng in relation to the Dinka people in present-day South Sudan. The Dinka concept of human relations is known as *cieng* which means "to live together" and centres around values such as integrity, honour, respect for self and for others, compassion, generosity and harmony. In short, *cieng* requires "positive assistance to one's fellow human beings" (Deng 1990, 266). According to Deng, "*Cieng*, as the Dinka see it, has the sanctity of a good moral order not only inherited from the ancestors who had in turn received it from God and clan spirits, but also fortified and policed by them" (ibid.). Violation of the principles of *cieng* is not only seen as an anti-social act, but also as a "violation of the moral code, which may invite spiritual retribution manifest in illness and even death, according to the gravity of the violation." Adhering to the principles, on the other hand, "received appropriate recognition and reward, both social and spiritual" (ibid.).

These accounts of African indigenous moral and social thought commonly suggest a "humanistic outlook that sees human dignity and honor as fundamental to individual and collective well-being" (Ibhawoh 2018, 42). According to Bonny Ibhawoh, similar humanist ideas can be distinguished in Islamic and Christian traditions on the continent. He specifically refers to the thought of 17th century Islamic thinker Ahmed Baba who was based in Timbuktu (in present-day Mali) and "challenged the legal and theological arguments used at the time to justify the practices of enslavement", and of 17th century Christian Ethiopian theologian, Zera Yacob, who "placed emphasis on human dignity, tolerance, non-violence and mutual responsibility" (Ibhawoh 2018, 43–44). It is these longstanding traditions of African moral thought and social practice that can be used in the process of inculturating human rights. However, both Deng and Atiemo point out that these traditions should not be romanticized. For instance, the Dinka social and moral order created inequities because of "the logic of the lineage system and its stratification on the basis of descent, age, and sex" (Deng 1990, 273). Atiemo acknowledges that Akan society violated the dignity of certain categories of human beings, such as babies born with deformities or albinism, as these were considered as "not properly human ... [but] as spirits that had come in that form to punish the parents for some offence" (Atiemo 2013, , 134). Such beliefs, he suggests, need to be corrected and transformed in the process of inculturation.

The belief that certain categories of human beings, from particular cultural or religious perspectives, are not "properly human" is of course highly critical in relation to human rights. As ter Haar argues, human rights debates have often concerned the "rights" aspect, but they also should consider the "human" aspect: "We have to ask ourselves not only what it means to have rights, but also what it means to be human" (ter Haar 2009, 62). Such a conversation about the fundamental question of anthropology – what makes a human being? – is of great contemporary relevance, for instance in relation to ongoing human rights violations of people with albinism, people accused of witchcraft and people perceived to be gay or lesbian. In each of these cases, the very humanity of the people concerned is called into question on the basis of certain physical or behavioural traits, which is then used as a reason why human rights do not apply to them. For instance, if one's full humanity depends on one's ability to reproduce offspring, then same-sex sexuality can be perceived as de-humanizing, leaving the idea of "gay rights" as unthinkable, as the Congolese Catholic theologian Bénézet Bujo (2009, 154–8) argues (but see van Klinken 2016 for a counter-narrative). The inculturation of human rights will require a cross-cultural conversation about these and other critical issues in order to rethink the subject.

Importantly, as much as the project of inculturation requires cultural sensitivity and an openness to learn from other cultures, it does not necessarily lead to cultural relativism. As ter Haar (2009, 66) puts it, "Whereas cultural sensitivity makes possible a process of dialogue that can be mutually enriching, cultural relativism leads to a separate development of human rights." In relation to the just mentioned example, a relativist argument might be that African societies do not have to recognize the human rights of sexual minorities because same-sex sexuality is not in line with African conceptions of personhood. However, cultures are never static, and neither are cultural conceptions of personhood and of sexuality. Thus, they may shift to accommodate a newly negotiated conception of universal human rights.

The premise of Western human rights thinking, which starts with and centres around the individual person, is different from the indigenous conception of human dignity as found among traditional African societies, which tends to have a strong communal dimension. It emphasizes that personhood is always about human existence in relation to others. As Josiah Cobbah puts it,

> The African worldview places the individual within a continuum of the dead, the living, and the yet unborn. It is a worldview of group solidarity and collective responsibility. In effect, in the same way that people in other cultures are brought up to assert their independence from their community, the average African's worldview is one that places the individual within his community.
>
> (Cobbah 1987, 323)

The point made here should, however, not be over-emphasized, as if African societies do not have a concept of the individual at all. Traditionally, African indigenous thought is concerned with balancing the development of individual personhood and the collective good, and negotiating the tension between the two such as through divination practice. In contemporary contexts, the question of the individual versus collective nature of human dignity and rights has repercussions for the conception of African human rights frameworks.

Feature: African Charter of Human and Peoples' Rights

The African Charter of Human and Peoples' Rights (ACHPR 1986) is the foundational document of Africa's continental human rights system. It came into force in 1986, after it had been ratified by the majority of member states of the Organization of African Unity (now known as the African Union). The oversight and interpretation of the Charter is in the hands of the African Commission on Human and Peoples' Rights (based in Banjul, The Gambia). The Charter opens with a Preamble that explicitly states a commitment to "the total liberation of Africa" vis-à-vis the historical and ongoing struggles against colonialism and neo-colonialism. In this light, the Charter can be seen as an African document resisting Western imperialism, including the imposition of Western ideas of human rights. Yet the document does not reject these ideas but instead presents a serious attempt at thinking about human rights in and from African contexts.

What is interesting in the light of the above discussion is that the Charter explicitly speaks not only of "human rights" but also of "peoples' right," emphasizing the collective dimension. Moreover, the Charter does not only speak about rights but also about duties, so as to emphasize the responsibilities that individuals have towards the community and society they are part of. Mutua (2002, 93) refers to the Charter as "the African fingerprint of human rights", and captures its significance as follows:

> The African Charter's duty/rights conception is an excellent point of departure in the reconstruction of a new ethos and the restoration of confidence in the continent's cultural identity. It reintroduces values that Africa needs most at this time: commitment, solidarity, respect, and responsibility. Moreover, it represents a recognition of another reality: individual rights are collective in their dimension.

Another interesting aspect of the African Charter is that it recognizes not only civil, political, economic and social rights, but also "cultural rights". This does not only mean that "every individual may freely take part in the cultural life of their community" (Art. 17.2) but also that each individual has the duty "to preserve and strengthen positive African cultural values (...) and, in general, to contribute to the promotion of the moral wellbeing of society" (Art. 29.7). It can be expected that, in the process of inculturating human rights, heated debates may emerge about what these "positive African cultural values" exactly are, and how they should be preserved and strengthened in contemporary societies.

Apart from guaranteeing freedom of religion and prohibiting discrimination on the basis of religion, the Charter says very little about religion. Compared to the document's positive reference to cultural values, it is remarkable that it does not explicitly call for the preservation and strengthening – or at least, the protection – of African indigenous religious beliefs and practices. As such, the Charter reflects what Mutua (2002, 103) describes as "the legal invisibility of indigenous religions" in contemporary Africa, where Christianity and Islam have become the dominant traditions.

Religion and African human rights struggles

Religious beliefs, practices and institutions have played, and continue to play, an ambivalent role in struggles for human rights in African societies (and elsewhere). This ambivalence is captured by Abdullah An-Na'im when he writes:

> As abstract ideals of human dignity and economic and social justice, human rights norms depend upon the religious vision and commitment of specific communities to give them content and coherence, and to motivate voluntary compliance with their dictates. Religious visions and commitments are also needed for generating the political will to enforce legal norms and implement concrete policies, as and when necessary for the protection and promotion of human rights standards. But many forms of religion, in Africa and elsewhere, seem to work contrary to the values of equality, justice and peace contemplated by a human rights paradigm.
>
> (An-Na'im 2002, 3–4)

Thus, religion can both motivate and hinder human rights efforts, and in many cases it does so in paradoxical – that is, not always consistent – ways. The current section reviews the ambiguous role of religion in relation to a number of particular human rights issues, both in recent African history and today.

Slavery

Historically speaking, 19th century campaigns against the transatlantic slave trade from West Africa have had a tremendous impact on the modern history of human rights. Although antislavery campaigners (or abolitionists) did not necessarily use the language of rights, their efforts "broadened the scope of individual rights and provided new international legal frameworks for their protection" (Ibhawoh 2018, 57). Indigenous slavery had been practised in some African societies within certain social and legal boundaries, but it became much more large-scale and exploitative in the 17th and 18th centuries because of overseas demand and foreign commerce. For Europeans involved in the slave trade, slavery was permissible because black Africans did not fully qualify as human (a view they justified with reference to the biblical story about the curse of Ham). Campaigns against slavery emerged in the 19th century under the influence of both European enlightenment thought and evangelical Christian activism. The end of the transatlantic slave trade in Africa was partly because of political and economic reasons, but also because of the "humanist and egalitarian impulse within indigenous ethics, Christian morality and modernist liberalism that sustained the work of African and transnational abolitionists" (Ibhawoh 2018, 65). One of the prominent figures in the campaign was the Yoruba Christian convert Samuel Ajayi Crowther who, as a former slave himself, in 1864 became the first African Anglican bishop in West Africa. He passionately advocated against slavery and for the emancipation of ex-slaves, on the basis of his Christian belief that every human being had "God-given liberties and rights" (Crowther, quoted in Ibhawoh 2018, 73). In Islamic Africa, abolition of slavery followed a different trajectory but there too, in the 19th century, the legality and morality of slavery became contested on the basis of emerging, alternative interpretations of the Quran and the life of the Prophet (Ware 2017).

Apartheid

The racist ideas about the inferiority of black African people and cultures that undergirded slavery were also the basis for European colonialism in Africa. The racist perceptions of colonized African subjects had their most extreme socio-political repercussions in the settler colonies of southern Africa, where policies of racial segregation were systematically developed and implemented by British, Dutch, German and Portuguese settlers. In South Africa, this culminated in the introduction of a system of racial discrimination – known as *apartheid* – by the Afrikaner nationalist minority government in 1948, with severe social, economic and political consequences for the majority black South African population as well as other racial minorities. Apartheid was inspired by a unique Christian version of white supremacist thinking, in which the Afrikaners (descendants of Dutch settlers) were the biblically "chosen people" of God who had a divine right to "the promised land", while under the name of "separate development" black African, mixed race (or "coloured") and Indian communities were economically and politically marginalized. The discriminatory apartheid regime became more and more repressive and violent, responding aggressively to organized forms of resistance, such as by the African National Congress (ANC) and other black liberation movements, which often framed their activities in a human rights discourse. Many activists and leaders of these movements "disappeared", such as black intellectual Steve Biko, while others, such as Nelson Mandela, suffered long prison sentences. When Mandela, after 27 years of imprisonment and strong international pressure, was finally released in 1990, he negotiated an end to apartheid and led the ANC in the first democratic elections in 1994. He then became the first black President of South Africa. Importantly, as much as apartheid was justified by a particular Christian theology and was condoned by the Dutch Reformed Church in South Africa, the resistance to apartheid was equally inspired by Christian thought, most famously the tradition of black South African theology, and many churches opposed Afrikaner nationalism (De Gruchy 2004). Muslim communities were also involved in the liberation movement, and a tradition of Islamic liberation theology emerged in South Africa (Esack 1997). Perhaps the most famous face of this religious resistance to apartheid is black theologian and Anglican clergyman, Desmond Tutu.

Feature: Archbishop Desmond Tutu and the philosophy of Ubuntu

Desmond Tutu (b. 1931; Figure 11.1) is a South African church leader and Nobel Peace Prize winning anti-apartheid and human rights activist. Ordained as Anglican priest in 1960, he served as General Secretary of the influential South African Council of Churches (1978–1984), as Bishop of Johannesburg (1985–1986) and as Archbishop of Cape Town (from 1986 till his retirement in 1996). Influenced by the tradition of black liberation theology, Tutu became a vocal critic of apartheid, the system of white-minority rule and racial segregation in South Africa (1948–1991).

After the end of apartheid, President Mandela appointed him as chair of the Truth and Reconciliation Commission (TRC; 1996–1998), which was assigned the task of promoting national unity and reconciliation in a society deeply divided and wounded after decades of systematic racial discrimination and violent repression. In that capacity, Tutu worked in the spirit of what he called *Ubuntu* and promoted this concept as an indigenous African philosophy and ethics that could enable restorative justice and healing.

Originating from the Bantu languages spoken in southern Africa, Ubuntu captures the idea that a person always exists in and through relation to others ("I am because you are"). In Tutu's own words, it means that "my humanity is caught up, is inextricably bound up, in your humanity" and "what dehumanises you, inexorably, dehumanises me" (Tutu 1999, 34–35). Applying this to the South African context, he argued that "the humanity of the perpetrators of apartheid's atrocities was caught up and bound up in that of his victim" (ibid., 35). This insight became the key principle of the public hearings of the TRC, where perpetrators could give testimony of their crimes, face their victims and ask for amnesty.

As much as Ubuntu is an indigenous African philosophy, for Tutu it also had explicitly Christian undertones: only in full community with others, human beings can truly bear the image of God. Tutu's philosophy and theology of Ubuntu can be seen as an example of the inculturation or vernacularization of human rights in Africa. Although contested by critics (who believe it is an elitist and romanticized idea and has failed to achieve justice in post-apartheid South Africa), others have argued that the TRC, thanks to Tutu's leadership and vision, "represents a uniquely South African normative contribution to the universal human rights idea and, specifically, the discourse on human dignity and transitional justice" (Ibhawoh 2018, 229).

Tutu himself has more recently become one of the few African faith leaders actively advocating for the human rights of sexual minorities. He believes that both racial and sexual diversity are part of the way God created humankind; neither race nor sexuality can therefore be grounds for discrimination.

Figure 11.1 Archbishop Desmond Tutu (© David Pearson / Alamy Stock Photo)

Women

One of the more successful human rights campaigns in Africa in recent decades is concerned with gender and the rights of women. The critical issues are diverse, ranging from women's political representation to their economic empowerment, legal and constitutional reform including the challenges women face vis-à-vis customary laws (e.g. regarding polygamy and widow inheritance) and traditional authorities, and issues of reproductive rights and gender-based violence. Partly, these campaigns have been inspired and/or driven by international feminist movements and external funders, but to a considerable extent African women's groups and gender initiatives have actively and creatively shaped their own agendas and found their own sources of inspiration. As part of this, "Contemporary movements in Africa have also drawn on their roots in indigenous women's strategies that pre-date Islamisation, Christianisation and colonisation" (Tripp and Badri 2017, 2). Also, Islamic and Christian groups on the continent actively engage with gender issues, for instance through Muslim and Christian women's movements, through faith-based programmes for women's empowerment and gender equality, and through campaigns addressing sexual and domestic violence against women (Abdullah 2002). At the same time, of course, religious beliefs – inspired by indigenous, Christian or Islamic traditions – are often used to justify and legitimize various forms of gender inequality, patriarchal structures and misogynistic practices.

One of the most critical gender issues in various African societies and cultures is the practice of female genital cutting (or mutilation), commonly abbreviated as FGM. The practice, also known as "female circumcision", involves the surgical removal of the clitoris, clitoris and labia minora, or a more radical process, infibulation, in which the vulva is sewn, leaving only a small opening for urine and menses. Rogaia Abusharaf captures the ambivalent role of religion with regard to FGM as follows:

> Not only is religion among those forces that both uphold and subvert the practice of FGM, but change is [also] facilitated by a double movement. Religious discourses and organizations both localize international human rights by linking them firmly to vernacular understandings of social relations and dissociate the practice of FGM and its connotations of fertility, chastity, and purity from their embeddedness in cultural traditions. Simultaneously opening prevalent practices to scrutiny in the light of ultimate values regarding the sacredness of the human body and validating alternative practices through the authority of religion is a uniquely powerful combination.
>
> (Abusharaf 2011, 148)

Female genital cutting is practised in at least 28 countries in Africa, in indigenous religious, Islamic and Christian communities, the motivation stemming from cultural and religious traditions. Since the colonial period the practice has become deeply contested, initially by European colonizers and missionaries who often tried to ban it (giving rise to socio-cultural conflicts, beautifully narrated by Kenyan literary writer Ngũgĩ wa Thiong'o in his 1965 novel *The River Between*), and more recently by government- and NGO-led human rights inspired campaigns. Although certain religious leaders have defended the practice, other clerics, such as Imam Demba Diawara in Senegal, and faith-based groups such as the All Africa Conference of Churches and the African Women of Faith Network, have critiqued FGM and argued that their faiths do not require it (Abusharaf 2011). It is one example of the critical role that religion plays in relation to gender issues and women's rights. Yet female genital cutting, like other harmful gendered practices, is also an example of a practice that can easily be misrepresented – when the different forms of the practice are overlooked and a monolithic account of FGM as "barbaric" is given – and misunderstood from modern human rights perspectives – when the underlying cultural-religious beliefs about fertility and purity are not adequately acknowledged and addressed.

Witchcraft

In many African countries, human rights organizations in recent years have become increasingly concerned with the violence resulting from witchcraft accusations. People who are vulnerable in society anyway, such as orphaned children or elderly women, are particularly prone to such accusations and the subsequent social and physical violence by relatives and community members (see Chapter 7). As ter Haar (2009, 67) writes, "People accused of practicing witchcraft run into deep trouble, as they are liable to be severely punished for their alleged antisocial behaviour. They may be maltreated, chased from their villages or otherwise banned from the community, and even killed." Various faith-based initiatives are offering support to people accused of witchcraft and suffering from the repercussions, such as the Gambaga Go Home Project of the Presbyterian Church in Ghana, which works in a "witch camp" in the northern Ghanaian village of Gambaga and seeks to reintegrate accused witches who sought refuge there with their families and communities.

Although it is obvious that witchcraft accusations are a serious human rights concern, not at least because the accused can often hardly defend themselves, the rationalist approach followed by many human rights activists who simply deny the reality of witchcraft, has been shown to be inadequate. It is inadequate exactly because it fails to acknowledge the spiritual worldview in which witchcraft is real and makes sense of people's insecurities and struggles. As Adam Ashforth (2015, 29) puts it, "The human rights approach to witchcraft accusations denies their validity and forecloses the possibility of a trial, fair or otherwise". Ashforth discusses several cases of magistrates in Malawi who do take these accusations seriously, and who conduct culturally sensitive witch trials enabling "restorative justice", through which the need for violence is averted.

Conclusion

This chapter has demonstrated that the question of religion and human rights in Africa is a complex one, partly because human rights itself is a complex idea with an ambivalent reception in Africa, and partly because religious beliefs, practices and organizations play a multifaceted role in critical human rights issues in African societies. Instead of simply arguing whether religion is "good" or "bad" for human rights in Africa, it is important, first, to acknowledge that religious beliefs need to be taken seriously in conversations about the meaning of human rights, which includes the question of the meaning of personhood; second, that the critical role of religious practices in human rights violations should be understood in a more nuanced way; and third, that religious communities and faith-based organizations should be actively involved in any human rights campaign that seeks to be locally relevant and effective.

Questions for discussion

- Reading the African Charter of Human and Peoples' Rights, what aspects make this document distinctly "African", and how does this relate to the idea of human rights as being universal?
- Do you think there is something like "African human rights", and if so, what does this concept look like, and how does it relate to the universalist premise of modern human rights?
- What do you perceive as the strengths and weaknesses of the approach of inculturating human rights in Africa?
- What difference do you think it makes for conversations about religion and human rights in Africa, to begin not with the question of "rights" but with that of "being human"?

References (*indicates recommended reading)

Abdullah, Hussaina. 2002. "Religious Revivalism, Human Rights Activism and the Struggle for Women's Rights in Nigeria." In *Cultural Transformation and Human Rights in Africa*, edited by Abdullah An-Na'im, 151–191. London: Zed Books.

Abusharaf, Rogaia Mustafa. 2011. "Gender Justice and Religion in Sub-Saharan Africa." In *Religion and the Global Politics of Human Rights*, edited by Thomas Banchoff and Robert Wuthnow, 129–156. Oxford: Oxford University Press.

African Commission on Human and Peoples' Rights (ACHPR). 1986. *African Charter on Human and Peoples' Rights*. http://www.achpr.org/files/instruments/achpr/banjul_charter.pdf.

An-Na'im, Abdullah. 2002. "Introduction." In *Cultural Transformation and Human Rights in Africa*, edited by Abdullah An-Na'im, 1–12. London: Zed Books.

Ashforth, Adam. 2015. "Witchcraft, Justice, and Human Rights in Africa: Cases from Malawi", *African Studies Review* 58/1, 5–38.

*Atiemo, Abamfo Ofori. 2013. *Religion and the Inculturation of Human Rights in Ghana*. London: Bloomsbury.

Bujo, Bénézet. 2009. *Plea for Change of Models for Marriage*. Nairobi: Paulines.

Cobbah, Josiah. 1987. "African Values and the Human Rights Debate: An African Perspective", *Human Rights Quarterly* 9/3, 309–331.

De Gruchy, John. 2004. *The Church Struggle in South Africa* (25th edition). London: SCM.

Deng, Francis. 1990. "A Cultural Approach to Human Rights among the Dinka." In *Human Rights in Africa: Cross-Cultural Perspectives*, edited by Ahmed An-Na'im and Francis Deng, 261–289. Washington D.C.: The Brookings Institution.

Esack, Farid. 1997. *Quran, Liberation and Pluralism: An Islamic Perspective of Inter-religious Solidarity against Oppression*. London: One World.

*Ibhawoh, Bonny. 2018. *Human Rights in Africa*. Cambridge: Cambridge University Press.

Mills, Scott. 2011. *Uganda: The World's Worst Place to Be Gay?* London: British Broadcasting Corporation.

*Mutua, Makau. 2002. *Human Rights: A Political and Cultural Critique*. Philadelphia: University of Pennsylvania Press.

Ter Haar, Gerrie. 2009. *How God Became African: African Spirituality and Western Secular Thought*. Philadelphia: University of Pennsylvania Press.

Tripp, Aili Mari, and Balghis Badri, editors. 2017. *Women's Activism in Africa: Struggles for Rights and Representation*. London: Zed Books.

Tutu, Desmond. 1999. *No Future without Forgiveness*. London: Rider.

Van Klinken, Adriaan. 2016. "Christianity, Human Rights and LGBTI Advocacy: The Case of Dette Resource Foundation in Zambia." In *Public Religion and the Politics of Homosexuality in Africa*, edited by Adriaan van Klinken and Ezra Chitando, 229–242. Abingdon: Routledge.

Ware, Rudolph. 2017. "Slavery and Abolitionism in Islamic Africa, 1776–1905." In *The Cambridge World History of Slavery: Volume 4, AD 1804–AD 2016*, edited by David Eltis, Stanley Engerman, Seymour Drescher and David Richardson, 344–372. Cambridge: Cambridge University Press.

12 Religion, illness and health in Africa

What does religion have to do with illness and healing?

In sub-Saharan Africa a person is considered first and foremost a relational being whose body, mind, and spirit are conditioned by critical relationships: the family (including the ancestors), the community (including witches and diviners who can affect the body by supernatural means), spirits, divinities and God (see Chapter 1; cf. Westerlund 2006). Ailments and afflictions are understood to be the result of a disturbance in this web of relations. Illness is therefore a spiritual or moral dilemma so symptoms cannot be treated as a medical matter alone.

The view of affliction and its treatment as a holistic matter, requiring spiritual intervention, is not limited to African indigenous religions, but shapes the pre-occupations of African Christians and Muslims as well. The search to restore the wholeness of body, spirit and heart, the original state of grace, is a biblical theme. The Qur'an refers to God's revelation itself as a healing for the suffering heart. The assertion by the Prophet, that for every illness Allah provided a cure, has inspired Muslims' pursuit of medical knowledge through the centuries. The faithful treat disease in the conviction that God is the ultimate healer.

Finding effective approaches to health care in the time of HIV and AIDS, Ebola, and Zika presents a profound medical and moral crisis for Africa and the entire globe. Faith-based agencies have a long history of intervening to alleviate human suffering in response to the charge that God mandates that we care for one another. In the past decade, in the absence of nationalized health systems in Africa, there has been a resurgence of faith-based health providers. In over a dozen countries, both Christian and Muslim faith-based hospitals and clinics are estimated to provide over 30 per cent of Africa's healthcare (Open Democracy 2015).

"Traditional" medicine

African healing practices are as varied as the many specific cultural contexts on the continent. They include midwifery, bone-setting and herbal tisanes, as well as spiritual techniques like the production and wearing of protective amulets ("gris gris"), purifying baths, and the recitation of religious scriptures. Most healers combine several practices. No single treatment modality could adequately characterize the range of views or the complexity of indigenous systems of diagnosis and treatment of disease. The term "traditional medicine", which implies the existence of a uniform system, is therefore questionable.

> Nevertheless, the term continues to be used and adopted by both the people who use traditional medicine (and in many rural areas of the Global South traditional medicine is often the only health-care choice) ... and also by policy-makers and international institutions such as the WHO [World Health Organization].
>
> (Bignante 2015, 702)

Moreover, healers themselves use the term. In French-speaking West Africa, one may see homemade signs posted along the road advertising the expertise of a local "tradi-praticien" (traditional practitioner) who treats ailments with herbs as well as spiritual techniques. These advertisements are usually illustrated, for the sake of the illiterate, depicting ailments and sometimes include imaginative portraits of bewitching entities (Figure 12.1).

Despite the nuances of the term "traditional", indigenous knowledge and practice are not timeless. They are constantly evolving in the face of "modernity": mobility, exchange and economic constraints of globalization, as well as the horrific new epidemics challenging the contemporary world. Therefore

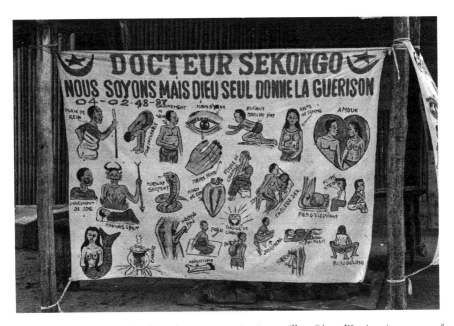

Figure 12.1 Indigenous healer advertisement in Jaqueville, Côte d'Ivoire (courtesy of Tommy Trenchard, 2010).

African healing practices do not necessarily compete with Western biomedicine, but complement it in order to address the full circumstance of disease: threats to personal security and the need for psychological wellbeing; misfortune and inexplicable suffering as a source of anxiety; social disruption or alienation that result in physical symptoms.

African "healthworlds"

The body is not a discrete and bounded entity. It is marked by its social context. From the effects of nutrition to the manipulations that inscribe cultural values on it (by genital cutting, for example), the body – its health and its "disease" – can be seen as a microcosm of the social body. Although banal ailments may be treated with medical remedies, chronic illness occasions an examination of the social and spiritual matrix upon which wellbeing depends. The afflicted may turn to diviners who identify the precise source of the conflict, traditional priests who can intercede with the ancestors who "remind" their descendants of neglected obligations by afflicting them with disease, or healers who can elicit spiritual protection against witchcraft attacks.

Paul Germond and James Cochrane (2010, 308) coined the term "healthworlds" to refer to the complex set of beliefs about health and behaviours that inform indigenous African healthcare. The concept was derived from *bophelo*, which in the Sesotho language spoken in Lesotho refers to the living context of existence as an organic unity that constitutes wellbeing. As elsewhere in Africa, "separate words for 'health' and 'religion' do not exist ... nor did their separation make sense to the worldview of the respondents" (Germond and Cochrane 2010, 309). Therefore, *bophelo* considers mind *and* body, person *and* society, as well as the ancestors' blessing as critical factors for health. "This injects a religious dimension ... there can be no *bophelo* without religious health" (309).

Given such nuanced and comprehensive ideas about health as integrated wholeness, Africans rely on a plurality of treatments, either as alternatives or as complementary therapies.

> The African of whatever faith description was born African ... and this simple truth means there are certain things which he or she takes in with the mother's milk. There is a world-taken-for-granted in his/her psyche which surfaces time and again ... That explains why some Africans will in one breath consult the Western trained medical doctor and in the same breath consult traditional shrines and healers.
>
> (Pobee, 2001, 61)

Because illness is socially constructed it must be treated in the collective domain. In Bantu languages spoken in eastern and southern Africa, the word *ngoma* means "drum" and also refers to a set of public performances intended to protect entire communities from spiritual danger. Ngoma ceremonies invoke ancestors or territorial spirits to cure diseases attributed to disembodied spirits. The afflicted are also actively re-incorporated into the community by singing together.

In other collective rituals the patient is symbolically associated with both community and cosmos to affect healing. The imagery reveals the logic of culture at work on the body.

Feature: Two cases of collective ritual for gynaecological healing

Given the premium placed on the wholesomeness of the community and its perpetuation, it is hardly surprising that much African ritual promoting healing focuses especially on fertility. *Isoma* is one such ritual. Performed by the Ndembu of Zambia and documented by Victor Turner (1969) in his classic work *The Ritual Process*, this rite addresses gynaecological disorders. "*Isoma*" means "to slip out of place or fastening", a reference to miscarriage and also to forgetting one's maternal ancestors whose neglect is presumed to be the cause (15). The curative rites "cause [patients and their family] to remember" their obligation to the ancestors and their moral mandates (13). *Isoma* uses medicines derived from the *mulendi* tree with a slippery surface, referring both to pregnancies that have "slipped out" prematurely and the potential to "slip out" of the ancestors' punishment that tied off fertility.

The *Isoma* site is set up near an ancestral stream. The husband builds a grass seclusion hut identical to the one used during puberty rites. Just as the patient was "grown into a woman" through initiation, she is "regrown" as a fertile woman in *Isoma* (21). A burrow of either a giant bush rat or ant-bear is excavated. The holes at each end stand for "'graves and for procreative power' – in other words, for tomb and womb" (28). The patient and husband are naked, "at once like infants and corpses" (31). The woman clasps a white hen supplied by her maternal kin against her breast, as one would a suckling infant. The couple cross the tunnel several times and at each end are splashed with medicines. The rite concludes with the sacrifice of a red cock whose blood is poured into the burrow (31).

Among the Yaka of the Democratic Republic of the Congo (DRC), too, "illness is considered to stem from a disturbance in the relationship between ... persons themselves and/or between them and the life-world" (Devisch 1993, 15). For the Yaka, the body is tightly interwoven with the threads of kinship, ancestors and cosmos; infertility is a tear in that fabric of life. The *khita* healing rite attempts to re-weave those threads to restore fertility by awakening a "vitalizing resonance" between the woman's body and the cosmic womb (Devisch 1993, xx). At the apex of the *khita* ceremonies, the patient is suspended horizontally by her arms and legs on a branch of a tree, likened to a woven fabric hanging from the loom, and brought home (183). She is then placed in seclusion, and made to re-experience the foetal condition (196). Identifying herself with an embryo, she undergoes self-generated healing that restores physical integrity.

Both healing rituals show that "gyn-ecology" concerns not only reproductive health, but also cosmic wholeness.

While biomedicine may eliminate symptoms of disease, a traditional healer addresses the deeper causes and ensures the long-term effects of the treatment. The overlapping modes of treatment are only one face of medical pluralism; African "healthworlds" are made more complex by the fact that the choice of therapy is often made by a sufferer's social entourage (extended family and friends), who act as intermediaries with the healer and participate in the treatment.

A vivid example of medical pluralism is the case of Maxwell Sarpong, a Ghanaian elder. In 2004, following a paralyzing stroke, Sarpong received medical treatment and Western pharmaceuticals at three separate hospitals. Each time he improved and was released, but his symptoms returned. For the Asante, an important ethnic group in Ghana, spiritual sickness (*sunsum yaree*) presents itself through biological symptoms but the cause is not treatable by Western biomedicine because the genesis is the rupture of relationships and justice in the kin group. Friends and kin therefore urged Sarpong to turn to traditional intervention. Sarpong made intercession with the deities at the witch-catching shrine. The shrine priest determined that the cause of his illness was a dispute over the succession to the office of chief to which Sarpong had a legitimate claim. The usurper presumably used witchcraft to prevent Sarpong from governing. The priest also prescribed a herbal remedy. Within two months, Sarpong was restored to full health and was ultimately able to assume his position as chief (Olsen and Sargent 2017, 61).

Other modes of healing are more intimate and "are built relationally in the patient–healer encounter" (Bignante, 2015, 698). In northern Senegal the most often cited reason for visiting a traditional healer was to get advice "on personal matters in order to find peace and emotional wellness" (706). Clients also cited the specialist's words and prayer, calming herbal remedies, protective amulets, and even the atmosphere in the healer's room as having healing effects. Therefore, from the most public ritual context to the most intimate, the relational dimension of traditional healing systems creates wellbeing.

Pathologies of power: structural inequality and disease

Increasing poverty and inadequate access to healthcare, wars causing death, famine and refugee flight and worldwide epidemics like AIDS, have all disproportionately affected Africa. Such real suffering is caused by structural inequality and the pathology of power relations in the world. Most people lack access to "modern" medical facilities, or cannot afford their costs. Hospitals and clinics are increasingly threadbare and understaffed. Surgical patients are commonly required to provide their own basic medical supplies as well as food and bedding during hospitalization. Medical staff do without basic equipment, such as protective gloves or medicine drips. The situation in Senegal is typical:

> Regional hospitals and district health centres are located almost exclusively in urban areas, while rural areas, home to 48% of the population of Senegal, often lack any health service at all, or rely only on health posts (with

three or four health workers) or health points (with a couple of health agents and a midwife). Nor is the situation in urban contexts any easier: often hospitals and dispensaries do not have enough medicines or tools or, if they do, patients cannot afford to pay for them.

(Bignante 2015, 703)

On the other side of the continent, in Tanzania, the situation is no better: "Quite simply, 'traditional medicine' is more accessible than biomedicine: it is estimated that the ratio of *waganga* [local healers] to population in Tanzania is 1:400, whereas for biomedical doctors it is 1:20,000" (Marsland 2007, 756).

The cause is linked to relations in the global community. In the 1980s, under international pressure led by the International Monetary Fund (IMF) and the World Bank, African states succumbed to "Structural Adjustment" (see Introduction). African currencies were devalued overnight, leaving economies bankrupt. Governments cut funding for public health programmes, medical services, drugs, equipment and personnel. Vulnerability increased just as the AIDS crisis was peaking (Schoepf 2017, 119). The introduction of these reforms had a devastating effect at every level of society.

Local peoples and elites alike regard their life courses as having lost the predictability and orderliness they may once have had. Under demanding conditions of modernity, they see plans for a child's school future, one's family and career, and for building material and spiritual capital, as constantly reversed by events and persons beyond one's control ... While many locals are aware that external and ultimately international factors (e.g. structural adjustment, fluctuating commodity demand) constrain their crop yields and prices, and their educational and socio-economic opportunities, this awareness is rarely enough to explain the uneven and apparent arbitrary nature of affliction. ... [It is this] decline in local trust that allows witch finders to flourish.

(Parkin 2013, 135)

In the capital of the DRC, Kinshasa, the Pentecostal churches that preach prosperity as divine blessing, repudiated the invisible force of affliction as witchcraft. A frenzy of accusations against children led to many being abandoned and shunned. Exorcisms allowed parents "to slough off unruly, burdensome, deformed or otherwise abnormal children", bringing new misery to the streets (Schoepf 2017, 128). This spiritual interpretation also masked "the true cause of misfortune, poverty, inequality and structural violence" (ibid.).

In the face of hard realities, medical pluralism is a simple matter of pragmatism. The array of treatments that Africans employ is a testimony to perseverance and creativity. Herbal medicine in particular has drawn attention as one possible way to compensate for shortfalls in available care. It also has the most potential to be integrated into Western healing systems as an effective and acceptable complement.

Herbalists and pharmaceuticals

Beyond merely filling gaps in healthcare, traditional healing practices are also often the first choice. Herbal remedies for minor illness are not only cheaper, many hold them to be more effective than Western allopathic medicines (Bignante 2015, 705). In cities like Zanzibar Town and Dar es Salaam (Tanzania) people rely on locally produced pharmaceuticals to treat common local ills including malaria, snake bite, and intestinal parasites (Olsen and Sargent 2017, 11).

In the 1970s the World Health Organization (WHO) and other development agencies called for collaboration with African "folk practitioners" to evaluate the pharmacological efficacy of traditional medicines. The interest coincided with hopes of many of the newly independent African states seeking to rehabilitate African medicine that, like most other forms of African traditional knowledge and practice, "had been denigrated and suppressed by the colonizers" (Schoepf 2017, 118). In 1978 an association of *nganga*, the *Traditional Health Practitioners Association of Zambia* (THPAZ), partnered with that country's Ministry of Health and WHO to identify active ingredients in local remedies and develop new commercial drugs (Sugishita 2009, 437). In Rwanda, 16 of the 25 most common herbal remedies tested were found to contain ingredients effective against gonorrhoea, meningitis and streptococcus, among other diseases. Many herbs contained salicylate, the active ingredient of aspirin (Schoepf 2017, 115). Such findings piqued interest in the possibility of an indigenous pharmaceutical industry that would help counterbalance the prohibitive cost of Western biomedicines. Tanzanian healers successfully developed a large-scale production of their pharmaceutical line, *Ngetwa*. "Ngetwa is a case of localising the global. It draws on modern technology used to mass produce pharmaceuticals, but unlike biomedical preparations, Ngetwa is not impersonal" (Marsland 2007, 762). Their medicine is advertised as a treatment for multiple ailments, like most traditional remedies, and Ngetwa's one-dose sachets bear the portrait of the healer who devised the original recipe.

A significant obstacle to collaboration has been the failure to appreciate the different ways that Western medical researchers and African traditional healers understand and protect knowledge. The former see medicine as "raw material" for patenting as intellectual property. African healers view their knowledge of plants' healing properties as secret, derived from "carefully cultivated … relationships with ancestors, spirits, gods, and other nonhuman actors", the true source of healing (Langwick 2017, 33). Invested in safeguarding their spiritual contracts and associated privileges, and protecting such knowledge from falling into the hands of those who would use it to cause harm (witches), traditional healers resist treating medicinal knowledge as a mere commodity. In Zambia, nganga–scientist collaboration almost failed because, in their effort to protect secrecy, the traditional healers "refused to specify the ingredients of medicines they had provided for chemical analysis" (Sugishita 2009, 444). As a result the two types of medicine merely coexist.

The integration of African medicines into healthcare systems is also problematic because some herbs can interfere with drugs' normal metabolism; side effects may be harmful or even lethal. An example is "cancer bush" (*Sutherlandia frutescens*) widely used in the treatment of HIV/AIDS and TB in Southern Africa; it "lowers the plasma levels when taken with the antiretroviral drug, *atazanavir*, reducing its anti-HIV efficacy" (Gouws 2018). Another problem is the potential loss of the relational dimension of traditional African modes of healing. Seeking greater professionalization and legitimacy some African healers formed guilds that imitate modern biomedical associations. They also adopted older Western attitudes that treated doctors' authority as sacrosanct, undercutting the therapeutic value of patients' participation (Parkin 2013, 126). Ultimately, because traditional healers consider both biochemical and occult causes of disease, full collaboration is impossible. African healers complain, "We refer [our patients] to hospitals but hospitals don't refer [them to] us" (Sugishita 2009, 438).

Feature: PRO.ME.TRA International ("Promoting Traditional Medicine")

Established as an international NGO in 1971 with headquarters in Dakar, Senegal, PRO.ME.TRA aimed "to preserve the knowledge of African traditional medicine, culture and indigenous science through research, advocacy and practice", to rehabilitate "traditional medicine, ancient religions and universal spirituality", and protect it as a "civilizational value" (Prometra.org 2018). Towards this end it has revived the ancient public divination ceremony of the Sereer people of Senegal, recognized by UNESCO as a cultural heritage. In addition to conducting scientific research on indigenous treatments for diseases including HIV/AIDS, Ebola and diabetes, PRO.ME.TRA trains traditional practitioners in critical healthcare matters such as nutrition, childbirth and family planning.

The president of the Uganda chapter, Dr. Sekagya, also directs the Institute of Traditional Medicine, known as the Buyija forest school. It instructs students about the medicinal properties of a shared repertoire of plants and teaches them how to develop and commercialize their products. At the same time the school trains them as "spiritualists", privileging this curriculum as the highest form of knowledge. Spiritualists obtain their diagnostic insights and healing knowledge from spirits in induced trance. This aspect of the training signals the school's double vision of healthcare as a spiritual endeavour as much as a scientific pursuit.

Islam and the assimilation of indigenous healing

In the Islamic world belief in the existence of *jinn* and other supernatural beings mentioned in the Qu'ran is widespread. Though not necessarily evil, *jinn* are thought to be able to possess both inanimate objects and animate beings and interact concretely. They may be sources of inspiration and uncommon insight, but are also considered responsible for various diseases and mental illness. Witches may invoke them to possess a chosen victim and cause suffering. Along the Swahili-speaking coast (Kenya, Tanzania and northern Mozambique) where Arabic influence is strong, belief in the *jinn* was assimilated with local belief about spirits and healing practices for exorcism. In Tanzania healers called *mganga wa korani* recite Qu'ranic verses as medicine or write them on paper that is incorporated into an amulet for protection from evil. Other healers (*mganga wa kibuyu*) conduct divination using a calabash to diagnose and make prescriptions for healing. Some combine both types. These specialize in symptoms of mental illness. The calabash reveals information on the client's life-force (*nyota*) and determines whether it is an illness caused by God or by "polytheism" (*ushirikina*), a Swahili term used to refer to indigenous African religions and the belief in witchcraft (Stroeken 2017, 165). In most cases they find it is the latter, in keeping with the traditional African view that humans and not God are the source of evil.

David Parkin (2017) relates the case of a boy brought to a healer in Mombasa, on the Kenyan coast, because he was having problems at school. The healer, Bwana Bwanadi, conducted divination by reading from "a small old book". He determined the cause was jealousy, implying he was victim of "the evil eye" (*husda*), a harm-inflicting glance. Bwanadi had the boy drink *kombe*, a medicine prepared by writing a Qur'anic verse on a plate in saffron and pouring rose water on it. He also performed an incense fumigation treatment called *zinguo la jahamu*, the "incense of consciousness" (Parkin 2017, 542).

> He sat him on a small stool facing west, covering him with a white cloth. He recited Qur'anic verses while spitting on the boy's head after each verse, repeating the action ten times. He took a small copy of the Qur'an in Arabic, moved it about the boy's head a few times.
>
> (Parkin 2017, 542)

Such practices may be seen to be in keeping with a body of Islamic alternative medicine known as *al-Tibb al Nabawi* (Medicine of the Prophet) that treats bodily ailment as a sign of the ill effects of evil forces on the soul (Tibbenabawi.org 2018). However Muslims influenced by Wahhabism denounce them as "superstition". In the last thirty years "magical" practices have come under increasing attack by "Wahhabi radicals who wish to eliminate spirit-based aspects of Muslim healing" as well as any diagnosis referring to witchcraft (Parkin 2017, 548). Nevertheless, most Muslims in coastal Eastern Africa consider the source of all healing to come from God and the spirit realm and view their practices as highly moral (543). (See Figure 12.2.)

Spirits not only cause illness, they can also be used to cure it. This is the case of the *bori* cult among the Fulani in Niger. A similar practice is found among their neighbours, the Tuareg.

Figure 12.2 Itinerant Muslim marabout conducting divination in Côte d'Ivoire (Laura Grillo, 2010).

Feature: Tuareg spirit possession as healing

The Tuareg live as nomadic herders and traders in the semi-arid Sahel region of West Africa (Niger, Mali, Burkina Faso as well as Algeria and Libya). They converted to Islam between the 8th and 11th centuries C.E. but local pre-Islamic religious culture still informs Tuareg belief and practice. The ancient ritual *Tende-n-Goumaten*, a "spirit possession and mediumship involving medico-ritual healing", is one of these (Rasmussen 2012, 190).

Tuareg in Niger believe that stress and depression cause spirits to enter the soul and manifest as mental instability. Close friends and relatives organize the *tende* for the afflicted, usually a woman, to exorcise the spirits. These spirits are pre-Islamic tree spirits and founding ancestresses, distinct from the *jinn*. Islamic scholars, popularly called marabouts, explain that women's spirits "require different types of cures" and refer patients for the *tende* if recitation of Qur'anic verses does not cure them.

The *Tende-n-goumaten* is conducted by mediums, women who consider themselves Muslims and whose songs may also address Allah. They play drums and sing to summon the spirit, which possesses the patient. During the possession-trance the spirit "may demand to wear clothes or use props appropriate to its ethnic and historical identity; may speak its own language, consume or avoid certain foods and drinks" (186). Once it is appeased, it permits the patient to recover. If the exorcism is not successful, the patient enters into "a therapeutic contractual relationship with the spirit" (186). She regains health on the condition that she becomes a medium herself. This "medico-ritual" exemplifies the blurred boundary between religion and medicine as well as between traditional African religious practice and Islam in an African context.

Christianity, African healing, and HIV and AIDS

Biomedicine was imported from Western Europe during the colonial period by administrators tasked with establishing material modernity, and by Christian medical missionaries intent on spreading the gospel by caring for the sick. The missionary movements' vision of holistic ministry remains the impetus for the many faith-based health care programmes on the continent today, serving many remote rural areas which might otherwise have no access to such services.

Much of the appeal of the Pentecostal churches in Africa since the 20th century has been their emphasis on the healing power of the Holy Spirit and repudiation of evil as the source of suffering. These themes, closely correlating with indigenous African preoccupations, gave rise to the African Independent Churches (AIC) which self-consciously integrate indigenous practices with Christian moral righteousness (see Chapter 5).

Healing is to search for the power of God and the goodwill of other spirit-beings who, under God administer various aspects of life and health. This mentality has seeped into the church. There is an AIC in Kumasi [that] Ashanti called "Christ Power Church". That name is eloquent of the power of Christ which that church enshrines and therefore, as the channel for effective cures.

(Pobee 2001)

In Zambia, the leaders of the Zion Apostolic Church are *ngangas* (traditional healers) who assume prophetic as well as healing roles, but claim to use only non-demonic spirits. "In effect, [the Churches] sanctify *ng'anga*" as Christian practitioners, as opposed to traditional herbalists (Sugishita 2009, 448).

The fervour of the Pentecostal and Charismatic churches that swept the continent since the 1980s is largely due to their active expression of the "gifts of the Holy spirit" (*charismata*), especially deliverance from evil and miraculous healing by the laying on of hands. "Born again" Christians see the Church itself as a place of complete restoration to God's grace. Healing services induce ecstatic states of trance, reminiscent of the phenomenon in African indigenous spirit-cults (see Chapter 5).

Sub-Saharan Africa was particularly hard hit by the HIV epidemic. Characteristic symptoms of AIDS, the diseases caused by HIV infection, such as wasting, persistent skin lesions, and dementia, are all associated in traditional African folklore with witchcraft attacks on the victim's soul. In some areas lack of education about the disease and superstition perpetuated the contagion and put young women at greater risk. In the DRC, for example, rumours spread that those infected could rid themselves of disease by rubbing their bodies with something "attractive", such as a bank note, and leaving it at a crossroads. The disease would supposedly transfer to the passer-by who would pick it up (Schoepf 2017, 125). The same principle of cure by contagion was behind another widespread but misguided idea that infected men could rid themselves of HIV by having sex with a virgin, and the mistaken belief that females could shed it through menstruation. "In the time of AIDS, this advice has … resulted in the rape of young girls and even babies in several countries, particularly South Africa" (ibid., 126). AIDS-related death is now "the second leading cause of death for young women aged 15–24 years in Africa" (UNAIDS 2017).

A denial of the existence of homosexuality in Africa, or rejection of it as a reversal of social order usually associated with witchcraft, coupled with conservative Christians' intolerance of homosexuality as immoral, led to an especially potent and dangerous refusal to face the HIV health crisis head on. In some cases AIDS is still so stigmatizing that families of those who have died from the disease prefer to ascribe the deaths to witchcraft. However, as AIDS in Africa has mostly spread through heterosexual contact, and left unprotected wives and their children especially vulnerable, attitudes about the disease and its treatment changed. This is clearly the case in the proactive way many churches have confronted HIV and AIDS as a problem of the whole person and whole community.

Feature: African churches confronting HIV and AIDS

Christian social values contributed to the rapid spread of the disease. To many Christians condom use suggested the promotion of promiscuity. Also because Christian women are supposed submit to their husbands' authority, many feel they do not have the power to insist on the use of condoms.

In Southern Africa, the sub-region most severely affected by the epidemic, Christian conceptions of health as holiness, and the condemnation of persons living with HIV as sinners meeting divine retribution, changed to accommodate the reality of the healthcare crisis. Churches re-organized programmes of public education to aim at prevention and re-shaped their social services to help infected people cope. Many such new efforts were inspired as much by opportunities for an infusion of funding from foreign donor agencies and eagerness to participate in "global modernity" as by their revised moral postures (Burchardt 2015, 72). Churches re-fashioned themselves as important players in civil society while making faith-based intervention the basis for a new "Christian modernity".

Church outreach to persons living with HIV draws on Christian notions of health and healing that include healing the soul. Participants narrate their lives as intimate self-disclosures in the style of confession, focusing on their diagnoses as the decisive moment of awakening and break with an unwholesome past. Although conventional Christian sexual morality condemns the sinner, these narratives unabashedly acknowledge the contemporary urban realities and sexual politics that victimized them. Rather than salvation, the HIV-positive recruit seeks first and foremost the recovery of personal dignity and social significance.

One of the most serious obstacles to addressing the epidemic effectively in South Africa is the continued insistence by some Pentecostal churches that biomedical treatment is incommensurate with faith in Jesus' healing power (Burchardt 2015). Their leaders may discourage members from using anti-viral medication, resorting only to prayer.

New hybrid programmes aim to address the epidemic more constructively. "Project Hope", an initiative of Hygerberg Hospital in Western Cape, South Africa, fostered unusual cooperation between government, churches and African indigenous healers (*sangomas*) (see Siyayinqoba Beat It! 2008). Its outreach and education draws on Africa's greatest strength, the understanding of health as a collective enterprise.

Conclusion

Far from being solely bio-medical concerns, illness and healing are experiences of crisis when those who suffer as well as those who care about and for them seek out the deeper meaning of the events. The spiritual domain is interpreted as a source of the disturbances, and is also the province that will deliver relief. Ultimately, from the viewpoint of religious practitioners, life and health is a gift from God.

Questions for discussion

- How might aspects of African explanations of illness or experiences of healing be considered commensurate with forms of Western psychotherapy?
- How is your own body a reflection of cultural shaping and religious practice?
- What recommendations would you make to an NGO seeking to address HIV and AIDS and wanting to engage religious practitioners (indigenous healers, Muslim marabouts, Pentecostal pastors, etc.)?

References (*indicates recommended reading)

Bignante, Elisa. 2015. "Therapeutic Landscapes of Traditional Healing: Building Spaces of Well-Being with the Traditional Healer in St. Louis, Senegal", *Social & Cultural Geography* 16/6, 698–713.

Burchardt, Marian. 2015. *Faith in the Time of AIDS: Religion, Biopolitics and Modernity in South Africa*. New York: Palgrave Macmillan.

Devisch, René. 1993. *Weaving the Threads of Life: The Khita Gyn-Eco-Logical Healing Cult among the Yaka*. Chicago: University of Chicago Press.

Germond, Paul, and James Cochrane. 2010. "Healthworlds: Conceptualizing Landscapes of Health and Healing", *Sociology* 44/2, 307–324.

Gouws, Chrisna. 2018. "Traditional African Medicine and Conventional Drugs: Friends or Enemies?" *The Conversation*. http://theconversation.com/traditional-african-medicine-and-conventional-drugs-friends-or-enemies-92695 (accessed 6 March 2018).

Langwick, Stacey. 2017. "The Value of Secrets: Pragmatic Healers and Proprietary Knowledge." In *African Medical Pluralism*, edited by William Olsen and Carolyn Sargent, 31–49. Bloomington: Indiana University Press.

Marsland, Rebecca. 2007. "The Modern Traditional Healer: Locating 'Hybridity' in Modern Traditional Medicine, Southern Tanzania", *Journal of Southern African Studies* 33/4, 751–765.

*Olsen, William, and Carolyn Sargent, editors. 2017. *African Medical Pluralism*. Bloomington: Indiana University Press.

Open Democracy. 2015. "Faith and Health Care in Africa: A Complex Reality." 9 April 2015. http://www.opendemocracy.net/openglobalrights/jill-olivier/faith-and-health-care-in-africa-complex-reality (accessed 20 March 2018).

Parkin, David. 2013. "Medical Crises and Therapeutic Talk", *Anthropology & Medicine* 20/2, 124–141.

Parkin, David. 2017. "Loud Ethics and Quiet Morality among Muslim Healers in Eastern Africa", *Africa* 87/3, 537–553.

Pobee, John. 2001. "Health, Healing and Religion: An African View", *International Review of Mission* 90/356–57, 55–64.

*Prometra.org. 2018. "PRO.ME.TRA International: Promotion of Traditional Medicine." http://prometra.org/ (accessed 5 March 2018).

Rasmussen, Susan. 2012. "Spirit Possession in Africa." In *The Wiley-Blackwell Companion to African Religions*, edited by Elias Bongmba, 184–197. Malden: Wiley-Blackwell.

Schoepf, Brooke Grundfest. 2017. "Medical Pluralism Revisited: A Memoir." In *African Medical Pluralism*, edited by William Olsen and Carolyn Sargent, 110–133. Bloomington: Indiana University Press.

*Siyayinqoba Beat It! 2008. *2004 Ep. 21 – Traditional Healers & HIV*. https://www.youtube.com/watch?v=nv8e950oZ-A (accessed 11 July 2018).

Stroeken, Koen. 2017. "The Individualization of Illness." In *African Medical Pluralism*, edited by William C. Olsen and Carolyn Sargent, 151–169. Bloomington: Indiana University Press.

Sugishita, Kaori. 2009. "Traditional Medicine, Biomedicine and Christianity in Modern Zambia", *Africa* 79/3, 435–454.

Tibbenabawi.org. 2018. "Tibb-e-Nabawi, Healing by ISLAM, both for the Body & Soul, for the Doctor & Patient, for the Sick & Healthy." http://www.tibbenabawi.org/ (accessed 3 March 2018).

Turner, Victor. 1969. *The Ritual Process: Structure and Anti-Structure*. Chicago: Aldine.

UNAIDS (Joint United Nations Programme on HIV/AIDS). 2017. "UNAIDS Data 2017." Geneva, Switzerland. http://www.unaids.org/sites/default/files/media_asset/20170720_Data_book_2017_en.pdf (accessed 11 July 2018).

*Westerlund, David. 2006. *African Indigenous Religions and Disease Causation: From Spiritual Beings to Living Humans*. Leiden: Brill.

13 Religion and Gender in Africa

What is "gender" and how does it relate to "religion"?

In popular usage "sex" and "gender" are often mistakenly used synonymously. But while sex designates a biological distinction, "gender" refers to cultural distinctions between men and women and to the traits and behaviours ascribed to them. Although these are not biological givens, they are often assumed to be "natural" and universal attributes. The factor that perhaps most deeply informs this impression is religion.

Sacred myths about the creation of human beings – and the religious doctrines, ethical norms and ritual practices that derive from them – consistently assign gender qualities and prescribe gendered roles to human beings. These teachings, considered by religious adherents to be revealed by God or handed down by the ancestors, systematically sanction the social arrangements that pattern gender relations, and make them appear timeless and inalterable. In Christian cultures, the biblical narrative of the creation of Adam as the primary human being and Eve as his "helpmeet" formed from Adam's rib is perhaps the most notorious case in point (Genesis 2:3).

From the 1970s, in the wake of the widespread feminist movement, scholars introduced "gender" as a critical and analytical category to challenge the foundation of many academic disciplines including religious studies. Initially, they called for more focus on women's lives and the experiences that shape the actual, lived reality of religions, as opposed to the study of texts and doctrines which were typically composed by male elites and served to further men's interests. This shift opened to view previously unexplored material, adding significant new dimensions to religious studies. But the plethora of contributions with a focus on women's experience led to a mistaken impression that "gender" pertains only to women. More recently there has been an emerging interest in the study of men and masculinity (the ideals and norms related to being a man). Studies in this area examine, for instance, the religio-cultural ideas informing masculinity in African indigenous religions (Dover 2005), the performance of masculinity in Islamic reformist movements (Wario 2012), and the impact of born-again conversion on men's self-perception of masculinity and gender in Pentecostal circles (van Klinken 2013; Lindhardt 2015).

Increasingly scholars have come to question the sex/gender divide. The view that sex is biological and gender is cultural ignores how much the body itself is culturally constructed and how meaning is inscribed in a corporeal way. For example, rituals of initiation, which are so common and fundamental to African indigenous religions, aim to "create" a man or a woman, often by genital cutting. In such a case sex is clearly not natural but culturally shaped, the physical manifestation of a religious ideal.

The sex/gender model was also challenged for recapitulating "crucial Western dualisms of flesh/spirit, body/soul, mind/matter [that] are undeniably gendered; the association of female with flesh, moral weakness, and irrationality and male with spirit, moral strength, and rationality has had a long history in the Western world" (Mikaelsson 2008, 295). Christian teachings endorsing these strong dichotomies sanction a gendered hierarchy as "God-given".

Religious myths of divine pairing and sexual union between the gods, and the prevalence of procreation as a recurring religious theme, privilege heterosexual coupling. Nevertheless, some religions do provide for gender variance, and even elevate ambiguously gendered persons to sacred status or enable them to serve as mediators of divinity (see Chapter 14). One influential scholar of gender studies, Joan Scott (1999), therefore emphasizes the need to study "[gender] discrepancy, even contradiction, in the cultural norms and social roles" within any given society, and advocates "reading for specific meanings rather than assuming uniformity in all spheres and aspects of social life" (206).

Most scholars today reject what they call "gender essentialism", the presentation of culturally prescribed attributes and roles as innate and fundamentally constitutive of maleness or femaleness. Feminism has been criticized for reducing all women's experience to a presumed universal condition and assuming that the experience of women in all times and places is the same as that of Western, white feminists. Scholars now employ gender as a category of analysis to disrupt such comfortable assumptions. Gender-critical thinking interrogates how gender functions, not as "an immutable fact of life or state of being, but rather [as] an expression of social processes" such as religion (Joy 2006, 14).

Judith Butler's (1990) seminal work *Gender Trouble* took these arguments against essentialism further, introducing the idea that gender is always "performative". Gender roles are assumed at will and enacted in conformity with social expectations or mandated behaviour. Gender is therefore more fluid than is often assumed. Under certain conditions the typical gendered roles of men and women become interchangeable. Therefore, gender should not be considered a *thing*, referred to with a noun, but understood as an *activity* in which ideas about what it means to be a man or woman are played out. Religion frames such activity, establishing the norms that govern the performance and as the context for gendered enactment. Religion therefore "engenders" adherents. From this point of view, religion and gender are not separate spheres, but are mutually reinforcing.

In what follows, we will consider the religions of Africa taking care to track how gender roles are inculcated through the imaginative processes of myth and ritual, how they have been legislated through religious institutions, and how they have changed with the social and political upheavals that have shaped the history of the continent.

Gender flexibility in African indigenous religions

In most African indigenous religions, powerful spiritual beings (God, divinities, primordial beings) are portrayed as surpassing gender and sex. Myths and icons depict them as hermaphroditic or sexually amorphous, or they are twinned as a male-female pair that only together bears the fullness of primordial power. Goddesses usually represent the primary sources of life, power and fertility. They are often considered to inhabit bodies of water, to possess cooling and healing qualities and to be the true source of children. This is the case of the Yoruba divinity Oshun, for example. However Yoruba mythology about the primordial couple, Obàtálá, the creator god and god of purity, and his spouse Yemòó depict the goddess as a fearsome power. Insatiably bloodthirsty, she prefers animal blood to the cool waters that are Obàtálá's domain. In traditional iconography, she is obese and bloated, "double the size of her husband" (Olupona 2011, 152). Moreover, she is associated with "the dangerous power of witches, who control the life force that blood symbolizes" (ibid.). This mythology subverts Western preconceptions about gender.

When the divinities manifest themselves through spirit possession, they can "mount" adherents of either sex, so goddesses as well as gods are said to possess "wives" (persons of either sex) who submit to their bidding. Among the Yoruba, the priests of Shango, the male god of thunder and righteous vengeance, "are transvestites who take on the role of male 'wives' of the deities by wearing female costumes and plaiting their hair in a feminine style" (Olajuba 2005, 3403).

In many indigenous African societies gender is performed according to one's position of responsibility and authority, and as a function of age. Such gender flexibility is most forcefully demonstrated by Ifi Amadiume's (1987) groundbreaking work, *Male Daughters, Female Husbands*. Writing about the Igbo people (in present-day Nigeria), she suggests that because there is no gendered pronoun in the Igbo language (as is the case for most African languages), the gender distinction between males and females is conceptually less determinative. To speak of a daughter or husband is to refer to a relative social position, which may be occupied by a person of either sex. In Igbo tradition "female husbands" are mature women who, by virtue of their acquisition of wealth and power are able to assume the role of protector and provider. A female husband does so for the sake of another woman (for example, a widow otherwise without resources whom she then married). The position of "husband" is freed from its gendered association with men. Likewise the role of "daughter" is loosed from the necessity of that role being occupied by a female. Thus rank and the social rights and obligations associated with it outweigh the importance of sex as the determinative factor. Behaviour similarly defies Western expectations. "Women as daughters also [play] male roles in ritual matters or in positions of authority over wives" but do so without becoming "man-like" (Amadiume 1987, 16–17).

As persons age they are believed to take on greater spiritual power. Female elders past menopause occupy a transcendent status as human beings who have surpassed gender. This widespread conception of their special nature is most clearly expressed in ritual performance.

Feature: Igbo indigenous religion, gender flexibility and "female genital power"

The Igbo culture is patrilineal, meaning that descent is traced from the male line, and its social order was founded on divine kingship. However, the Igbo town of Nnobi was originally the seat of worship of the river goddess Idemili, whose all-encompassing religion surpassed the importance of the cult of the ancestors (Amadiume 1987, 21). The central shrine was occupied by a titled woman called "The Great Woman" (*Agba Ekwe*), who symbolized concepts of womanhood derived from the goddess (54). She was also known as *Eze Nwanyi* (female king) (174). In pre-colonial times Idemili religion bound the region under one law overseen by the *Agba Ekwe*, whose political and judicial determinations were never disputed (55). She also oversaw the Women's Council, a powerful institution with its own rules that adjudicated all matters concerning women, to safeguard their rights and protect women against abuse. The meetings of the Women's Council were conducted in secrecy and were "feared and respected by the men-folk" (66). Their strongest weapon was a collective ritual in which the female elders would assert their prerogatives as the bearers of supreme moral authority. They "attacked viciously any decision or law which denied them, or interfered with, their means of livelihood" (66–67). Waging spiritual battle, the female elders stripped naked (or "half-naked") and struck the ground with old pestles in the gesture of a curse; they marched together to besiege the home of the offender or headquarters of the government deemed guilty of corruption or abuse of power, to aggressively assert their demands – even to the point of the destruction of property – until they obtain satisfaction.

In *An Intimate Rebuke*, Laura Grillo (2018) situates the Women's Council's collective mobilization and ritual curse as an example of an ancient and widespread phenomenon still practised throughout West Africa today, the deployment of what she calls "Female Genital Power." Post-menopausal elders, referred to as "the Mothers", are considered the living embodiment of the ancestors, the guardians of the moral order, and conduits of the paramount spiritual power to protect the community. The seat of this power is the female sex. No longer defined by their repro-ductive function, they defy classification by biological sex. The focus is, therefore, not the womb, organ of reproduction, but the genitalia as an emblem of "matrifocal morality", the primary bond on which society established its foundational moral mandates. Appealing to their genitals as a living altar to their innate force, these women ritually elicit the most perilous of curses against any evil that threatens the community (Grillo 2018, 2). They strip, pound the ground, and slap their genitals as they curse the enemy. This act of spiritual combat is a dangerous taboo for men to view. It is performed both as a spiritual rite to counter witchcraft, and as a form of political activism against governmental corruption and violence. Through their performance, these elders engender power in a unique way, unified in their self-understanding as the supreme embodiment of the moral code.

Gender and power in African secret societies

More overtly "religious" in nature than the Women's Councils are the secret societies, whose membership is restricted to one sex. Throughout Africa secrecy is a means of ensuring the proper management of knowledge by restricting it to those prepared to handle it. Initiation transmits spiritual knowledge and inculcates its supporting values. Sanctions against disclosing secrets are severe. However, it is well known that the collective initiation into secret societies at puberty is the occasion for instructing youth about sex and sexuality, teaching them about gender ideals and social etiquette, and for "making" a gendered person in ritual.

One of the best-known societies of this kind is the ancient, widespread, and enduring male masking society, Poro, and its arguably more important female counterpart, Sande (also known as Bundu), found in Mande-speaking societies in West Africa. The head of the Sande society is called Sowei, like the mask that represents female power. She is not only inducted as a member of Poro, but holds its highest office. The practice of placing a matron at the head of a male secret society is common.

Sande presents a rare instance in which women make and don the masks that represent them. The iconography of the principal mask (Sowei) communicates ideals of womanhood and female power. The elaborately plaited coiffure identifies women with Great Mother Earth and her abundant flora. The fleshy neck coils render homage to the river goddess and suggest that women are spiritual beings who rose from that sacred source. The face portrays downcast eyes and small closed mouth, an image of containment and "cooling" power. The archetypal carvings at the crest, comprised of three or five segmented petals protrude unabashedly like the spread vulva. (See Figure 13.1.) The female sex is thus glorified as the sacred locus of female power (Grillo 2018). However, an integral part of Sande is excision, a genital operation that slices away the clitoris and labia minora, known as female genital mutilation (FGM) (see below). The pain of the operation supposedly bonds women of the society, enhances their political power, and instils supernatural empowerment (MacCormack 1979).

Figure 13.1 The Sande Sowei (Bundu) mask representing ideal qualities of womanhood
(courtesy of the British Museum)

Female genital mutilation as cultural rite or human rights crisis

"Excision" refers to a ritual operation on the female genitals that profoundly
and irreversibly alters their appearance and function. The word, derived from
Latin, does not exist in African languages. The Igbo (Nigeria) call it "having a

bath" (*Isa aru* or *Iwuaru*). The Bambara (Mali) refer to it as "washing of one's hands", while in Soninke (Senegal) it is *saline*, "cleansing in order to access prayer" (Zabus 2007, 10). These euphemisms connote that the intention is to purify the female body, to make it holy and acceptable before God, and underscore that the genital cutting is intended as a religious act. To Muslims it suggests the requirement that one must perform ablutions, or ritual bathing, before coming to prayer. However these phrases hide the truth: that excision is a painful, dangerous and traumatizing operation with serious life-long ramifications for a woman's health and well-being. Even when they do not suffer shock or die from infection or haemorrhage, women regularly experience severe complications like incontinence, fistulas, keloid scarring and painful intercourse. Excision is of three types:

> The first ... involves a partial clitoridectomy, often understood as the removal of the prepuce or hood of the clitoris. Second, excision per se, also called clitoridectomy, involves the removal of the said prepuce and the clitoris itself and is often accompanied by partial or full labiadectomy. Third, infibulation, or "suturing," consists of the complete removal of the clitoris, the labia minora, and the labia majora and the stitching together of the two sides (the cut edges) of the vulva so as to cover the urethra and vaginal opening, leaving a very small aperture to permit the flow of urine and menstrual discharge.
>
> (Zabus 2007, 11)

This most radical form is usually not part of an initiation or religious rite of passage. Mostly practised in Somalia and the Sudan, it is called "Pharaonic circumcision," but is a far cry from male circumcision that neither deprives males of sexual pleasure nor precludes normal, pain-free sexual function. The woman's body is aesthetically fashioned, closed by sealing the wound with thorns used like skewers. Infibulation later requires that the sutures be cut opened for intercourse or childbirth.

The origin of excision is unknown, but was likely a pre-Islamic practice of ancient Nubia, now Sudan. Considerable evidence indicates it was practised in Egypt by the first millennium BCE. Its geographical distribution corresponds with the Arab caravan and slave-trading routes across Africa from Yemen to Senegal, down the Nile from Egypt to Tanzania. Evidence suggests it was adopted as a means to guarantee the virginity of female slaves as prized goods. Excision is not mentioned in the Qu'ran, leading some Muslim theologians to view it as a barbaric "innovation" (*buda'*) that defies the sanctity of bodily integrity (Zabus 2007, 148).

Operations on the genitalia of both sexes are performed throughout sub-Saharan Africa during initiations in order to construct unambiguously gendered bodies. They remove the vestiges of the presumed original hermaphroditism, which according to cosmogonic myths is the natural human condition. Excision and male circumcision recapitulate the common mythic theme in which a blood sacrifice of a primordial being establishes the world and infuses its vital force. An example well known in ethnographic literature is the mythic tradition of the Dogon of Mali, in which God (Amma) sacrifices the Nommo, the twin of the primordial trickster, Ogo, to purify the world and set right the disorder that Ogo's disobedience had loosed on creation.

Believing that excision makes a woman feminine, cultivated and honourable, women perpetuate the practice. Yet the severe pain, psychological trauma and disastrous physical ramifications of excision have led to international efforts to eradicate excision altogether. In Khartoum in October 1984 Africans from 14 countries formed the Inter-African Committee on Traditional Practices (IAC), to advocate eliminating "female genital mutilation" but noted that it "can only be changed through coordinated collective action by practising communities" (IAC 2018). It is worth noting that referring to genital cutting as "mutilation" condemns this operation without applying the same judgement to male circumcision. The World Health Organization calls FGM a violation of human rights of global concern (WHO 2018). In 2017 the United Nations Secretary-General António Guterres renewed the Sustainable Development Agenda that promises to end the practice by 2030 (UN News 2017).

Veiling (hijab) and the gendered performance of Islam in Africa

The genders are mutually constructed, largely in relation to power. Therefore "how one exercises or relates to authority is always shaped by one's gender, even if this fact is more obvious in the case of women than it is for men" (Frede and Hill 2014, 132). This is especially evident in the phenomenon of women's veiling, generally referred to as hijab.

The place and role of women is central to the moral imagination in Muslim societies, and veiling as its symbol has become the focus of highly visible political and cultural contests around the globe today. In Africa, stylized rehearsals of gender norms have been rapidly changing in response to pressures to veil. Increasingly as a way to signal religious identity and commitment Muslim women wear headscarves in public, veil the face, or adopt an Arabic-style dress that covers a woman's entire body, with each representing a different degree of the principle of veiling (hijab). Such dress is a performance of gender, a very public spectacle of shielding from view of that which is most prized: the contained female body, and women's humility and deference in male-dominated Islam.

While Western feminists interpret veiling as a sign of internalized repression, self-denial and seclusion, Muslim women do not necessarily view themselves as marginalized or powerless. Some claim to derive "prestige and authority from upholding prevalent norms of feminine piety" (Frede and Hill 2014, 149). In Mali women played an active part in an Islamic moral renewal movement by advocating strict dress codes as "the embodied performance of virtue" that would set them apart as devout adherents (Schulz 2008, 21). In Côte d'Ivoire as well, women who became active in Islamic revival abandoned the *boubou*, the ample garment traditionally worn by Muslim women in the region, and adopted the strict Arab-style dress code as a signal of Muslim piety, even using it for proselytism. Young women made neighbourhood rounds to supervise others' behaviour and encourage Muslim women to adopt Arab-style dress. By "dress [ing] like a good Muslim", women are able to maintain a visible presence in public spaces and circulate freely rather than remain restricted to the private domestic sphere (Leblanc 2014, 176). Veiling is a public performance of gender that allows women to shift "from being 'objects of religious regulation' to 'agents of religious transformation'" (189).

Nevertheless many mainstream Muslim women reject the idea that the hijab is empowering. They charge that compulsory veiling is an oppressive imposition of a cultural standard dating to the Ottoman Empire that signals the resurgence of the Islamic State and its repressive gender ideology. They underscore that veiling is not mandated by the Qu'ran or hadith as a religious requirement.

Detractors note that the word "hijab" is also used to refer to the hymen, as the "veil" of virginity, thus associating veiling with infibulation as parallel means of exerting male control over access to women's bodies, agency, sexuality and reproductive capacity (Zabus 2007, 106). The recent demand that Muslim women veil is therefore necessarily linked to "the notion that 'the woman is *awrah*', or forbidden, an idea that leads to the confinement, subordination, silencing and subjugation of women's voices and presence in public society" (Nomani and Arafa 2015).

En-gendering African Christianity

A strong priority of the earliest missions in West Africa, both Protestant and Catholic, was the making of Christian families as patriarchal units (Toungara 2001, 41). Records of the Anglican Church Missionary Society (CMS) dating back to 1804 show that a very particular ideology of gender was imposed through the mission schools – one that reflected the Victorian ideals of the white middle class. Their expressed aim was to provide suitable marriage companions for the young male converts by inculcating ideals of feminine virtue to African girls: "domesticity, conjugal fidelity and selflessness" (Leach 2008, 335). Nakedness was considered lewd and associated with promiscuity, therefore sewing was a key component of girls' education. Sewing produced modest clothing to contain if not control female sexuality. Gendered dress encouraged gendered roles and vice versa.

Both colonial administrators and missionaries promoted patriarchy:

> Under the guise of protection, family codes reinforced patriarchal authority over women and children, and, in some cases, left women with less power than they had exercised under customary law with regard to their property rights and traditional economic responsibilities.
>
> (Toungara 2001, 54)

By restructuring African women's lives to conform to Western gender ideals, missionaries undermined customs that protected women's autonomy, especially strong in matrilineal societies. The Christian model of the family restricted females to subservient domesticity while in many West African indigenous societies, women played active roles outside the household (Bastian 2000, 152). Traditional women could become priestesses, prophets, healers/diviners; they could take up roles as "market queens" or be members of other titled societies. Women belonged to self-governing secret societies. By contrast the Christians remained isolated in marriage (149). Christian values contravened customary expectations that young women conceive a child before marriage as an essential proof of fertility. The missionaries condemned the promiscuous behaviour of such "shameless women".

The "modern" mission schools that inculcated 19th century gender ideology remained "remarkably unchanged well into the twentieth century" (Leach 2008, 336). Patriarchal civil codes displaced many matrilineal traditions and Africans today increasingly make sexist assumptions about women's "natural" subservience. African Christian feminist theologians are now reclaiming pre-colonial traditions to promote gender equality in church and society (Oduyoye 1995).

Although Pentecostal-Charismatic movements are even less accommodating to African Indigenous Religions than mainline churches, there is great potential for this form of Christianity to support gender equality on the basis of the idea that the gifts and power of the Holy Spirit are distributed among women and men equally. Several Pentecostal churches have been founded and/or are led by women pastors, and women play prominent roles in prophecy and healing. In this sense, these churches reclaim the role that women enjoyed in indigenous religions as mediators of the sacred.

However, the experiences of exceptional women on the charismatic scene do not necessarily empower women more generally, as Jane Soothill (2010) demonstrates in her study of the prominent role of the powerful pastor's wife and of women's leadership in a female-founded church in Ghana. In the case of Francisca Duncan-Williams, this wife of a charismatic pastor played the classic role of subservient "helpmeet" and garnered visibility and power only by extension of her husband's patronage. When she divorced her prominent husband, the once adulated Francisca was ejected from the ministry and "vilified as a bossy and adulterous wife" (91). Like wives of many African politicians, pastors' wives recapitulated the "First Lady Syndrome", in which political wives and their elite entourage "serve male dictatorships whilst advancing conservative gender ideologies to the detriment of democracy and gender equality" (89). The case of Rev. Christie Doe Tetteh, the most renowned charismatic female preacher in Ghana, proved equally disappointing. Far from offering new avenues for gender equity and female empowerment, Rev. Tetteh followed a traditional model of "'big man' politics" (93). She demanded loyal allegiance, and promised to bestowed spiritual power in return. Moreover, she appeared to act in the mode of the so-called Mothers, post-menopausal elders who "control the influence of witchcraft", but who equally threaten to curse their foes (92).

Where Soothill suggests that the fascination with the spiritual realm and its gifts does not necessarily translate into gains in the social world, other scholars argue that Pentecostalism does, in fact, bring about some form of social, economic and political empowerment. They point, for instance, to the ways in which churches encourage economic entrepreneurship among women and help them develop the necessary skills (Parsitau 2012). Another area of gender transformation is the domestic sphere, where women benefit from the new concepts of masculinity promoted in Pentecostal churches. Ultimately, Pentecostal gender ideology and politics appear to be complex and paradoxical, making it difficult to offer a straightforward appraisal.

Feature: Pentecostal and Catholic masculinities in Zambia

In *Transforming Masculinities in African Christianity: Gender Controversies in Times of AIDS*, Adriaan van Klinken (2013) explores how churches in Zambia address the epidemic by transforming conceptions of masculinity. He focuses on Zambia, a country heavily affected by HIV, and presents two case studies, of a Pentecostal church and of a Catholic parish, both located in Lusaka, Zambia's capital. Aware that prevalent notions of masculinity in Zambian society played a critical role in HIV transmission, gender-based domestic and sexual violence and other social problems, both churches were involved in efforts to work with men to instil alternative, more constructive gender ideals. In both cases this typically happened in a discourse of "irresponsible" versus "responsible" forms of masculinity.

In the Pentecostal case, men's irresponsibility tended to be explained with reference to "African culture", suggesting that men are in bondage to traditional definitions of masculinity from which they need to be delivered. This reflects the wider Pentecostal theme of "making a break with the past". The bishop delivered a series of sermons about "Fatherhood in the 21st century", in which he emphasized that Jesus Christ could liberate men from sinful, irresponsible forms of masculinity, and promoted instead an ideal of "biblical manhood". He argued that male headship does not mean aggressive dominance, but that men should take their "God-given responsibilities" and demonstrate "servant leadership" in their families and in society at large. Men attending this Pentecostal church who shared their born again conversion stories tended to present themselves as former "bad boys" who had become responsible husbands and fathers.

The Catholic parish did not emphasize discontinuity or "breaking with the past". Instead, in line with the Catholic idea of "inculturation", they experimented with reclaiming traditional initiation rites that prepared men to become good husbands (and women good wives). Moreover, rather than preaching an ideal of "Catholic manhood", the role model for Catholic men was presented in the figure of St Joachim who, according to Catholic tradition, was the father of Mary and grandfather of Jesus. Adopted by the parish men's organization as their patron saint, St Joachim presented a model of marital love and faithfulness, family responsibility and religious piety. Members of the organization typically wear a blue and white uniform, whose colours symbolize his spiritual faith and moral purity. Although a Catholic figure, St Joachim reflects the traditional ideals of adult masculinity in Zambia, defined by maturity, responsibility, wisdom and respectability.

In both churches, men's involvement was motivated by the HIV epidemic. Many of them had seen their peers become infected and die of AIDS, making them determined to adopt an alternative masculinity. Although feminist-minded scholars may well argue that these Christian versions of masculinity are still based on patriarchal notions such as male headship, for the men involved, these alternative visions of masculinity are truly "transformative" and "redemptive".

Conclusion

These examples serve as a caution to outside observers not to assume that there is any universal or essential understanding of gender identity, and not to impose desired patterns of gender relations on their subjects. Similarly, one cannot assume that gender roles and relations are consistent within a religious tradition, even a "world religion". Instead these case studies point to the need for deeper reflection on how to analyze unfamiliar dynamics of power, including gender relations, in their own contexts. African gender studies make substantial contributions to debates on the distinction of sex and gender and on gender as a cultural performance.

Questions for discussion

- Today, as efforts to abandon genital modification are gaining ground in Africa, young girls and women in the United States and the UK are now seeking out female cosmetic genital surgery (FCGS), and "labiaplasty" is a fast-growing medical specialty. What might be driving this effort to make the most private, and essentially invisible, parts of the body conform to an imaginary gender ideal? Is FCGS the same as FGM?
- How might an increased knowledge of African matrilineal traditions among African Christians and Muslims influence gender relations today?
- How is the HIV epidemic changing gender relations and sexuality in Africa?
- Racist and sexist stereotypes about Africans endure in the west. Do you think that they affect academic research on gender in Africa? How?

References (*indicates recommended reading)

Amadiume, Ifi. 1987. *Male Daughters, Female Husbands: Gender and Sex in an African Society*. London: Zed Books.

Bastian, Misty. 2000. "Young Converts: Christian Missions, Gender and Youth in Onitsha, Nigeria 1880–1929", *Anthropological Quarterly* 73/3, 145–158.

Butler, Judith. 1990. *Gender Trouble: Feminism and the Subversion of Identity*. New York: Routledge.

Dover, Paul. 2005. "Gender and Embodiment: Expectations of Manliness in a Zambian Village." In *African Masculinities: Men in Africa from the Late Nineteenth Century to the Present*, edited by Lahoucine Ouzgane and Robert Morrell, 173–188. New York: Palgrave Macmillan.

Frede, Britta, and Joseph Hill. 2014. "Introduction: En-Gendering Islamic Authority in West Africa", *Islamic Africa* 5/2, 131–165.

*Grillo, Laura. 2018. *An Intimate Rebuke: Female Genital Power in Ritual and Politics in West Africa*. Durham: Duke University Press.

IAC (Inter-African Committee on Traditional Practices). 2018. "FGM," http://iac-ciaf.net/fgm/ (accessed 11 July 2018).

Joy, Morny. 2006. "Gender and Religion: A Volatile Mixture", *Temenos* 42/1, 7–30.

LeBlanc, Marie Nathalie. 2014. "Piety, Moral Agency, and Leadership: Dynamics around the Feminization of Islamic Authority in Côte d'Ivoire", *Islamic Africa* 5/2, 167–198.

Leach, Fiona. 2008. "African Girls, Nineteenth-Century Mission Education and the Patriarchal Imperative", *Gender and Education* 20/4, 335–347.

Lindhardt, Martin. 2015. "Men of God: Neo-Pentecostalism and Masculinities in Urban Tanzania", *Religion* 45/2, 252–272.

MacCormack, Carol. 1979. "Sande: The Public Face of a Secret Society." In *The New Religions of Africa*, edited by Bennetta Jules-Rosette, 27–37. Norwood: Ablex Publishing.

*Mikaelsson, Lisbeth. 2008. "Gendering the History of Religions." In *New Approaches to the Study of Religion*, edited by Peter Antes, Armin Geertz, and R.R. Warne, 295–316. Berlin: De Gruyter.

Nomani, Asra, and Hala Arafa. 2015. "As Muslim Women, We Actually Ask You Not to Wear the Hijab in the Name of Interfaith Solidarity." *Washington Post*, sec. Opinion. https://www.washingtonpost.com/news/acts-of-faith/wp/2015/12/21/as-muslim-women-we-actually-ask-you-not-to-wear-the-hijab-in-the-name-of-interfaith-solidarity/ (accessed 11 July 2018).

Oduyoye, Mercy Amba. 1995. *Daughters of Anowa: African Women and Patriarchy*. Maryknoll: Orbis.

Olajuba, Oyeronke. 2005. "Gender and Religion: Gender and African Religious Traditions." *Encyclopedia of Religion*. Detroit: Macmillan Reference USA, 3400–3406.

*Olupona, Jacob. 2011. *City of 201 Gods: Ilé-Ifè in Time, Space, and the Imagination*. Berkeley: University of California Press.

Parsitau, Damaris. 2012. "Agents of Gendered Change: Empowerment, Salvation and Gendered Transformation in Urban Kenya." In *Pentecostalism and Development: Churches, NGOs and Social Change in Africa*, edited by Dena Freeman, 203–221. New York: Palgrave Macmillan.

Schulz, Dorothea. 2008. "(Re)Turning to Proper Muslim Practice: Islamic Moral Renewal and Women's Conflicting Assertions of Sunni Identity in Urban Mali", *Africa Today* 54/4, 21–43.

Scott, Joan Wallach. 1999. *Gender and the Politics of History*. New York: Columbia University Press.

Soothill, Jane. 2010. "The Problem with 'Women's Empowerment': Female Religiosity in Ghana's Charismatic Churches", *Studies in World Christianity* 16/1, 82–99.

Toungara, Jeanne Maddox. 2001. "Changing the Meaning of Marriage: Women and Family Law in Côte d'Ivoire." In *Gender Perspectives on Property and Inheritance: A Global Source Book*, edited by Sarah Cummings, 33–51. Oxford: Oxfam.

UN News. 2017. "UN Urges Renewed Fight to End Female Genital Mutilation as Populations Grow Where Practice Occurs." UN News. https://news.un.org/en/story/2017/02/550882-un-urges-renewed-fight-end-female-genital-mutilation-populations-grow-where (accessed 11 July 2018).

*Van Klinken, Adriaan. 2013. *Transforming Masculinities in African Christianity: Gender Controversies in Times of AIDS*. Farnham: Ashgate.

Wario, Halkano Abdo. 2012. "Reforming Men, Refining Umma: Tablīghī Jamāᵇat and Novel Visions of Islamic Masculinity," *Religion and Gender* 2/2, 231–253.

WHO (World Health Organization). 2018. "Female Genital Mutilation." WHO Media Centre, http://www.who.int/mediacentre/factsheets/fs241/en/ (accessed 17 April 2018).

Zabus, Chantal. 2007. *Between Rites and Rights: Excision in Women's Experiential Texts and Human Contexts*. Stanford: Stanford University Press.

14 Religion and sexuality in Africa

Introduction

Opening this chapter, it is important to reiterate a point made by Sylvia Tamale, that discourses on and research into sexuality in Africa have often been part of and shaped by colonizing agendas. "African bodies and sexualities became focal points for justifying and legitimising the fundamental objectives of colonialism: to civilise the barbarian and savage natives of the 'dark continent'" (Tamale 2011, 14). This legacy continues to influence certain writings about sexuality in Africa. It is time, according to Tamale (2011, 22), for "rewriting and rerighting African sexualities", which includes highlighting positive aspects of sexuality in African cultures such as its associations with pleasure, eroticism and desire. This chapter aims to present a nuanced and critical account, acknowledging the complexity of African sexualities, and to do justice to both positive and negative aspects.

Religion, sexuality and fertility

Any discussion of the relation between religion and sexuality in Africa may need to start with the acknowledgement that African religions, in a certain way, are "fertility religions", meaning that they are concerned with human procreation (which does not mean, as discussed later, that sex *only* serves procreative purposes). On a practical yet fundamental level, this concern can be seen as a response to socio-economic needs:

> Throughout Southern, East and Central Africa for the past two thousand years the political economy was profoundly shaped by labor shortages at key points in the production cycle. In a relatively precarious environment and climate, this could endanger the survival of the society. Survival then constituted a powerful incentive to maximize family size, to construct gender relations that emphasized fertility, to conflate sexuality with procreation, and to anchor religio-political institutions within and around fecund, stable heterosexual relationships.
>
> (Epprecht 2012, 516)

However, there may be more to this. According to Laurenti Magesa, African indigenous religions centre on what he calls the "vital force of life", that is, the mystical power of divine origin through which God, spirits, ancestors and human persons are interconnected. One of the consequences of this belief is a strong "emphasis on fecundity", because it is through procreation that the life force is transmitted to the next generation and the possibility of becoming an ancestor is opened up (Magesa 1997, 53). Against this background, Magesa explains the significance of traditional initiation rites where detailed instruction is given about sexuality:

> Instruction in this area is exhaustive as the transmission of life and the preservation of the life force depends on sexuality. Coded language is almost always used, but there is little doubt about its meaning; sexual enjoyment is good, but it must be accompanied by sexual responsibility.
>
> (Magesa 1997, 98)

The question of ethics, how "sexual responsibility" is perceived, is also shaped by the belief in the force of life. Basically, acceptable sexual relationships are those which contribute to the flourishing of human life in relation to the ancestors and spirit world. This allows for a significant level of sexual freedom, on the one hand, as sex is something to experiment with – especially during one's youth – and to enjoy. For example, writing about the Makhuwa people in Mozambique, Signe Arnfred (2011, 260) observes how young women during initiation rites are "instructed in the art of lovemaking", as women are "expected to be proficient in the erotic arts". Yet it also means, on the other hand, that certain sexual taboos, such as on sex during women's monthly periods, must be strictly observed. Although both blood and semen are regarded as powerful carriers of the force of life and of one's lineage, menstrual blood has a negative connotation because an excessive flow of blood is associated with death; thus, menstruation leaves the woman ritually "cold" and therefore she cannot be in contact with the "heat" of semen.

Sex before marriage – a major taboo in the Abrahamic religions – was not so much an issue in African traditional societies. In fact, sexual experimentation was encouraged, and often there were structures in place to facilitate this. An example of this is the *maji* house in Sukuma communities (in present-day Tanzania), where girls after their first menstruation would stay together, and would at night be visited by young men in the village – an institution that the Christian missionaries saw as immoral (Allen 2000). Sexual relations outside marriage were also not necessarily frowned upon, as long as there was a certain level of discretion and they would not result in pregnancies. Even among the nomadic Tuareg people in the Sahara, who have long practised Islam, there was a relative "freedom of sexual action" for both women and men, with both partners allowed to have affairs before and even in the first few years of marriage (Bledsoe and Cohen 1993, 58).

Referring to examples like these, Arnfred (2004, 16) concludes that "marriage in Africa in precolonial days dealt with control of fertility, more than with control of sexuality as such". This is not to say that marriage was not important. Many of the ceremonies around marriage in African cultures serve to create the right ritual and social context for the force of life to be transmitted, as it is through procreative sex that not only two individuals are connected but two lineages. As Magesa (1997, 120) puts it:

> The sexual, reproductive, and relational ethics of African marriage must be located and viewed within the context of relationships that affect the life of two families and communities involved in the marriage union. By "life" is understood not only biological life, but life in its comprehensive sense of the strength of vital forces. It involves love and fidelity, faith and trust, and the promotion of everything that fosters an ever-closer union between the spouses. This is important because it prevents dissension and promotes harmony in a marriage and in this way protects the vital forces.

Considering the enormous concern with transmitting life, one can imagine that infertility poses serious problems. Barrenness among women and impotence among men are widely abhorred and are often explained in relation to spiritual causes. Indeed, this observation about the Karanga people in Zimbabwe applies more generally in Africa: "Infertility is viewed as a curse from the spirits" (Shoko 2007, 23). Yet paradoxically, Magesa (1997, 146) observes that in some parts of the continent, barren and impotent people are sometimes believed to "possess special mystical powers that can be used for the good of the society. Divination, rain-asking, and mediumship are powers that these people are said to hold." This reflects a principle that can be observed in many religions, that any aberration is often held to be simultaneously taboo *and* sacred.

As much as the concern with fertility is informed by African indigenous religions, it can also be commonly found in Christian and Muslim communities. Thus, among Muslim Hausa communities in Northern Nigeria, high fertility rates are considered to be vital to "the survival of family names", "the immortality of lineages", as well as to "securing the future of Islam", with large families being seen to symbolize "wealth, influence, respect and fame" (Izugbara and Ezeh 2010, 197–8, 196). In cases of fertility problems, the Tuareg people in West African countries such as Mali and Niger traditionally resorted to the ritual assistance of *marabouts* (Muslim spiritual leaders), who are believed to hold sacred blessing powers known as *albaraka* (Rasmussen 2004). Similarly, writing about contemporary Pentecostal churches in Ghana, Kwabena Asamoah-Gyadu (2007, 440) observes an understanding that "biological infertility, sterility or barrenness is a spiritually caused condition" – an understanding which, he argues, "sustains ideas that are also prevalent in traditional thought". Several of these churches run ministries of healing specifically aiming at securing "fruits of the wombs", and ministries of deliverance specifically seeking to break the "bondage of barrenness". Childlessness is believed to be caused by demons, evil powers or witchcraft, and pastors perform the role traditionally occupied by diviners and healers, of providing a spiritual solution. When fruitfulness does not come naturally, it will be achieved miraculously through the intervention of pastors and their mediation of divine power. Where most of these ritual activities in the area of fertility do specifically target women, who traditionally bear the brunt of the accusations and blame for childlessness, more recently men have been targeted too.

Feature: Pastors blessing penises

In 2016, Pastor Daniel Obinim of the International God's Way Church in the Ashanti region in Ghana, sparked controversy. Locally, the pastor was already known for various rather extreme practices, such as stepping on a woman's belly as part of a deliverance ritual, and publicly flogging a young couple who had got pregnant out of wedlock. But this time Obinim received international headlines, such as in British boulevard newspaper *The Sun*, reading: "Shocking video shows con-artist Bishop blessing men's PENISES to make them grow bigger" (Cambridge 2016). The newspaper reports how the pastor in his church performed a ritual on men in order to enlarge their penises through spiritual power. It includes videos, originally published on (but now removed from) the church's online TV channel, depicting large numbers of men of various ages, expectantly lining up in front of the church to be administered by the self-proclaimed man of God, who one by one lays his hands on the private parts of the faithful while praying over them. Obinim reportedly said, "If you have a small manhood, I can change them all when I come to the spiritual realm."

It is easy to dismiss Obinim as a con pastor who is trying to make money out of his desperate followers. Yet his case does not stand on its own. For instance, in 2017 there was a similar case in Zambia, with Prophet Bernard Siame claiming that he had miraculously doubled the size of the penis of a man who had come for help after his wife had left him because of his small penis. When Siame was criticized by another Pentecostal leader for his intervention being "un-biblical" and a "magical stunt", he retorted by saying that it is better for a person to seek manhood enlargement services from a pastor, who has received healing powers from God, than go to a witch doctor (The Church Newspaper Zambia 2017).

Anyone travelling in Africa may have seen posters put on walls or trees, or may have been handed leaflets, advertising penis enlargement and potency enhancement (Figure 14.1). Usually these services are offered by people presenting themselves as "traditional healer" or "herbalist", and sometimes as "doctor" or "professor", but the above cases demonstrate that more recently Christian figures have also engaged this market. Moreover, there are similar examples of Muslim *marabouts* in West African countries such as Benin, often presenting themselves through social media such as Facebook (cf. Observers 2014). These healers (whether fake or not) tap into widespread concerns that are related to what anthropologist Paul Dover describes as "the expectations of manliness" centring on male virility. Dover's argument about the culture of the Goba people (in present-day Zambia) applies to many other African peoples: "The big man is a virile man. In Goba culture, the phallus defines masculinity: potency, fertility, and male strength are combined. ... The phallus is therefore not just a symbol of authority, it 'stands' for life-giving creative power" (Dover 2005, 182). Against this background, one can understand the concern about small penises and impotence, as well as the popularity of religious rituals addressing such concerns.

The fact that African cultures are characterized by a concern with fertility should not be taken to imply that sex only serves procreative purposes or is not linked to desire, pleasure and romance. There is a long tradition of Western writing suggesting that romantic love did not exist in pre-colonial African societies, and that sexual relationships in Africa are purely instrumental. Yet more recent scholarship challenges such assumptions and draws attention to the complex links between sex and love. "Even in the most conservative Islamic communities that systematically practiced arranged marriages, Africans often exhibited a great degree of freedom in making decisions based on emotional attachment" (Decker 2015, 2). It is acknowledged, however, that notions of romantic love are affected by broader dynamics of social, cultural and religious change, such as caused by colonialism, the spread of Christianity and Islam,

Figure 14.1 Tree with penis enlargement adverts in Lusaka, Zambia (Adriaan van Klinken, 2013)

globalization and popular culture (Cole and Thomas 2009). Nowadays, modern notions of romantic love are actively promoted, not only through films produced in Nollywood (the film industry in Nigeria) and elsewhere on the continent, but also in popular gospel songs and by churches offering services for dating as well as pre-marital counselling.

Religion and same-sex intimacy

Against the background of the concern with fertility, one can understand that homosexuality as it is known in Western societies today – as a distinct and exclusive sexual identity – is difficult to imagine and accept in African cultures. As Magesa puts it in his book about African indigenous religions:

> Active homosexuality is morally intolerable because it frustrates the whole purpose of sexual pleasure and that of a human person's existence in the sight of the ancestors and God. ... It is clear how such an expression would be directly antagonistic to what the ancestors and the preservation and transmission of life stand for.
>
> (Magesa 1997, 146)

However, this way of putting it may be a bit too black-and-white, and is perhaps informed by Magesa's own position as a Catholic priest representing the view of his church. As Marc Epprecht (2012, 516) suggests, indigenous religions "were in fact less dogmatically intolerant of, and indeed sometimes more respectful towards, sexual difference than is frequently claimed." The crucial point is that the concern, in African religions, is not so much with sexual morality as such, but with fertility. What follows from this is that an individual does not necessarily have to suppress same-sex desires and behaviour, but "that she or he never allows such desires to overshadow or supplant procreation" (Murray and Roscoe 1998, 273). In other words, as long as one lives up to the important obligation of transmitting the force of life to a next generation, there is a certain level of freedom to pursue other interests and desires. Epprecht (2012, 522), writing about the Shona people in present-day Zimbabwe, observes "a tradition of great public discretion about sexual matters" including same-sex practices. He suggests that this culture of discretion "meant that acts which were forbidden in theory could be tolerated as long as the community was not compelled to pay explicit attention" (ibid.).

Indeed, there is substantial archaeological, historical and anthropological evidence of same-sex relationships being practised in various forms across the African continent, often in combination with levels of gender ambiguity and fluidity, such as in the cases of boy-wives, female husbands and ancestral wives (Murray and Roscoe 1998; cf. Chapter 13).

With regard to indigenous religions, what we today would describe as homosexual orientation or transgender identity could in some cases be associated with particular spiritual powers and/or as the result of spirit possession.

For instance, Epprecht presents the case of male diviners in southern Africa, specifically Angola and Namibia:

> These men, described as "passive sodomites" by early European explorers and traders, were reputedly possessed by especially powerful female spirits. They were said to have dressed as women except with a loincloth open at the back to invite anal penetration. They would entice men into sex, charging a fee for the service. The active partner either gained by contact with the spirit (good crops or hunting, health, protection from evil spirits and so on) or realized his own homosexual preference.
>
> (Epprecht 2012, 524)

Along similar lines, in South Africa there is the phenomenon of male and female *sangomas* (traditional healers or diviners in Zulu indigenous religion) involved in same-sex relationships under the alibi of ancestral possession. This alibi is considered acceptable because "a *sangoma* acting on the dictates of his or her possessing spirit is not acting out of personal desire; thus the community will not hold the *sangoma* responsible for transgressing limits and rules that are believed to maintain moral order in society" (Buijs 2007, 98). Although there is a long history of same-sex practising *sangomas*, the phenomenon has recently become more widely known as some of them have come out publicly, adopting a modern lesbian or gay identity.

Feature: Lesbian sangomas in South Africa

One example of an openly self-identifying lesbian *sangoma* is Nkunzi Zandile Nkabinde, who in 2008 published her autobiography under the title *Black Bull, Ancestors and Me: My Life as a Lesbian Sangoma*. Here, Nkabinde (2008, 4) presents herself as "a Zulu woman, a lesbian, and a sangoma", and she narrates how she received her name from the ancestor, Nkunzi (meaning "blackbull"), who called her to become a *sangoma*. Although Nkabinde experiences possession by various ancestral spirits, both male and female, Nkunzi is her dominant ancestor. As such his spirit inhabits her body and defines her personality as well as, it turns out as the story unfolds, her sexual desire. According to her own childhood memory Nkabinde has always been a "tomboy", yet it is only after her calling and initiation into *sangoma*-hood that she experiences new levels of gender fluidity. Not only does she dress and behave in ways that in Zulu culture are perceived as typically male, yet also the physical working of her body has changed: "Since I started to have the spirit of Nkunzi in me I hardly menstruate. I only menstruate when I have a female ancestor in me. With Nkunzi I can stay up to a year without menstruating" (Nkabinde 2008, 19). The pausing of menstruation could possibly be explained in relation to the earlier discussed perception of menstrual blood as "cold" and "impure". In the absence of menstruation, Nkabinde maintains her ritual purity and can continue to engage in divination practice. Yet possession by Nkunzi's spirit does not only affect Nkabinde's monthly periods, but also her sexual desire and even her orgasms. Throughout the book, Nkabinde uses the phrase "he uses my body", suggesting that Nkunzi – who was known for his high sexual appetite – possesses her body in order to satisfy his sexual desires. Thus she narrates:

> Nkunzi loves women, especially young women. If I am with a woman of 21 or 22, normally Nkunzi will want to have sex with her. … He takes control of my body and even the sounds I make are different. … When I come my partner will say, "In that moment you were not yourself. What was happening?" I will make a sound like a lion roaring. That is how I know that Nkunzi is satisfied.
>
> (Nkabinde 2008, 68–9)

What is fascinating is that for Nkabinde there is no tension between being a *sangoma* and a lesbian. Instead, both identities are integrated through the motif of Nkunzi's spirit possessing her. It is through the active deployment of the indigenous religious notion of ancestral possession that she is able to legitimize her same-sex desire and adopt a lesbian identity, in a way that is culturally and religiously acceptable. She even suggests that for her practice as a *sangoma* it is, in fact, essential that she does not sleep with men, as this would contaminate her body and affect her ritual purity. Her account demonstrates that the Western dualism between body and mind is not adequate to understand African sexualities in which spirituality, erotic desire and sexual experience are closely intertwined (van Klinken and Otu 2017).

Same-sex sexuality is also practised in Christian and Muslim communities on the continent, in spite of the reputation of these religions being anti-homosexuality. Writing about the ancient Islamic sultanate of Kano, in the Hausa-speaking region of northern Nigeria, Rudolph Gaudio (2009) documents the existence of a relatively visible community of *'yan-daudu*, a term referring to feminine performing men who engage in sexual relationships (often of a commercial nature) with other, conventionally masculine men (not seldom business men, politicians and other "big men"). Although the *'yan-daudu* obviously transgress the gender and sexual norms of Islamic law, they used to be tolerated in society; only in recent decades, with the emergence of Islamic reform movements in northern Nigeria, their existence has become contested and they have become subject to persecution. Yet the *'yan-daudu* themselves identify as Muslim and take their practice of Islam seriously, for instance by saving money for pilgrimage to Mecca. Indeed, they believe that Allah created them the way they are, and that even their "womanlike behaviour is a personality trait bestowed by God" (Gaudio 2009, 122). The same belief that their sexuality is part of the way God created them can be found among Christian people identifying as gay or lesbian, who in recent years have become more visible in several African countries (Chitando and van Klinken 2016).

Religion and modern politics of sexuality

With colonization and missionary Christianity, European Christian lines of thinking were introduced and sexuality became more disciplined, especially for women. Writing about the Owambo people in Namibia, whose traditional *efundula* initiation rite for women became fiercely contested by Christian missions, Heike Becker captures these changes as follows:

> Earlier, the initiation was central to the definition of female identity. It legitimatised women's adulthood, sexuality and fertility … Christianity entailed a new set of ideas about "legitimate" sexuality. It tied sexuality and motherhood down within the framework of a Christian, monogamous marriage whereas in earlier times initiation had provided the transition to full female adulthood, and had legitimised fertility and full heterosexual relations for young women and their male sexual partners.
>
> (Becker 2004, 37)

Importantly, Becker points out that it is questionable whether Christian norms have completely replaced older local traditions. This creates a complex moral field in which patterns of continuity and discontinuity regarding sexuality have to be constantly navigated. The same applies to Islamic contexts in sub-Saharan Africa, although here the situation might be even more complex as Islamic norms have to be negotiated both vis-à-vis traditional cultures and Christian colonial modernity. Some interesting differences have been observed between the ways in which Christianity and Islam engaged in sexual politics during and after the colonial period:

> First, whereas European colonial officials and missionaries often blamed social problems – such as homosexuality, premarital sex, and female promiscuity – on indigenous African cultures, Muslim Africans tended to associate these and other practices that challenged the prevailing social order with colonialism and Westernization, especially in areas affected by European tourism. Second, from the precolonial era to the present, many Muslims in Africa have had more fluid ideas about love, sex, and sexuality than popular discourses associate with either Islam or Africa. And third, campaigns to promote the acceptance of non-heteronormative approaches to love and sex in Islamic Africa stress the need to reconcile personal experiences with local articulations of Islam and, in doing so, draw on both historical traditions and current global politics.
>
> (Decker 2015, 1)

What is true for both Christian and Muslim societies in Africa, is that sexuality has become a deeply politicized terrain, not only during the colonial period but also in the post-colonial era. As Basile Ndjio (2013, 127) argues with specific reference to Cameroon, but with wider relevance to post-colonial Africa, after independence many post-colonial governments continued the "civilizing mission" of the colonial powers and Christian missionaries, which centred on "transforming the sexuality of the African natives, by taming what they viewed as licentious behavior and immoral sexual practices from an early age". Interestingly, much of this civilizing agenda, consisting of promoting heterosexuality, monogamous marriage, and nuclear family life, in the post-colonial era became associated with "African culture" and "African values", as a way of resisting the increasingly liberal sexual culture of secularizing Western societies. Ndjio (2013, 128) refers to this process as the "nationalization of sexuality", through which governments sought to "draw boundaries between Africans and westerners, insiders and outsiders, citizens and strangers, authentic and deracinated Africans, good and bad citizens, loyal and disloyal subjects". In the period immediately after independence this process manifested itself in attempts to control public morality, such as in Zambia where the government introduced a moral code banning nude pictures and policing the dress of girls and women. In more recent decades, this process has become most apparent in the explicit campaigns against homosexuality and lesbian and gay rights, with these phenomena being widely depicted as "un-African" and, depending on the context, as "un-Christian" or "un-Islamic" (van Klinken and Chitando 2016). The latter phrases demonstrate how both Christianity and Islam have been utilized strategically in the nationalization and politicization of African sexuality, in order to promote a much more rigid heteronormative culture than previously existed on the continent. In relation to Christianity, Pentecostal movements in particular have played a prominent role in this process, while the same applies to Islamic reform movements in relation to Islam. With the support of religious leaders, several African governments introduced new anti-homosexuality legislation, most famously the Ugandan Anti-Homosexuality Act (2014) and the Nigerian Same-Sex Marriage (Prohibition) Act (2014). Both bills were an addition to the anti-sodomy laws already existing in many African countries since the colonial period. The colonial laws, it should be added, were specifically designed to address male homosexuality, as female same-sex intimacy was considered unthinkable; to date, much of the anxiety in Africa seems to be about male same-sex relationships, in particular anal sex which is considered a cultural taboo.

Although religion has been part and parcel of anti-homosexuality campaigns across the continent, it should also be acknowledged that emerging lesbian, gay, bisexual and transgender (LGBT) communities often identify with religious traditions and make strategic use of religious symbols, beliefs and practices as part of their activism. For instance, the music video *Same Love* that in 2016 was released by a group of Kenyan activist-musicians concludes with a quotation from the Bible and with the statement "Love is God and God is Love" (Art Attack 2016). A collection of Kenyan LGBT life stories, *Stories of Our Lives*, demonstrates that many of the more than 200 people participating in this project identify as Christian or Muslim and find ways of reconciling their sexuality and faith (The Nest 2015). In various parts of the continent, faith-based groups have emerged that advocate for inclusion of sexual minorities and for the recognition of their human dignity and rights. Examples are the South African Muslim organization The Inner Circle, and the Christian organisation Fellowship of Affirming Ministries that is active in several East African countries.

Sexual politics of HIV and AIDS

Contemporary politics of sexuality in sub-Saharan Africa have been shaped by the realities of the HIV epidemic. Since its emergence in the early 1980s, the epidemic has taken millions of African lives, leaving Africa the continent worst affected by this global pandemic. Because HIV is a mostly sexually transmitted virus, the high prevalence rates in Africa have frequently been explained with reference to "promiscuous" African sexual cultures. In religious settings the epidemic has been explained as a punishment from God for "sexual immorality" (as well as, in popular discourses, as a result of witchcraft). Such narratives, which reinforced the stigmatization of people living with HIV, ignore the complex colonial histories and post-colonial social, economic and political structures that allowed HIV to become such a devastating epidemic on the continent. One consequence of the epidemic has been that sexuality, thus far often a taboo subject in religious communities, became much more openly discussed as part of HIV prevention campaigns (Trinitapoli and Weinreb 2012). Also, under the threat of HIV and AIDS, more people than before may have felt compelled to take seriously the moral teachings of their religious leaders on matters of sexuality. However, HIV prevention also gave rise to controversy in religious circles. While health organizations promoted what they coined as the ABCs of prevention, religious leaders debated whether they should prioritize A (Abstinence), B (Being faithful) or also C (Condoms). Many Christian and Muslim leaders did not want to promote the use of condoms, arguing that this would allow for sexual promiscuity. Condom use may also be hindered by deeply rooted religio-cultural perceptions that sex, and in particular male sexuality, is about transmitting the vital force of life, as a result of which "live sex" (that is, sex without a condom) is preferred (Silomba 2015). Other religious leaders adopted the more pragmatic approach that saving lives is more important than maintaining moral taboos. In 2002, even an African Network of Religious Leaders Living with and Personally Affected by HIV and AIDS (ANERELA+) was established by Ugandan Anglican priest, Gideon Byamugisha, which now has thousands of members across the continent from Christian, Muslim and other faith backgrounds (Byamugisha and Williams 2005).

The enormous amounts of money from international bodies put into HIV prevention in Africa have created a new moral economy of sexuality, especially because the US government through its PEPFAR (President's Emergency Plan for AIDS Relief) programme decided to focus on "behavioural change" and to prioritize collaboration with faith-based organizations, often of an evangelical Christian nature. According to Lydia Boyd's study in Uganda, PEPFAR was a programme of unequalled scope, seeking to "intervene in behaviors and beliefs about sexual relationships, medicine, and family life", based on the model of the "accountable subject", that is, emphasizing individual responsibility for disease prevention rather than addressing "broader structural, economic and social factors that might also contribute to wellbeing" (Boyd 2015, 3). This approach coincided with the emphasis on born-again conversion and a subsequent radical change in lifestyle preached by Pentecostal churches. Yet this is not necessarily the most culturally sensitive approach nor best suited for many people whose socio-economic circumstances make it difficult to exercise physical and sexual autonomy and independence (see Chapter 12).

Conclusion

Traditional ways of perceiving and organizing sexuality, relationships and family life in Africa have undergone substantial change. This is partly due to processes of religious change but is also a result of wider processes of social and economic change such as through urbanization, migrant labour, neoliberal policies, global human rights discourses, and the rise of HIV and AIDS. The subsequent moral uncertainties of these changes often translated into renewed fears of witchcraft (see Chapter 7). As observed in post-apartheid South Africa, in a context where "harmonious conjugal sexuality and supportive kinship are moral ideals rather than normative expectations", discourses that link witchcraft and sexuality can be read as reflecting "micro-political struggles in the domestic domain" (Niehaus 2002, 293–4). In other words, people may resort to blaming witchcraft for the suffering caused by many complex, overlapping social factors that are rapidly changing ways of life. The same moral uncertainties regarding sexuality may explain the popularity of revivalist religious movements, both within Christian and Muslim settings in Africa. At the same time, as has become clear, deeply rooted cultural and indigenous perceptions of sexuality continue to shape people's practices and experiences. Thus, sexuality can be seen as one of the key sites manifesting the complex religious dynamics in post-colonial African societies.

Questions for discussion

- What does Sylvia Tamale (2011, 22) mean by "rewriting and righting African sexualities", and how do you think this chapter has (or has not) achieved this?
- In which key ways are religious belief and ritual practice intertwined with the sexual cultures in African indigenous religions as well as Christianity and Islam?
- How do you explain the popular idea that homosexuality is "un-African", and how would you respond to this idea?

References (*indicates recommended reading)

Allen, Denise. 2000. "Learning the Facts of Life: Past and Present Experiences in a Rural Tanzanian Community", *Africa Today* 47/3–4, 2–27.

Arnfred, Signe. 2004. "Re-thinking Sexualities in Africa: Introduction." In *Re-thinking Sexualities in Africa*, edited by Signe Arnfred, 7–29. Uppsala: Nordiska Afrika Institutet.

Arnfred, Signe. 2011. *Sexuality and Gender Politics in Mozambique: Rethinking Gender in Africa*. London: James Currey.

Art Attack. 2016. "Same Love (Remix)." YouTube. https://www.youtube.com/watch?v=8EataOQvPII (accessed 25 March 2018).

*Asamoah-Gyadu, Kwabena. 2007. "'Broken Calabashes and Covenants of Fruitfulness': Cursing Barrenness in Contemporary African Christianity", *Journal of Religion in Africa* 37/4, 437–460.

Becker, Heike. 2004. "Efundula: Women's Initiation, Gender and Sexual Identities in Colonial and Post-Colonial Northern Namibia." In *Re-thinking Sexualities in Africa*, edited by Signe Arnfred, 35–56. Uppsala: Nordiska Afrika Institutet.

Bledsoe, Caroline, and Barney Cohen. 1993. *Social Dynamics of Adolescent Fertility in Sub-Saharan Africa*. Washington DC: National Academy Press.

Boyd, Lydia. 2015. *Preaching Prevention: Born-Again Christianity and the Moral Politics of AIDS in Uganda*. Athens: Ohio University Press.

Buijs, Gina. 2007. "Sexual Orientation and Gender Identity among Zulu Diviners." In *Medical Identities: Healing, Well-Being and Personhood*, edited by Kent Maynard, 84–100. New York: Berghahn.

Byamugisha, Gideon, and Glen Williams, editors. 2005. *Positive Voices: Religious Leaders Living with or Personally Affected by HIV and AIDS*. Oxford: Strategies for Hope Trust.

Cambridge, Ellie. 2016. "Place Your Hands. Shocking Video Shows Con-artist Bishop Blessing Men's PENISES to Make Them Grow bigger", *The Sun*, 5 December. https://www.thesun.co.uk/news/2335849/shocking-video-shows-con-artist-bishop-blessing-mens-penises-to-make-them-grow-bigger/

Chitando, Ezra, and Adriaan van Klinken, editors. 2016. *Christianity and Controversies over Homosexuality in Contemporary Africa*. Abingdon: Routledge.

Cole, Jennifer, and Lynn Thomas, editors. 2009. *Love in Africa*. Chicago: University of Chicago Press.

Decker, Corrie. 2015. "Love and Sex in Islamic Africa: Introduction", *Africa Today* 61/4, 1–10.

Dover, Paul. 2005. "Gender and Embodiment: Expectations of Manliness in a Zambian Village." In *African Masculinities: Men in Africa from the Late Nineteenth Century to the Present*, edited by Lahoucine Ouzgane and Robert Morrell, 173–188. New York: Palgrave Macmillan.

*Epprecht, Marc. 2012. "Religion and Same-Sex Relationships in Africa." In *The Wiley-Blackwell Companion to African Religions*, edited by Elias Bongmba, 515–528. Malden: Wiley-Blackwell.

Gaudio, Rudolf Pell. 2009. *Allah Made Us: Sexual Outlaws in an Islamic African City*. Malden: Wiley-Blackwell.

Izugbara, Chimaraoke, and Alex Ezeh. 2010. "Women and High Fertility in Islamic Northern Nigeria", *Studies in Family Planning* 41/3, 193–204.

Magesa, Laurenti. 1997. *African Religion: The Moral Traditions of Abundant Life*. Maryknoll: Orbis.

Murray, Stephen, and William Roscoe. 1998. "Diversity and Identity: The Challenge of African Homosexualities." In *Boy-Wives and Female Husbands: Studies in African Homosexualities*, edited by Stephen Murray and William Roscoe, 267–278. New York: Palgrave Macmillan.

Ndjio, Basile. 2013. "Sexuality and Nationalist Ideologies in Postcolonial Cameroon." In *The Sexual History of the Global South: Sexual Politics in Africa, Asia, and Latin America*, edited by Saskia Wieringa and Horacio Sivori, 120–143. London: Zed Books.

Nkabinde, Nkunzi Zandile. 2008. *Black Bull, Ancestors and Me: My Life as a Lesbian Sangoma*. Auckland Park: Fanele Books.

Niehaus, Isak. 2002. "Perversion of Power: Witchcraft and the Sexuality of Evil in the South African Lowveld", *Journal of Religion in Africa* 32/3, 269–299.

Observers, The. (2014). "Behind the Scenes of Benin's Online 'Healing' Scams." http://observers.france24.com/en/20140820-benin-online-healer-scam-marabout (accessed 26 April 2018).

Rasmussen, Susan. 2004. "These Are Dirty Times: Transformations of Gendered Spaces and Islamic Ritual Protection in Tuareg Herbalists' and Marabouts' Albaraka Blessing Powers", *Journal of Ritual Studies* 18/2, 43–60.

Shoko, Tabona. 2007. *Karanga Indigenous Religion in Zimbabwe: Health and Well-Being*. Farnham: Ashgate.

Silomba, Samuel. 2015. "Perceptions of Condom Use and Sexual Risks among Out-of-School Youths in the Nakonde District, Zambia." In *Perspectives on Youth, HIV/AIDS and Indigenous Knowledges*, edited by Anders Breidlid, Austin Cheyeka and Alawia Ibrahim Farag, 113–128. Rotterdam: Sense Publishers.

*Tamale, Sylvia. 2011. "Researching and Theorising Sexualities in Africa." In *African Sexualities: A Reader*, edited by Sylvia Tamale, 11–36. Cape Town: Pambazuka Press.

The Church Newspaper Zambia. 2017. "Manhood Enlargement 'Pastor' Speaks out as Bishop Joshua Banda Says its Magic", Facebook, 27 February. https://www.facebook.com/ChurchNewspaperZambia/photos/a.213576908847792/596415740563905/?type=1&theater

The Nest. 2015. *Stories of Our Lives*. Nairobi: The Nest Collective.

Trinitapoli, Jenny, and Alexander Weinreb. 2012. *Religion and AIDS in Africa*. Oxford: Oxford University Press.

van Klinken, Adriaan, and Kwame Otu. 2017. "Ancestors, Embodiment and Sexual Desire: Wild Religion and the Body in the Story of a South African Lesbian Sangoma", *Body and Religion* 1/1, 70–87.

van Klinken, Adriaan, and Ezra Chitando, editors. 2016. *Public Religion and the Politics of Homosexuality in Africa*. Abingdon: Routledge.

15 Religion, media and popular culture in Africa

How is media and popular culture a matter that concerns religion?

The inextricable relation between religion, media and popular culture may come as a surprise to those who have been taught to think of religion as an eternal truth regarding spiritual reality, or as a sacred domain separate from concerns of everyday life. Solemn religious doctrine and piety seem far removed from contemporary media technology, and even further from the seemingly frivolous matter of entertainment that dominates popular culture. In fact, communication and transmission are at the core of any religious tradition.

Religion is necessarily "mediated" – through words, but also through ritual and the arts (performance, spectacle, music and dance) intended to reveal its truths. As we have seen, in Africa multimedia performances such as traditional masquerades and their accompanying festivities, deliver critical values and ideals of indigenous religions (see Chapter 1). Pageantry, pilgrimage, feasting and fasting are common "media" of Christianity and Islam as well. Religion in Africa today cannot be understood, however, without taking into account contemporary media technology that has been an integral part of its distinctive dynamic character and the rapid development of a new religious climate.

Although mass media – TV and radio – were introduced in colonial times as extensions of the British Broadcasting Corporation (BBC) and Radio France International, it is only since the 1990s that the independent media landscape in Africa began to flourish. Initially, after independence, broadcast stations were under the control of the new African governments and essentially served to promote state policies and their programmes of national unity. The end of one-party rule, economic liberalization and expansion of democracy in many African nations brought media deregulation. The commercialization of media opened new opportunities for entrepreneurs, such as private radio stations and satellite TV programmes. A proliferation of new *information and communication technologies* (ICTs) emerged, ranging from mobile telephone networks with capacities for text messaging (SMS), to the worldwide web offering instant information sharing, user-generated audio-visual material via YouTube, and social media sites like Facebook. Religious leaders and practitioners seized on these powerful new media to serve their mission and recruit converts.

A medium is not just an envelope in which to deliver a message, however. When transmitted through these new media, the experience and expression, practice and perception of religion are transformed. How are contemporary media and the ICT revolution transforming the understanding of religion and its practice in Africa now? How have religious leaders and communities adopted new media and how have media reshaped their missions? How have religious media influenced popular culture and vice versa? This chapter will address such questions by exploring various interfaces of religion, media and popular culture in Africa.

Microphones and loudspeakers in religions' sound-wars

Loudspeakers and microphones are not cutting edge media technology, but they are a ubiquitous feature of worship in Africa, amplifying fiery sermons and song, and making competing religious presences ever more palpable. The services of African Pentecostal-Charismatic mega-Churches, whose congregations number in the thousands, are literally electrifying. Pastors shout into microphones to enjoin their enthusiastic prayers. The volume alone conveys the power of God that is the subject of preaching and prayer:

> Loudness – to such an extent that participants' bodies vibrate from the excess of sound – and also pastors' use of microphones in rhythmic sayings induce a certain trance-like atmosphere that conveys a sense of an extraordinary encounter with a divine force:
>
> (Meyer 2011, 24)

In urban contexts where religious communities vie for dominance, volume has also been used as a political weapon. Amplified sermons, hymns and all-night prayer vigils impose on public space and demand the attention of all within hearing range. Often the electronics distort and muffle speech, making the meaning indecipherable. In such cases the actual message may be less important than the resounding projection of the performance of faith. The auditory assault is not necessarily only deployed against competing religions, but "can be even more intense when different churches ... begin to compete with each other" (Larkin 2014, 1004). In 2009, the Governor of Lagos (Nigeria) called for a "war" on noise pollution, citing "places of worship" as their primary source.

Meanwhile, the amplified *azan*, the traditional Muslim call to prayer, in simultaneous diffusion from multiple minarets contributes to the cacophonous soundscape. In Nigeria "Muslim movements sponsor cars with large loudspeakers fixed to the top, relaying their *wa'azi* (preaching) as they drive slowly from street to street" (Larkin 2014, 991). Loudspeakers have thus become weapons in soundwars, a subtler form of aggression and competition to dominate social space. In the city of Jos in northern Nigeria, the war escalated to violence. Mosques and churches there were accused of inciting riots and, when the houses of faith became the targets of attack, calling adherents to battle (1000). Loudspeakers were so implicated in interreligious violence that the governor banned their use.

Radio, cassettes and CDs: disembodied voices and religious authority

The loudspeaker can be interestingly contrasted with the use of another older medium: the cassette tape. For Pentecostal-Charismatic Christians as well as Muslims engaged in the Islamic renewal, religion is increasingly understood as a matter of deep personal calling and moral piety. In Africa cassette recordings of sermons and other inspiring religious teachings circulate within religious communities for the purpose of spiritual edification (Figure 15.1). While the loudspeaker can be used to perform religious adherence simply by imposing sound volume, a radio sermon or an audio recording of it is only as powerful as its ability to move and persuade the hearer.

The recirculation of radio sermons on cassette tapes creates "novel forms of religious sociability" shaping both Christianity and Islam in Africa (Schulz 2012, 24). In particular, this new, intimate means of sharing and exchanging religious teaching has challenged the nature of religious authority.

Feature: Female voices and moral authority in Mali

Cassette or audio-CD recordings of radio sermons are commonly circulated among Muslims for private listening to encourage piety. In Mali, a number of elderly and learned Muslim women capitalized on the expansion of private radio stations dedicated to religion to broadcast lectures on morality, piety and Arabic literacy. The broadcasts, and the circulation of audio recordings of them, extend the reach of the women's edifying speech beyond its traditional confinement to women's secluded circles.

Although these broadcasts enjoy great popularity, they created controversy about who had a legitimate authority to serve as Muslim preachers. One opponent sarcastically referred to them as "radio *hadjas*", using the title meant to venerate women who made the pilgrimage to Mecca. He warned that their "sweet and alluring" voice was not to be trusted (Schulz 2012, 24). Both disembodied speech and the seductive sensuality of the female voice bear "the potential for delusion" that can misguide the hearer (28). The women, however, appeal to the traditional precept that trustworthy speech is recognized when it elicits a moving, heart-felt response. Their broadcasts and recordings promote just such an affect in pious listeners.

Their followers, in turn, consider that the very process of listening to their lectures on radio or cassettes is a moral exercise. The care and reverence with which followers handled fragile cassettes demonstrate the authority they attribute to their female teachers. In their eyes the cassettes offer "palpable proof of the leader's special calling by God" (Schulz 2012, 37). They are not just technological vehicles of a religious message, but are seen to have certain holy attributes themselves. Here the medium itself becomes a "material token" of the moral lesson and a tangible presence of its teacher.

Figure 15.1 Devotional listening (courtesy of Joseph Kebbie)

In Côte d'Ivoire and its neighbouring francophone countries, listening to sermons was also a standard feature of Muslim practice. Audiences expected them to entertain as well as edify, and their local form would often "bear striking resemblance to Mande epic recitation" (Launay 1997, 446). Traditional stylistic devices included musical interludes, or pious chanting and punctuated responses from the audience. By contrast, Muslim clerics trained in Saudi Arabia were scripted and formal and "would make dull tapes indeed" (451).

In Cameroon, as well, the traditional Muslim religious leaders (*marabouts*) preaching in local languages and using indigenous oratory styles initially had greater appeal to the majority of listeners than the pedantic Arabic-speaking scholars. These were also often pegged as "fundamentalists" by wary states (Adama 2015, 141). With the advent of new information and communication technologies, however, the younger generation tuned in to more "interactive Islamic programs broadcast by private FM radios and hosted by charismatic young Muslim scholars" (144) who entertain lively exchanges on timely subjects. These shows are supplemented by blogs and list-serves that address topics more relevant to young audiences, like sexuality and marriage, and widen their reach. The popularity of these "new ulama" (scholars of Islam) marginalized traditional clerics.

From local billboard to global internet

Travelling through any African city today, one would notice roadside banners and looming billboards advertising Pentecostal-Charismatic churches and featuring their pastors at revival meetings and international summits or conferences (Figure 15.2). A common theme is prosperity, which according to the gospel they preach is God's reward to his faithful servants. "The material

Figure 15.2 Roadside banner of a Pentecostal ministry in Eldoret, Kenya (Hassan Ndzovu, 2018)

signifiers of this prosperity and well-being are the flamboyant outfits of the pastors and their wives, in particular, and the jewellery displayed in various images" (Asamoah-Gyadu 2005, 345).

Pentecostalism has attracted large numbers with such images. By the early 1990s, they were edging out the once ubiquitous hand-painted billboards of local diviners and healers, signalling a significant shift in religious culture. While banners still triumphantly hail the active presence of Christian ministry, local print advertising is now extended and surpassed by new electronic media with more powerful and dynamic imagery and a global reach.

Within the relatively brief span of the last two decades the technological capacity in Africa increased exponentially. Exposure to the global "market-place" of religious options and styles influenced the African churches, which adopted the idea of re-conversion as a "born-again" experience (Hackett and Soares 2015, 5). The new generation of Pentecostal-Charismatic Christians that emerged from this exposure has been especially keen to embrace the media's power. Mega-churches stream services on the internet. Websites offer blogs and interactive discussion boards, fostering a sense of intimate contact while simultaneously expanding their outreach to global scale.

Worship via the worldwide web conforms to the Pentecostal-Charismatic vision of a world connected by the Holy Spirit, and of Christianity as a "world religion" that supposedly transcends culture. The internet affords a viable arena for religious participation for those who envision religion as a matter of individual spirituality, unfettered by traditional duties or community ties. It encourages the "complete break with the past" that is the clarion call of many African Christians.

Texting: instant virtual community, omnipresent piety

As mobile phones and SIM cards became more affordable and the number of phone service providers increased in Africa, the use of short message service (SMS, or "texting") grew, especially among youth. In Nigeria, Ghana, Cameroon, countries with the largest Pentecostal assemblies in the West African region, the diffusion of SMS messages within actual and virtual Christian communities has become a common means of encouraging daily piety.

Posts offer admonitions, Bible quotes, or requests for prayer. Innocent Chiluwa (2013, 25) provides a poignant example: "The world doesn't reward your efforts or struggles only your success. Today I pray GOD will reward your efforts and struggles in JESUS name". Imprecations (religious curses) against enemies are also common. Some imitate the style of psalms, diffusing anxiety with the faith that the wicked are punished and Christian righteousness will prevail: "Surely, hardship & difficulties shall follow all our enemies, every seconds of their lives, & dey will receive 10,000 bullets each in their foreheads, which will result 2 their death forever, Amen" (Taiwo 2015, 197).

Even though the flow is from one to many – from pastor to worshippers – and not interactive, SMS can be a meaningful way to influence people's lives and provide a sense of spiritual bonding. SMS has fulfilled such an important social function among Nigerian Christians that at Christmas and Easter, providers offer free service to allow for seasons' greetings (Taiwo 2015, 199).

Control over religious media outlets and Christian video production

Unlike most churches, the Pentecostal-Charismatic churches that emphasize prosperity typically "have the financial resources to produce their own programs and pay for airtime on radio and television, as they attract many upwardly mobile professionals" from whom they exact ten percent of their income as a form of tithing (de Witte 2015, 210). Many wealthy producers and even owners of private media outlets are church members. Therefore, Pentecostal Christian broadcasting has dominated the media scene: radio broadcasts of sermons and gospel music permeate public and private life, and TV programmes featuring energetic preachers, turn them into "religious superstars" (Asamoah-Gyadu 2005, 347). Figures like the Nigerian Prophet T.B. Joshua, through his Emmanuel TV channel, reach homes in countries virtually all over the continent and beyond. Christians have also created a private industry of religious video production.

African Christian leaders were introduced to religious video-tapes brought from the United States in the 1980s, and quickly recognized the potential of the VCR as a new instrument for proselytization:

> Neo-pentecostalist pastors not only introduced ... the culture of viewing religious films in the form of video cassettes, recorded sermons and songs, they were also instrumental in the subsequent popularisation of video tapes of their own preaching and other religious events. These tapes were duplicated and copies sold to members of their congregations who were often exhorted to watch them since they contained seeds of blessings and divine inspiration.
>
> (Ukah 2003, 211)

Like the cassette tapes of Muslim women for their pious listeners, the videotapes of Christian preaching were themselves "vaunted as 'points of contact' with the divine, as purveyors of miracles and fortunes ..." (Ukah 2003, 211). Christian actors, including pastors who appear in them, claim that their performances are inspired by the Holy Spirit and refer to the experience as "entering the costume" (Oha 2002, 128). For audiences, too, watching the spectacular imagery may be akin to a revelation. The sound quality of popular video films is usually so poor that dialogue becomes entirely secondary to the spectacular character of the movies showing the occult world in action.

Christian video extended from instruction to entertainment. Because they considered secular films instruments of the Anti-Christ, mega-churches, like Deeper Life Bible Church and Mount Zion Faith Ministries International (MZFMI) "set out to provide 'healthy drama' and 'safe films' for a Christian public" (Ukah 2003, 216). They produced their own amateur narrative videos. These are mostly of poor quality but have guaranteed audiences:

> Video films, which are cheaply produced mainly by drama wings of Christian Churches and ministries, and marketed in video shops and by mobile vendors, are often played on some local television stations in Nigeria on weekends, especially on Sundays ... They are also played at Christian revival rallies.
>
> (Oha 2002, 128)

The plots may be hackneyed and the quality poor, but Christian narrative video has become a lucrative industry. Many churches expanded from low-budget, amateur video production to commercial enterprises:

> [In Nigeria] Mega-churches like the Redeemed Christian Church of God (RCCG), the Redeemed Evangelical Mission (TREM), and Winners' Chapel are all involved in the burgeoning production, circulation and consumption of video-films ... Often, Pentecostal pastors are key in both the

acting and production. Religious sites are major distribution centres for these video-films

(Ukah 2003, 215).

African indigenous religions in Christian video and self-representation in media

Not coincidentally, "the growth areas of Christianity" in Africa are among "denominations, congregations, pastors and media that demonize African traditions" (Hackett 2003, 70). The Pentecostal-Charismatic churches' enthusiastic claim to spiritual power and working miracles of deliverance are built on casting African indigenous religions as evil. The mega-churches owe their popularity to the central place they give to public confession of witchcraft and to aggressive practices of exorcism. For example, the ministry of the Mountain of Fire and Miracles Ministry (MFM) in Nigeria's capital, Lagos, focuses on "deliverance" from connection to traditional religious belief or practice, objects or places where "evil spirits" are deemed to dwell.

Christian videos depict African indigenous religions (AIR) as "juju" with sensationalist imagery of frightening "fetishes", like skulls of supposed human victims of sacrifice, to feed congregants' horror and convince them of their need for protection through Christ. Ironically, their characterization simultaneously acknowledges the existence and efficacy of indigenous spiritual practices including witchcraft. Far from dismissing them as superstition, they portray them as Satanic. One of the foremost producers of Christian video-film in Nigeria, Helen Ukpabio, claims to have a divine mandate "to unveil the secrets of witchcraft and to deliver those who are under the oppressive burden of demon possession" through her videos (Ukah 2003, 219).

In contrast with Pentecostal-Charismatics, practitioners of African indigenous religions (AIR) shun self-representation in the media. They are aware of their demonization and are wary of mass media's exoticizing gaze. More importantly, shrine priests and other ritual specialists are concerned with the proper management of knowledge and reserve spiritual "secrets" for initiates. Exposure through mass media is incompatible with the traditional mode of transmission. Ultimately, virtual space cannot substitute for concrete material substance that, in AIR, mediates spiritual presence in the world.

By the same token, practitioners are under increasing pressure to counter African Christianity's marked hostility for indigenous religions (Meyer 2011, 208). In large measure, it was this that motivated Kwabena Damuah to found Afrikania, a neo-traditional movement that recast AIR in Christian terms (see Chapter 4). Subscribing to the Western model of world religion, it aimed to show AIR as comparable in terms of structure, philosophy, moral value and import to Christianity. It is also imitating its mediatization: "Competing with what is known as 'Pentecostal noise-making,' Afrikania has readily embraced the use of a public address system … establishing a sonic presence in Sunday's battlefield of religious sound" (de Witte 2015, 215). Especially because it is eager to present AIR as a universal philosophy, Afrikania has been particularly vigilant that the media not film rituals of animal sacrifice that would only feed the public's stereotypical image of African tradition as dirty, bloody and evil.

Building their reputations by word of mouth as "strong" and effective practitioners, most healer-diviners scoff at those who rely on self-aggrandizing advertisement. Nevertheless, "increasing numbers of 'traditional' healers and diviners in many places in Africa have sought to enhance their credibility through an online presence – for example, in websites and on YouTube and through radio advertising and publicity" (Hackett and Soares 2015, 7). One contemporary "fetish priest", Kwaku Bonsam, earned popular notoriety in Ghana by savvy use of the media, establishing a website through which he offers his healing services, and arranging for TV appearances in which he makes a spectacular show of his powers. Fighting fire with fire, Bonsam employs the media to decry self-proclaimed Christian prophets as "fake men of God". In particular, he denounced the renowned Nigerian founder of Synagogue Church of All Nations (SCOAN), T.B. Joshua, claiming that such preachers seek him out for spiritual services only to denigrate him in public: "Apart from the pastors, many prominent business people and celebrated church founders in Africa frequent my shrine for my services and if they deny, I am going to name them", he said (GhanaWeb 2017). Recently, Bonsam was featured in a movie-themed music video, shown singing the latest song release of the Ghanaian pop star Shatta Wale. It "garnered an impressive number of views" on social media (Yengh 2018).

Religion in African popular culture

Popular ("pop") culture is a constantly shifting ensemble of beliefs, practices and material objects that express the contemporary ideas and feelings of members of a society, and that in turn influence them. It increasingly circulates via mass media – TV, radio and online. Platforms like AfroPop Worldwide and New African Woman magazine, or blogs like Ms Afripolitan, spotlight music, art and fashion and feature social commentary from Africa-centred perspectives (AWDF 2014). Religion features in all these media. "Wherever one looks, religion has appeared more and more in entertainment and popular culture" (Asamoah-Gyadu 2016, 647).

One of the most powerful purveyors of popular culture is cinema. The burgeoning centre of African filmmaking today is Nigeria, and the industry is known as "Nollywood". Economically independent of government funding, and not answerable to any religious entity, Nollywood is a global force in its own right. It is hard to overestimate its impact. The low-budget melodramas have an avid international audience, not only in West Africa but also around the world. "There are cable channels in Ethiopia, South Africa and Kenya dedicated solely to Nollywood movies" (Abah 2009, 735). They are just as popular among African immigrant groups worldwide. Nigerian films are mediating local culture, including the African religious scene, to a global public.

Following independence, many African states attempted to use select symbols, practices and artifacts of indigenous religions to consolidate identity and forge national pride. Governments promoted African "heritage" as worthy of honour and selective preservation. Pentecostal churches, especially, crusaded against this view of heritage, casting it as demonic and a dangerous portal for evil. Calling for the nation to be "exorcized" of such projects Nigerian church leaders even attempted to ban the pouring of libation at state functions. The African film industry capitalized on this portrayal of African tradition, producing a genre of religion-based and witchcraft films known as "juju" movies. The story lines follow "tales and gossip that frequently circulate at all levels of African life" about witchcraft as the source of personal and social suffering, and depict Christian "spiritual warfare" against African tradition (Meyer 2011, 25). For many, such films featuring bizarre rituals were seen as revelations that lent "visual credibility" to rumours on the street (25).

Leading Nigerian filmmaker Tunde Kelani, however, took a different path. Forging a transition from Yoruba traveling theatre to movies, Kelani founded Mainframe Film and Television Productions, "a company dedicated to promoting Nigeria's 'rich cultural heritage and moral values both within the country and the outside world at large'" (Klein 2012, 138). His films include local "cultural imagery, music, dance, poetry, proverbs, humor, drama, magic" and relay stories that treat tensions between tradition and "modernity" (ibid.). "Arugba" is based on the life of a real woman that Kelani met while filming a documentary about a festival for the river Goddess Oshun. The story relates the struggle of Adetutu, selected by the king and oracle God Ifa to be an "Arugba", a ritual specialist with powers to ward off evil. Adetutu struggles to fulfil her duty while maintaining her life as a university student in theatre arts. The film features the Oshun Osogbo festival as a backdrop, while the traditional Yoruba songs and dances for the goddess "provide the spiritual structure that grounds the film's main characters" (Klein 2012, 140). Such feature films, modelled on traditional theatre performances, reflect traditional aesthetics, and provide moral lessons to new audiences. As Klein notes, "The fictional university students in Arugba are inspired by the aesthetics of a globalized hip-hop and rap culture" but the performances depicted honour the goddess. The film aims to appeal to this same pop audience even as it produces and circulates a depiction of a traditional and uniquely African moral world.

Since 2000 a new genre has emerged. "Epic movies" feature African heritage in a romantic light and represent them visually in a style considered "pan-African", one which does not refer to any actual history or existing ethnic tradition. This "repackaging" of African heritage depicts it as an imagined pre-Christian past from which to draw pride and inspiration. Epics represent a "revaluation and new aesthetics of African tradition among young urbanites" (de Witte and Meyer 2012, 53), and pose an alternative to the diametric opposition between tradition and Christianity.

Music is another critical form of African pop culture. Its distinctive, vibrant styles reflect its youth, vitality and innovative reworking of tradition. Music –

even pop music – also conveys religious messages, and for many listening is a devotional act. A number of well-known musicians switched from secular music to gospel or other religious genres to cater to an expanding "worship industry" (Ukah 2003, 204). In Kenya, popular hip hop artist Julius Owino blends religious language into his music in order to appeal to Christian audiences, thus creating a new hip hop gospel youth culture (Ntarangwi 2016). In Nigeria, "cross-over artists" include Sunny Okosun, famous for anti-apartheid titles like "Fire in Soweto". Since he became a Pentecostal pastor with his own church, his music is Christian-themed. In the 1990s, he also released an album singing the praises of Mohammed to appeal to Nigeria's Muslim population (Ukah 2003, 228 n2). In Senegal, hip hop rapper Thieuf collaborates with a *marabout*, Seydina S. Se'ne in "Adouna", a song that calls listeners to turn from earthly pleasures and focus on Muslim ideals and the afterlife (Niang 2009, 67).

Interactivity, empowerment and self-authorization on the internet

The internet allows for the marketing of religion and for users to explore new forms. Interactive features – chat rooms, discussion forums and answers to Frequently Asked Questions – allow individual seekers to engage with an invisible community that constellates around the website. Despite low bandwidths and problems of connectivity, blogging is a growing medium where young people share information and resources in the safety of anonymity. Among notable blogging themes is religion. Bloggers tend to be highly educated urban-based professionals and do not represent the majority (Somolu 2007, 482). Nevertheless they are building community and enabling social change by giving voice to those not usually heard, such as young African women.

The internet plays an increasingly prominent role in promoting and sustaining religions in the globalized world for expatriates seeking to stay connected to their religious communities at home. For example, followers of the Mouride Sufi order based in Senegal sustain community by watching videos of pilgrimages to the order's sacred sites (Hackett and Soares 2015, 6). Practices that once required an intimate setting of close contact, like divination, are now available digitally. The famous Nigerian form of divination, Ifa, can be readily accessed on the internet now. On one hand, the Internet may only allow for

> the acquisition of religious and ritual knowledge [that] is "disembedded" from its local and original social context … on the other hand, [for some] the Internet is just about the only chance to be "re-embedded" into that original cultural and religious context.
>
> (Krueger 2004, 188)

The web has also been a conduit for the promotion of African indigenous religions in the diaspora, whose presence has grown exponentially in recent decades. For example, Afro-Cuban religion, Santería (Lucumi) that blends Yoruba religion with Spanish Catholic veneration of the saints, has attracted followers around the globe.

Ordinarily, religious authority is derived from ritual mastery attained through real-life instruction, gradual initiation and experience. But wherever the internet has replaced the local community with a virtual one, religious authority has become as much a matter of visibility and persuasive power as the pedigree of formal training and initiation, education or licensing. It is based on what Krueger (2004, 190) calls "inter-subjective consensus" of the virtual community, validated by online activity. In such cases, the "new state of spiritual identity" is attained through self-initiation (192). Ability to control media – a website homepage and its links that create the virtual community of users (VCU) or computer-supported social network (CSSN) – can be the determinative factor for self-authorized religious ordination. For example, Mensa Otabil, the founder of International Central Gospel Church in Ghana, has only secondary school training and an honorary doctorate. He created his religious following through TV and radio followed by social media, including Facebook and Twitter, and is considered one of the most influential personalities in Ghana.

Mediating African religion to New Age surfers

For many who feel themselves alienated from mainstream religious organization, the internet is a resource for seekers of alternative spiritual spaces. Cyberspace has also afforded "religion surfers" access to neo-traditional African religious ideas and practices, marketed to Western New Age seekers. African religions are often marketed online as a "mysterious", "occult" tradition with "powerful" mediators, called "shaman". The case of Credo Mutwa is an example of this phenomenon.

Feature: New Age neo-shamanism authorized by internet

Credo Mutwa, a Zulu neo-traditional "shaman" from South Africa, was initiated as a young man as a diviner/healer (*sangoma*). After failing to establish a cultural village at home, and reviled there as a fraud, Mutwa made effective use of the media to gain a worldwide following, and establish notoriety if not legitimacy as an authentic spiritual guide. "Celebrated within the global network of contemporary neo-shamanism", he presents himself as the keeper of an ancient African tradition (Chidester 2008, 141).

Mutwa preaches that the disembodied space of the media is more akin to the dream-world, the traditional domain of spirit-human mediation. According to Mutwa, extra-terrestrial aliens have established contact with humans and use media to communicate with them just as the ancestors used dreams. Mutwa claims to have been abducted and tortured by aliens from outer space after which he began to experience intense psychic impressions. His "vivid accounts of his encounters with extra-terrestrials ... circulate through videos, DVDs, and the Internet" (Chidester 2008, 137). Ironically, Mutwa views the media with ambivalence, holding that electronic transmission and reception of media blankets psychic power and thwarts the work of the sangoma. But he believes mass media are urgently necessary to help humanity realize the fact that the aliens are provoking humanity's self-destruction by warfare.

Among Mutwa's disciples are displaced South Africans longing to be re-grounded in the space of home and to claim an authentic African identity. One is David Cumes, a white South African urologist with a practice in California who underwent an abbreviated initiation as a Zulu sangoma. Cumes draws an analogy between the invisible communications networks of shamanic "psychospiritual technology" and media (151). In fact, Zulu dreaming has "gone global" on the Internet. "Zulu dreams visions, and mysteries ... [are recapitulated] through film and video, musical CDs and DVDs, and the expanding global dreamscape of neo-shamanism on the Internet" (Chidester 2008, 138). The case of Mutwa and his following demonstrates how media can transmute local, embodied and material religion to a globalized phenomenon, dis-connected not only from indigenous tradition and the material world, but from earth itself.

Where once initiation into a spiritual tradition required being embedded in an actual community and under the supervision of elders, the internet and its associated interactive technologies have facilitated virtual communities composed of cyber connections. Religious authority and legitimacy is as obtainable as access to electronic media:

> Literally anybody who feels called by God, possesses the necessary charisma, and can mobilize some material resources can found a church. These independent reverend doctors, pastors, prophets, bishops, and archbishops, as they designate themselves, then take to the mass media and preach the word without theological accountability to any ecclesial institution or authority.
>
> (Asamoah-Gyadu 2005, 343)

In the virtual realm "the possibility of immediate checks and balances [on the authenticity of practice or legitimacy as a religious leader] ... all but disappear online" (Wood 2016, 450). In this new situation a practitioner's reputation for authenticity and trustworthy guidance is "the new currency" on which circulation in the marketplace of religious ideas depends (449). But while websites and Facebook pages offer insubstantial pedigree for the exercise of religious authority, one may take some comfort that the transparency of the internet also makes public scrutiny and feedback global, and evaluation certain.

Questions for discussion

- Which medium best serves each of Africa's religious traditions and why? What does it convey about the nature of each?
- Find a website representing religion in Africa (Christianity, Islam or AIR) and assess its value for (a) understanding the tradition and the place of that particular community or practitioner in it; (b) recruiting new practitioners/ adherents; (c) establishing "legitimacy" of religious authority. On what basis are you making your assessments?
- How has this chapter changed your view of the intersection of media and/ or pop culture with religion in your own society?

References (*indicates recommended reading)

*Abah, Adedayo Ladigbolu. 2009. "Popular Culture and Social Change in Africa: The Case of the Nigerian Video Industry", *Media, Culture & Society* 31/5, 731–748.

Adama, Hamadou. 2015. "Islamic Communication and Mass Media in Cameroon." In *New Media and Religious Transformations in Africa*, edited by Rosalind Hackett and Benjamin Soares, 137–156. Bloomington: Indiana University Press.

*Asamoah-Gyadu, Kwabena. 2005. "Of Faith and Visual Alertness: The Message of 'Mediatized' Religion in an African Pentecostal Context", *Material Religion* 1/3, 336–356.

Asamoah-Gyadu, Kwabena. 2016. "Comments on 'Sensational Movies'", *Religion* 46/4, 644–653.

AWDF (The African Women's Development Fund). 2014. "'Why Popular Culture Matters for African Feminism' (on Something Other than Beyoncé) Part 1". http://awdf. org/why-popular-culture-matters-for-african-feminism-on-something-other-than-beyon ce-part-1/ (accessed 5 July 2018).

Chidester, David. 2008. "Zulu Dreamscapes: Senses, Media, and Authentication in Contemporary Neo-Shamanism", *Material Religion* 4/2, 136–158.

*Chiluwa, Innocent. 2013. "Community and Social Interaction in Digital Religious Discourse in Nigeria, Ghana and Cameroon", *Journal of Religion, Media and Digital Culture* 2/1, 1–37.

De Witte, Marleen, and Birgit Meyer. 2012. "African Heritage Design: Entertainment Media and Visual Aesthetics in Ghana", *Civilisations* 61/1, 43–64.

De Witte, Marleen. 2015. "Media Afrikania: Styles and Strategies of Representing 'Afrikan Traditional Religion' in Ghana." In *New Media and Religious Transformations in Africa*, edited by Rosalind Hackett and Benjamin Soares, 207–226. Bloomington: Indiana University Press.

GhanaWeb. 2017. "TB Joshua Is My Boy! – Witch Doctor Kwaku Bonsam", GhanaWeb, 2 February 2017. http://www.ghanaweb.com/GhanaHomePage/religion/TB-Joshua -is-my-boy-Witch-doctor-Kwaku-Bonsam-506879 (accessed 9 July 2018).

Hackett, Rosalind. 2003. "Discourses of Demonization in Africa and Beyond", *Diogenes* 50/3, 61–75.

*Hackett, Rosalind, and Benjamin Soares, editors. 2015. *New Media and Religious Transformations in Africa*. Bloomington: Indiana University Press.

Klein, Debra. 2012. "A Political Economy of Lifestyle and Aesthetics: Yorùbá Artists Produce and Transform Popular Culture", *Research in African Literatures* 43/4, 128–146.

Krueger, Oliver. 2004. "The Internet as Distributor and Mirror of Religious and Ritual Knowledge", *Asian Journal of Social Science* 32/2, 183–197.

Larkin, Brian. 2014. "Techniques of Inattention: The Mediality of Loudspeakers in Nigeria", *Anthropological Quarterly* 87/4, 989–1015.

Launay, Robert. 1997. "Spirit Media: The Electronic Media and Islam among the Dyula of Northern Cote d'Ivoire", *Africa* 67/3, 441–453.

Meyer, Birgit. 2011. "Mediation and Immediacy: Sensational Forms, Semiotic Ideologies and the Question of the Medium", *Social Anthropology* 19/1, 23–39.

*Niang, Abdoulaye. 2009. "Preaching Music and Islam in Senegal: Can the Secular Mediate the Religious? The Case of Rap and Mabalax Music", *African Communication Research* 2/1, 61–84.

Ntarangwi, Mwenda. 2016. *The Street is my Pulpit: Hip Hop and Christianity in Kenya.* Urbana: University of Illinois Press.

Oha, Obododimma. 2002. "Yoruba Christian Video Narrative and Indigenous Imaginations: Dialogue and Duelogue", *Cahiers d'Études Africaines* 42/165, 121–142.

Schulz, Dorothea. 2012. "Dis/embodying Authority: Female Radio 'Preachers' and the Ambivalences of Mass-Mediated Speech in Mali", *International Journal of Middle East Studies* 44/1, 23–43.

Somolu, Oreoluwa. 2007. "'Telling Our Own Stories': African Women Blogging for Social Change", *Gender and Development* 15/3, 477–489.

Taiwo, Rotimi. 2015. "Religious Discourse in the New Media: A Case Study of Pentecostal Discourse Communities of SMS Users in Southwestern Nigeria." In *New Media and Religious Transformations in Africa*, edited by Rosalind Hackett and Benjamin Soares, 190–204. Bloomington: Indiana University Press.

Ukah, Asonzeh. 2003. "Advertising God: Nigerian Christian Video-Films and the Power of Consumer Culture", *Journal of Religion in Africa* 33/2, 203–231.

Wood, Funlayo. 2016. "Cyber Spirits, Digital Ghosts: African and Diasporic Religions in the Age of Collaborative Consumption", *Cross Currents* 65/4, 448–456.

Yengh. 2018. "Kwaku Bonsam Shows Massive Support for Shatta Wale as He Jams to His Latest Song in New Video", GhanaSummary, 6 May. https://ghanasummary.com/yengh/6674/kwaku-bonsam-shows-massive-support-for-shatta-wale-as-he-jams-to-his-latest-song-in-new-video (accessed 9 July 2018).

Index